Rassie

About the Authors

Rassie Erasmus is the former head coach of the South African Rugby Union team. Well known for his outspoken opinions and tactical nous, under his leadership the Springboks won the 2019 Rugby World Cup in Japan against all expectations. Erasmus had a successful coaching career at club level in South Africa and Ireland. He was the head coach of South Africa's Cheetahs and Stormers, as well as Ireland's Munster, leading the team to the Pro12 final. As a player, he was a leading flanker for South Africa and several club teams, including South Africa's Free State Cheetahs and the Cats. He retired from playing in 2004 due to injury, and since then he has dedicated himself to coaching. *Rassie: Stories of Life and Rugby* is his first book.

David O'Sullivan is a writer and award-winning broadcaster. He has presented a weekly rugby show and live rugby matches on SABC TV, and has covered news and sport over the years for South Africa's Capital Radio, 702, Hot91.9, Power FM and Kaya FM.

Rassie

Stories of Life and Rugby

RASSIE ERASMUS

WITH DAVID O'SULLIVAN

MACMILLAN

First published 2023 by Pan Macmillan South Africa

This edition first published 2023 by Macmillan
an imprint of Pan Macmillan
The Smithson, 6 Briset Street, London EC1M 5NR
EU representative: Macmillan Publishers Ireland Ltd, 1st Floor,
The Liffey Trust Centre, 117–126 Sheriff Street Upper,
Dublin 1, D01 YC43
Associated companies throughout the world
www.panmacmillan.com

ISBN 978-1-0350-2939-6 HB
ISBN 978-1-0350-2940-2 TPB

1 2 3 4 5 6 7 8 9

A CIP catalogue record for this book is available from the British Library.

Editing by Sean Fraser; proofreading by Wesley Thompson; transcribing by Vivien Wray;
indexing by Christopher Merrett; design and typesetting by Triple M Design, Johannesburg

Printed and bound by CPI Group (UK) Ltd, Croydon, CR0 4YY

Visit **www.panmacmillan.com** to read more about all our books
and to buy them. You will also find features, author interviews and
news of any author events, and you can sign up for e-newsletters
so that you're always first to hear about our new releases.

To my mother Maria, my sisters Martlie and Gerda, my wife Nikki,
and my children Nikki, Carli and Jani.

Glossary

ag: oh

aikona: never (isiZulu and isiXhosa)

boepens: beer belly

boerseun: farm boy

boykie: lad

braai/braaivleis: barbecue

dikbek: sulky

dominee: priest

dompas/se: official document/s black people in South Africa had to carry to prove their identity and where they could live or work. The pass laws were repealed in 1986.

dop/s: drink/s

down-down: drink rapidly in one go

dronkgat: drunkard

fok: fuck

gatvol: had enough

gees: vibe

hartseer: heartsore

hoendervleis: goose bumps

hoërskool: high school

Jik: brand name for bleach

jol/jolling: party/partying

kak: shit

kontiki/'s: post-match fines meeting, usually involving drinking alcohol as a penalty

kouekoors: fever

kuier/kuiering: settle/settled in for a party

k-word: a derogatory word used to insult a black person, considered to be extremely offensive hate speech

laaitie: young boy

lekker/lekkerest: nice/nicest

moering: hitting hard

oom: uncle

opfok: fuck up

ou tannie: old auntie

pap/papper: weak/weaker

plankiesteaks: barbecued steak sliced and served on a board

sokkie/s: dance/s

stoutgat: badly behaved person

takkies: sneakers

tannie(s): auntie(s)

troep(s): soldier(s) with no rank

volkslied: folk song

windgat: a show-off

Preface

PEOPLE THINK THEY KNOW ME. And I understand why. I've lived my life in the public eye ever since I started playing rugby for Free State back in 1994. I come from Despatch, an Eastern Cape town with humble beginnings, where my world was incredibly small. And then, as my rugby prowess grew, I was suddenly being featured on the sports pages of newspapers and in rugby magazines and being talked about on the radio and appearing on TV. The matches I played were live in people's homes.

The public gaze increased dramatically when I became a Springbok and later a coach who won the Currie Cup twice. And when I coached the Boks and won the 2019 World Cup, the scrutiny became almost unbearable.

When social media arrived, I was quick to get on board. I've always been slightly ahead of the game when it comes to technology. I used Twitter a lot, sometimes fuelling Twitter storms and Twitter wars, and that simply increased the public's access to what I was doing and saying. People read and commented on what I had to say and watched videos of me dancing and enjoying life. So many saw that now-infamous video of me criticising a referee. It's all out there for the public to view and judge.

People think they know me, and so they form their own opinions of me. I've got no problem with that. People can and must have their own views. Of course, I would prefer that those views and opinions were based on fact, but I know the facts aren't always available. So people sometimes make up their minds about me based on something that simply isn't true.

To be honest, a lot of the public opinion about me is way off the mark. I may come across as a loudmouth, opinionated, arrogant, unrepentant. That I'm not very serious, like I enjoy to jol a little too much. I might appear troubled, complicated and angry. The list of perceptions is long. And while some of this criticism is understandable, even justified, a lot of it is just plain wrong.

People think I'm extroverted, but I'm not. I find social occasions difficult, and I'm uncomfortable engaging with people I don't know. When I speak at news conferences, I'm nervous and way out of my comfort zone. Of course, I'm used to it by now and try to put on a smile, but that doesn't mean the situation gets any easier to handle.

I speak my mind when I believe I can make a difference. I express my view when I think people may otherwise misunderstand what's going on. I put myself out there. But that doesn't mean I like the limelight. Actually, behind it all, I'm a quiet, uncomplicated person. I can count the number of close friends on one hand. I prefer to be private. I don't want to be the centre of attention. But that's not the life I can lead with the career I've chosen for myself, and I can live with that.

People think they know me, but they don't.

You want to know who the real Rassie Erasmus is? Let me tell you …

1

THE NAME RASSIE CAME LATER. For the first 18 years of my life I was simply Hannie, the shortened version of the name on my birth certificate: Johan. That's me – simply Johan Erasmus. No other names.

My old school friends and people who knew me as a laaitie still call me Hannie.

Despatch, where I grew up in the Eastern Cape, is a small working-class town, home to 40 000 people, about 30 kilometres from Port Elizabeth (PE; now Gqeberha). I was born on 5 November 1972 in the provincial hospital of the neighbouring town of Uitenhage just across the bridge over the Swartkops River. Despatch didn't have a hospital. It's that small.

Most of the people who lived in Despatch worked at the Goodyear factory or at Volkswagen in Uitenhage. They're proud people and they work hard. Never windgat. You couldn't be windgat in Despatch, because there was nothing to be windgat about.

I am the youngest of three. My eldest sister is Martlie, eight years older than me. She and her husband Bert and their two children have lived in England for the past 20 years, where she works as a social worker for the National Health Service. Despite the distance between us, we are still very close.

Then there's my other sister Gerda, three years older than me, who lives with her husband Willie and their two children on a farm in Baviaanskloof. When I was growing up, that farm belonged to my grandparents, and we would go there every single holiday. The tradition continues to this day, and I try as often as I can to go to the farm to get away from the stress of my job. Gerda and I have a wonderful relationship because we are closer in age. When I started high school, she was in Standard 9 (Grade 11).

After Gerda was born in Caledon, my parents moved to Despatch. They moved around a bit before finally settling in a small house at 98 President Reitz Street. I remember that house so well. So many good things happened there. And some bad things.

When I look back on my life in Despatch, I can say I was a happy boy in that small town, with lots of friends; I enjoyed school and was success-ful playing sport. I had a loving, supportive mother and two wonderful sisters. My father was difficult, but I loved him all the same.

Let me tell you about my complicated father, Abel Hermanus Erasmus. While he did play a bit of rugby at school and at teachers' training college, he was more artistic and an incredible musician. My sisters inherited those talents. I got my sporting abilities from my mom.

My father came from Sunland, 25 kilometres from Kirkwood and around 45 kilometres from Despatch, in the Sundays River Valley. Abel's father, my grandfather, had an unusual job. He was known as the *waterfiskaal* (water-fiscal), the guy who regulated the water flow through the irrigation systems for the citrus farms on the banks of the Sundays River. I used to love visiting him in his office, with its 30-plus large stopwatches – big, silver government-issued *nekhorlosies* (necklace watches) that were used to time how long the irrigation sluices would be open to irrigate the land. For example, a farmer would get water for two hours, timed to the last second by those big stopwatches the workers wore on a strap around their necks.

My dad's younger brother, Erik Erasmus, known fondly as Oom Moos, loved to tell the story of how my father arrived home one evening with his clothes torn and covered in blood and mud. He was shaking in fear. Moos, who was about 10 years old at the time, thought it was a monster at the gate and fled. It turned out my father had been hit by a train, which

4

must have either been going very slowly or hit him with no more than a glancing blow. He wasn't badly hurt, more shaken up by the experience. Even after my dad passed away, Moos was still laughing at the story of the day he thought his older brother was a monster at the gate.

My father could play just about any musical instrument: *trekklavier* (piano accordion), concertina, electric guitar, banjo, ukelele, you name it. He was so talented. If it was new to him, he would learn to play it within half an hour. He played in a band and was often the master of ceremonies at weddings and dances in the town hall. He was a very clever man; he went to school at the age of four, could play the piano when he was four, and finished school when he was 16.

One of my favourite memories is when my father would gather the family together on a Sunday and play music. It didn't happen very often, but it was so special when it did. My two sisters are very musical. Martlie can sing, and Gerda can play the organ and piano. My mom and I have no rhythm and we can't sing, so we would get the tambourine and the shakers, and my dad would be on the electric guitar. We'd then have our own concert. Those were happy times, but sadly they were rare.

My father had his demons, and his main demon was alcohol.

He would come home from work, open a bottle of Mainstay cane spirits, and drink until he passed out. We had a laundry room next to the kitchen where my dad kept his Mainstay, or *bloukop-soldaatjies* (blue-helmeted soldiers), as my mom called them because of their blue bottle tops. There were so many of those bottles, mainly empty. When my father was sober, he'd joke that he could make a lot of money by returning the empties.

At about six in the evening, he would take a beer glass – the one with a short stem – and half-fill it with cane spirits. No ice, no water, no mixer. Just straight cane. He would down it and then go to the lounge to watch TV. Twenty minutes later, he'd be back in the laundry pouring another.

He would walk around in his underpants, with his boepens sticking out, from the lounge to the laundry room and back, until the bottle was empty or until he was so drunk that he couldn't get out of his chair, until he couldn't talk and couldn't argue.

It was nerve-wracking to have him walking around in his underpants, in case somebody outside of the family saw him. We hid him from visitors, and my sisters never wanted to bring boyfriends back to our house.

He never physically assaulted us, but his drinking scared me. If he wanted to pick an argument when he was drunk, we knew to just walk away. If you want to argue with a drunk, you're just going to get into an even bigger argument. My parents slept in separate rooms, and the best thing to do was get him into his room.

But he wasn't completely safe there. When we got him to his room, he would – every night, without exception – lie on his side and start beating himself on his legs. He'd slap himself very hard, over and over again. Then he would rub his legs and repeat the slapping. On and on it would go. It upset me and I tried to stop him. I wanted to protect him, so I would lie next to him and hold his hand to stop him hitting himself. I tried putting some towels over his legs so it wasn't that hard a slap. I would also lie behind him and hold him, which sometimes worked. All I wanted to do was comfort him because I could see he was in anguish.

I'd have to play mind games too. I'd say, *'Pa, kan ek hier by Pa lê? Ek voel alleen'* (Dad, can I lie next to you? I feel so alone). I wouldn't say, *'Pa, ek wil jou beskerm,* (Dad, I want to protect you). I would just lie behind him so that he could feel like it's a hug.

He wouldn't let me into the room if I said, *'Pa, ek wil jou help'* (Dad, I want to help you) or *'Pa, moet asseblief nie vir Pa so slaan nie'* (Dad, please don't slap yourself like that). Slapping wasn't a decision he made. He couldn't help himself. Some nights you felt he was never going to stop. Many times I just stood and watched.

I remember one night my friend David Malan was visiting and he could hear my father slapping himself in his bedroom. I confided in David and explained what was happening. David tried to lighten the terrible situation by saying, 'No, no, it's mosquitoes – your dad is hitting mosquitoes against the wall.'

When my father drank at functions at which his band was playing, I was always nervous he'd have too much. The band would start up and they would slowly drink more and more. My dad would get tipsy and close his eyes while he was playing. It was like he was in another world, as if the music and the drink took him away from his troubles.

I remember a friend asking, 'Why does your dad close his eyes when he plays?' I told him, 'When you're really good, you don't have to look at your instrument.' But I knew what was really going on, and I would worry that he would get too drunk. I hated that. I didn't want him to embarrass me. Or embarrass himself.

On some occasions we tried to stop the drinking early so that it wouldn't spiral out of control. Soon after he started drinking, we would get him into his room and lock the door. But then all hell would break loose. He would bang on the door until we opened it. Then he would walk to the laundry room, fill up his glass and sit back down in front of the TV, and repeat the process until the Mainstay bottle was empty.

Once we had to rush him to hospital because he mistakenly took a big slug from a bottle of Jik. Somebody had put the Jik bottle in the fridge and my father, in his drunken state, thought it was milk and took a huge gulp. He started vomiting. I was 14 years old and had to jump in the car and race, with the hazards on, to my cousin, and they took him to the hospital.

On Sundays, we often visited my grandparents in Kirkwood. I remember an incident when I was about 10 years old. Even though it was a Sunday, my dad was already drunk and wanted to go to Kirkwood, but my sisters and mother refused to go with him. I heard my father say I was the only person who could drive him.

As bizarre as it sounds now, it was much safer that way. For me, it was lekker to drive and be safe with my family alongside me. At the age of about 10, in Standard 4 (Grade 6), I started driving us to my maternal grandparents' farm in Baviaanskloof or my paternal grandparents' home in Kirkwood. I had to because my father would be just too drunk. He insisted I drive, not my mother or sisters. We had an automatic Ford Cortina. I would take a big pillow and sit on it so I could see over the steering wheel. My father sat next to me, with my mom and sisters in the back. I know now that it's insane, but we didn't think it at the time. I was a good driver. I also learnt to drive the tractor and the lorries on the farm, so driving the Cortina wasn't a big deal and everyone felt quite safe.

On this particular day, I didn't want to go with him to Kirkwood. I didn't want him to find me to ask me, so I hid. But he knew I was somewhere in the house.

My sisters came to warn me. '*Pa soek jou*' (Dad is looking for you). So I said, '*Nee, ek gaan nie nou saam met hom ry nie*' (No, I'm not going to ride with him). They told him, '*Johan is nie hier nie – hy gaan nie saam nie*' (Johan isn't here – he's not going with you).

So he went to his room, picked up his .303 rifle and came looking for me. '*Hy is hier!*' (He is here!)

My sisters rushed to me. '*Kruip weg – hy soek jou. Hy't 'n geweer*' (Hide – he's looking for you. He's got a gun). They were clearly very scared, and if they were scared, I was certainly not going to confront him. I remember that I wasn't afraid. I knew he wouldn't really shoot me.

I climbed onto the roof of our house and lay there until my sisters told me he had passed out. I remember one of our neighbours spotting me on the roof and asking what was going on. I told them I was looking for my tennis ball. Then I just lay there, bored, waiting for him to pass out on his bed.

My father never physically hurt me, but he would say things to hurt me. My mother also suffered that mental abuse. He knew how big rugby was for me, and after my team lost to Framesby High School, he'd say something like, '*Ja, jy met jou dun nekkie, jy sal nêrens kom nie – julle kan nie eers vir Framesby wen nie'* (Yes, you with your thin little neck, you'll never amount to much – your team can't even beat Framesby).

That hurt me 10 times more than him wanting to shoot me.

I remember when my dad was driving us to Port Elizabeth and he was drunk. My friend David Malan was with me in the back and my mom was in the passenger seat. As he turned onto the N2 highway to PE, he ended up on the wrong side of the road, heading straight into the oncoming traffic. My mom was too afraid to say anything, and David eventually nudged me and said, *'Jou pa ry nie aan die regte kant van die pad nie'* (Your dad isn't driving on the correct side of the road).

My dad called me Kwedin (isiXhosa for 'small boy'). So I said, *'Pa, kan Kwedin nie bestuur nie?'* (Dad, can't I drive?) He pulled off the highway, and I got behind the wheel and drove.

Even though he had been a teacher, he didn't take an interest in my schoolwork. He came to some of my rugby matches when I was in primary school because they started early, around 8am or 9am, but when I was in high school and playing for the first team, the games would start at 11am or 12pm. He would watch for a short while and then drive off to someone's house to start drinking again.

It was embarrassing when the headmaster and the dominee came to the house to say, *'Ons is hier vir julle. Ons weet waardeur julle gaan'* (We are here for you. We know what you're going through). They could come round for a chat, but they would do fuck-all to help us. I was embarrassed for my mom. And my dad. I didn't want the headmaster and the dominee to know anything about us. Just go away, we'll be okay. I hate it when somebody says 'I'm there for you'. Rather say nothing. Just be there. Really be there.

I don't think people at his work knew my dad was an alcoholic. He woke up every morning at 5.30am, and before he drove off to work, he drank a glass of soda water. Then he would get into his government-spon-sored Mazda 323 and head off to Port Elizabeth where he worked for the

Department of Bantu Administration (later, with the demise of apartheid, it was abolished and some of its functions shared among various departments). He never missed a day's work and was never drunk at work.

The thing that gets me is the way he sobered up after I left home at the age of 18 and was in the army. My mom had made the decision to stay with him for as long as the children were still in the house. Then, after Martlie left to study at the University of Port Elizabeth and Gerda later moved to Bloemfontein, she told herself to hang in there because she knew I didn't want her to leave my dad. As soon as I left for the army in Bloemfontein, she filed for divorce. My father's parents took him home to Kirkwood, where they looked after him and helped him manage the withdrawal symptoms. They kept him in his room away from alcohol until he was able to control his addiction and stop drinking.

If only that had happened years earlier. If my father had received proper help in the early 1980s, when he started drinking, he might be alive today. When I was young, alcoholics were seen as bad people who had chosen this life for themselves. No one helped us as the family, and we couldn't help ourselves because we didn't know what to do.

My mom is Maria Elizabeth Erasmus (née Terblanche), and she was the sporty one in the family. She was a sprinter and she played netball. I get my sporting abilities from her. She's in her eighties now. She was my biggest supporter when I played sport at school. She still is my biggest supporter. She would throw a tennis ball for me for hours, not only for me to practise but because we both loved it.

We made up our own games. Our kitchen chairs had metal legs with rubber plugs on the bottom, and I would tilt a chair onto its front legs and bounce-bounce-bounce, balancing on the two legs. My mom would count how many times I could bounce without falling over. We'd count up to 130, and the next day she'd say, 'Come, let's go again,' and I'd bounce, bounce to 140. I loved that game.

My mother worked at the local municipality. She knew every plot number in Despatch. If you showed her where someone lived, she could tell you their plot number and if they paid their rates and taxes on time.

My primary school, Susannah Fourie, was right next door to the municipality. From her office window, my mom could see the school gate and the sports fields. She would watch me playing rugby from her office. She would watch all my games, either through her office window, or standing at the side of the field. She still watches cricket, netball and rugby and has plenty to say about the way the games are played. She has strong views about the tackle laws. She'll say: '*Niemand kan sonder sy bene hardloop nie. Jy moet vir daai Springbokspan sê*' (No one can run without their legs. You must tell that Springbok team). And I tell her: '*Ja, Ma, ek sal vir hulle sê*' (Yes, Mom, I'll tell them).

My parents met at the teachers' training college in Graaff-Reinet. My father became a teacher in Port Elizabeth when he was only 18 years old, and, for a brief period when he was 24, he was an acting headmaster at a school in Graaff-Reinet. He, however, eventually gave up teaching because it didn't pay the bills. Those were the days before he started drinking.

Many of my family went into teaching, including Oom Moos and my father's sister, Tannie Tilla. My mom's sister was a teacher and my sister Martlie taught art for a while before moving into social work. I had plans to become a Physical Education teacher, but that didn't work out.

On my mother's side, there was my grandfather, Daniel Johannes Terblanche. We called him Oupa Bokkedaat – it has no meaning, it was just a nickname. He and my grandmother, Ouma Marta, had three children: my mom, my Tannie Taniela and my Oom Boetie.

Oupa Bokkedaat was a rich, successful farmer in the Baviaanskloof. His farm was our holiday spot every holiday. It still is. My oupa tried his hand at anything. He farmed goats, cattle and sheep, and grew tobacco, pumpkins and onion seed. He eventually owned four or five farms. He was strict too. He allowed no alcohol in the house. He was even against having a glass of wine with a meal, so my father would sneak a drink behind the barn. I never saw him drunk in front of my oupa.

Let me tell you about my life growing up surrounded by the people of Despatch.

The Human family lived next door. Oom Piet and Tannie Leah and their five children: Gerhard (nicknamed Pote), Dawie, Herman (nicknamed Harry), Siegie and Leah. The boys all played rugby. Pote, who is 13 years older than me, was the most successful. He played over 200 provincial rugby matches for Eastern Province and Free State and coached the Bulls. He now coaches the Houston SaberCats in the USA. In 2006, Pote and I were the opposing coaches of the teams that shared the Currie Cup after the final ended in a 28–all draw. That was an impossible dream to consider when we lived next door to each other in Despatch.

The Humans were a second family for me. They looked after me. A simple fence separated our houses, with a hole that I could crawl through. I spent most of my time with them. Often, when I was in trouble, I would escape to their house and hide. They understood my family and what was going on.

Harry walked me to school on my very first day. It was something he and Siegie did often when I was young because school was close by. I walked to school until the age of 16 when I got a 50cc motorbike.

I used to wear the clothes the Human boys had outgrown, not because my mother couldn't afford new clothes – it was just what you did in Despatch. If clothes could still be worn and they fit, why not wear them? School uniforms would pass down from successive Human boys to me.

I remember that the Humans had boxing gloves. We would fight each other in their front yard, challenging anyone who walked past to a fight. They would come in, try their luck against the bigger Human boys, maybe get knocked down, and then just carry on walking. Despatch people have a knack for fighting. The town is a tough place. If there's a brawl, few will stand back. Not because they're troublemakers, but people don't just say, 'Ag, well,' and walk on. They'd get stuck in.

Our garden fights were proper. We would box against each other for three rounds, really moering each other – but with boxing gloves on. Even Pote, so much older than me, would fight me. And he wouldn't just come out and flatten me, even though he could. It was never vicious, but it was hard.

On the corner lived Willie and Gerhard Meyer. Willie, who is five years older than me, would later become a Springbok teammate and play 26 Test matches.

Rugby was our favourite sport. To get a game going, all I had to do was walk into the street and whistle to call my friends. Nobody ever phoned each other. We just had to whistle loudly. I would whistle and then the Humans would whistle, the Meyers would whistle, and my friends Conrad Fouche and Pieter O'Neill (who later played SA Schools and for Boland) and his brother Paul would whistle. And Riaan Scholtz and Werner Terblanche. The whole street would be filled with whistles. We're in, we're in, we're in – and very quickly a group of players had formed.

Sometimes we played in someone's yard until it got dark. Most often we would head to an open piece of land, a barely used park, about 800 metres from my house and close to the church, where we would measure out a rugby field and play.

Right across from Susannah Fourie Primary School is Despatch High School, also known as Hoërskool Despatch, and further along is the main rugby field. That's where I played my first-ever game of rugby, not counting the private social games in the park. These days, alongside that field is the Rassie Erasmus Pavilion. Every time I go to Despatch, I visit the field. I feel very proud and quite overwhelmed that the pavilion is named after me. It's lekker to show my kids the pavilion, but when my name was unveiled I wasn't sure if I deserved the honour for doing something I loved and for which I got paid.

Pote and Siegie were my first rugby heroes because they played for Despatch Rugby Club as well as Eastern Province. But my main hero was another Despatch local, the Springbok legend Danie Gerber. The sports complex at Despatch High is named after him.

I didn't have to go too far to see him. His grandmother lived up the road and I would see him when he came to visit her. Danie was a super-star. He's still regarded as one of the best centres in the world ever to play Test rugby. He scored 19 tries for South Africa in 24 Test matches and played 179 provincial games for Eastern Province, Western Province and Free State. I was seven years old when he made his international debut. In my small world, the fact that he played for Despatch Rugby Club was a very big deal. I never missed a single home game.

Danie and Pote went on training runs through the streets of Despatch. They were incredibly tough. They would load their floppy green rucksacks with a couple of bricks and then go for an eight-kilometre run, carrying the rucksacks on their backs. Afterwards, when they took the rucksacks off, they would show us the chafe marks. That impressed us so much.

My friends and I would ride our bikes alongside them or run with them, just to be near them. They would run through the cemetery and on the outskirts of the township. I was shit-scared of that cemetery, but the township intrigued me. At that young age, I didn't question why black people lived there. It was just the way things were.

I played a lot of sports, both for my school and for the Despatch Sports Club – rugby in winter, cricket in summer. Tennis as well. My friends and I would play rugby and afterwards we would switch on the lights at the club's tennis courts and play until late into the evening.

I won my age group in Standard 7 (Grade 9) and then gave up tennis. But two years later I decided to have another go and won my age group without any training and using an old tennis racket. I remember that my opponent in the semifinal was a boy called Morne Mostert. He went on to have a hugely successful career. Not as a tennis player, but as an academic.

That came as no surprise because, while I was academically quite bright, averaging around 75%, Morne would be getting 95%. He is now Dr Morne Mostert, serves on the National Planning Commission, and is Director of the Institute for Futures Research at Stellenbosch University. He teaches us how to think about things that haven't happened yet. We always knew Morne would go places with his way of thinking. He is incredibly smart, but he remains a down-to-earth, lekker guy today. He comes from Despatch, after all.

In summer I played cricket. From primary school to high school, I was often the opening batsman and opening bowler. Oom Moos, my father's brother, lived with us, and he and I played cricket in the backyard. We placed various objects, like a bin, in the garden to be the fielders. If you hit the object, you were caught. The wicket stretched the length of the driveway, with the house wall on one side and the neighbour's wall on the other. If you hit the wall, or hit the ball back past the bowler, it was a four. I had to bowl one over spin, one over fast, one over medium, until I got 10 wickets. Tannie Tilla kept score.

I was good enough to play Nuffield Week trials in matric but didn't make the Eastern Province team. I didn't enjoy cricket as much as rugby. It didn't feel like a team sport to me. Whether you were batting, bowling or fielding, I always felt you were on your own.

I also tried my luck with cycling. In my final year at primary school, I decided to enter a cycle race sponsored by the *Oosterlig* newspaper. I can't remember how far it was – I think it was 45 to 65 kilometres. I had skinny legs and I didn't really have a proper racing bicycle. The route took us through Uitenhage, out towards Jeffreys Bay, and back to Port Elizabeth. There are quite a few hills just before you get to St Albans Prison (which is where Charles Wessels, our current Springbok team manager, was detained as a political activist in the 1980s).

A photo appeared in the *Oosterlig* of me on one of those long hills, wearing tracksuit pants my mom had made for me. I didn't give her time to buy any of the proper kit my friends were wearing. Those pants were made from wool, which chafed me and made me very hot. I think I wore my school shoes. The caption read: '*Sjoe, hierdie bult is steil, dink Johan Erasmus*' (Shew, this hill is steep, thinks Johan Erasmus), and there's another photo of me pushing my bike while a female competitor – a young girl – rides past me.

Rugby was my main sport. I started playing at pre-primary school, Despatch Voorbereidingskool, where Frikkie Meyer – a legend in the town – was our coach. I still remember our little green jerseys with brown collars when I was in the under-9 A team. I carried on playing when I went to Susannah Fourie Primary School and was one of the fastest runners so I played flyhalf. At Despatch High, you had no choice – if you were a boy, you played rugby. We had to bring a certificate from the doctor if we missed practice. I was quite chubby at first, until about Standard 5 (Grade 7). In high school I became tall and thin and played flyhalf up to the age of 16 because I was quite fast, but as I got older and taller, my coaches realised I was better suited to being a fast loose forward. I was also the captain of the team.

From a young age, I could instinctively analyse a rugby game and played better when I relied on those instincts. The moment I had time to think about the situation, I'd overdo it. If I knew we were doing a particular move from a lineout, but play was delayed by an injury, I would overthink the move and end up cancelling it because I knew I would mess it up.

Tennis was always a challenge because I had time to overthink the situation between games. I was good at rallies, though, because then everything happened fast and instinctively.

At that age, I didn't really know that I was good at rugby. But then one day in primary school one of the coaches, Pypie van Vuuren, was dividing us into groups and said to me: '*Okay, Tiger, staan daar*' (stand there). I wasn't sure what he meant and thought he was teasing me. I said, '*Wie is jou Tiger?'* (Who's your Tiger?) He said he meant I was tough, that I never stopped running, and I tackled everyone. I was delighted and wanted to stay Tiger, but the nickname didn't stick. I was still Hannie to everyone.

Our main rivals were Uitenhage's Hoërskool Brandwag, which we always beat, and Hoërskool Daniel Pienaar, which were much tougher opponents. When I was in matric and captain of the first team, Pote Human was playing for Free State and he organised for Despatch High to play against the country's premier rugby school, Grey College in Bloemfontein. I knew nothing about them.

I was amazed at the size of their players, the size of the school, the traditions and the war cries. Just before we ran out, I had to go to the toilet. I didn't like to use the change-room toilets so I went and found the normal school toilets. As I was having a pee, I could hear someone locking the door to the toilet block. I tried calling out, but the person just kept on walking.

These were the days before cellphones. I knew the teams were about to run on to the field and they'd be waiting for me to lead Despatch out. But I was locked in. The windows were too high and too small for me to crawl through. I shouted and shouted for help, but there was nobody in the school buildings. They were all at the rugby field. I got quite desperate and kept yelling.

Finally, a teacher heard me. I shouted that I was captain of Despatch and was needed on the field. The rather-surprised teacher had to find the caretaker and I was eventually freed. I sprinted to the field where the impatient players were waiting, and we ran out with the match slightly delayed by the visiting captain's pee.

Grey College has the most amazing home record in rugby. Since 1855, they have won 91% of their home games. But then they came up against little Despatch High. At halftime we were ahead 7–4 (in the days when a try counted for four points). People were starting to get excited. Could Despatch do the unthinkable and beat the mighty Grey College? I would love to tell you that the story has a great fairy-tale ending of triumph against all odds. But it doesn't. Back then, I didn't know Grey College has a reputation for coming back in the second half. They ran riot over us. We didn't score another point and lost 7–50.

In 1990, my matric year, I played in the Eastern Province trials for Craven Week, the premier interprovincial schools rugby competition. The trials were held in Uitenhage, and I had a good tournament. The team to represent Eastern Province at Craven Week in Durban was to be announced in the *Oosterlig* newspaper, so when the paper hit the streets just after midnight, my mom slipped out without me knowing to get a copy. She was so keen for me to make the team that she couldn't wait until morning when it would be delivered to our front door.

It wasn't a big deal for me to make Craven Week. Because my world was small and I was happy in that world, I wasn't ready to travel to Durban. Apart from visiting Bloemfontein and Baviaanskloof, I'd barely been out of the Eastern Cape. I didn't have an adventurous streak that made me want to travel. I hate embarrassment and I was worried that I wouldn't be able to cope. If I didn't make the side, I knew life would just go on. Craven Week wasn't an obsession.

But it was a big deal for my mom. It made me nervous because she was so nervous. The *Oosterlig* was produced and printed in PE, but she found out where it would be dropped off for distribution in Despatch and went to get a copy just after midnight. When I woke up the next morning, she played it cool and asked me to get the newspaper from the front door. She already knew I had made the team, selected as eighthman. She was unbelievably happy and proud – and so was I.

I can't remember my father's reaction. I don't recall him saying anything to me, but he must have been proud because they both drove up from Despatch to Durban to watch the tournament while I flew to Durban with the team. At the age of 17, it was the first time I had ever been on an airplane.

I was nervous about playing Craven Week, but my anxiety was not about the rugby. I was anxious about embarrassing myself. There were so many things I didn't know. What's it like in a hotel? I'd never stayed in one. When I went on tour, we always stayed at other people's homes. I'd never been in a team where you shower after the game and get dressed in the change rooms. I always showered at home. Do I take my own soap or is the soap there? Do I take a towel, or do they give us towels? I was worried about which knife and fork to use at functions. These small things bothered me. The outside world was nerve-wracking.

But on the field I was not nervous for one second. I just played to enjoy the game. I didn't worry about making the SA Schools team, which is selected at the end of Craven Week. I didn't even know such a team got selected. That's how narrow my world was. I thought there would be a grand final, but there isn't one at Craven Week. I don't remember much about the games, but I think we lost to Northern Transvaal. I remember that some of my teammates did really well for themselves. Michael Catt, from Grey High in PE, went on to have a successful career with England, playing 75 Test matches. Our flyhalf, Greg Miller, eventually played for Border.

From the opposition, I remember Western Province's eighthman, Dion O'Cuinneagain. He was from Rondebosch Boys' High and an incredible sportsman. At the end of Craven Week, he was selected for the SA Schools team as eighthman, not me. I wasn't disappointed, though, because I didn't really expect to make the Schools team as Dion was certainly the better player.

I would come up against Dion in Currie Cup games when I played for Free State and he represented Western Province. Later we met in a Test match when Dion made his debut for Ireland (his dad was Irish) against South Africa in a vicious encounter at the Free State Stadium in Bloemfontein. We were both on the flank, and the Springboks won 37–13.

Rugby was a very big deal in Despatch. The sport and the town were intertwined. You couldn't avoid it, and there was nothing to beat it. Sometimes you could get over a thousand people going to watch the Despatch first team training. About 2 000 would watch the Saturday club game. We idolised the players. I didn't miss a training session or a match. It took me five minutes to run from my house to the rugby club, and I'd be the ball boy and take sand out for the kickers.

When I got my 50cc motorbike at 16, I used to ride to the stadium on a Saturday for a big match, with the school mascot, a huge teddy bear, on the back of my bike. I would ride down the main street, resting my back against the bear. For me, it was the lekkerest ride.

I had close connections with some of Despatch Rugby Club's first team. My high-school headmaster, Jan Hurter, was the coach there; my school rugby coach and maths and accounts teacher, Koenie Strumpher, played hooker, Oom Moos played prop and my sister's best friend's boy-friend, Hennie Bezuidenhout, played fullback. Also in the team were some of the big names in Eastern Province rugby, like Elandré van der Bergh and Frans Erasmus (both Springboks), Mynhardt le Roux, Giepie van Zyl, Neels Lombard, and the big winger Kallie Grobler.

The player who had the biggest impact on my life was the Despatch first-team captain Gideon van Rensburg, leading the team when Despatch twice won the National Club Championships. His day job was working for the municipality, where he knew my mother. Gideon made sure the municipality ran efficiently and was the go-to guy when things went wrong if there was a power outage or a water leak. And, because he was the captain of Despatch, he was a big deal in town. Certainly not a windgat, though.

He had seen me playing at school in my matric year and one day he told me I needed to get stronger if I wanted to be more successful with my game. Without me asking, he started to come to my house every morning at 5am to take me to the local gym to train with him. There was only one gym in town and Gideon had the key. It was quite a primitive set-up compared to the facilities I have access to today.

I never found out why he decided to help me. At first, I was worried that my mom had asked him to help because of my dad's situation, but I like to think he did it because he saw something in me and believed I could play for Despatch one day if I trained properly. I never asked my mom and I never asked Gideon. I don't want to know the truth if it wasn't that. All I know is that he did it for a whole year and it made a big difference because that was the year I made the Craven Week side. To this day I find it the most selfless thing for him to have done. Why would the Despatch captain drive to the house of a 17-year-old laaitie, take him to gym, teach him strength exercises and then drop him off again – and tell no one about it? It's unbelievable for me to think he would make such an effort. At the time, I thought he would maybe do it once or twice, but he did it for the whole bloody year. I remain so grateful.

A few of the Despatch first-team players got some money from a local lawyer, Piet Hancke, who helped fund the Despatch Rugby Club. To be a Despatch rugby player and get a little bit of extra money was unbelievable.

When I was 12 years old, Despatch won the prestigious National Club Championships in Durban for the first time, beating some highly fancied clubs that had better resources. It was the biggest thing to happen to Despatch – until they won it again three years later, and then two years after that.

One of my longest excursions out of Despatch was to the club champs in 1985 with one of my best friends Murto Loots and his father. I had known Murto from Grade 1, and his family would sometimes come on holiday with us to Baviaanskloof. They were probably the only friends my dad had. Tragically, Murto died of a heart attack when he was just 19 years old. It was shattering for me. He had battled with heart problems and during one operation something went wrong and he was never really the same. He had to go to a special school just outside Port Elizabeth, but we stayed as close as we could.

I will never forget that adventure to the club champs, made more special because Despatch won. I knew all the players. Danie Gerber was the captain, Siegie Human was my next-door neighbour, Gerhard Meyer lived up the road, Koenie Strumpher was my accounts teacher, Frans Erasmus owned the local garage.

At that young age, my dream was to play for Despatch Rugby Club. I never dreamt of playing for the Springboks. Despite what I was able to achieve in my career as a rugby player, I only managed to play one game for Despatch. It happened when I was in the army in 1992 and was in Despatch on a weekend pass. In those days there was a first team, a first reserve team, then a second and third team. There were no reserves for the first team. No Bomb Squad. Instead, the first reserve-team players would play against the opposition reserves and then sit on the sidelines for the main game in case someone was injured. My army pass coincided with a Despatch home game and I finally got to play fullback for the reserve team. At the time I was playing Free State under-20, but I never got to play for the Despatch first team.

For the first 12 years of my life, my universe was very small – Despatch and Baviaanskloof. We'd never go to Port Elizabeth, which was just 30 kilometres away, to visit a restaurant or go to the beach. Sometimes I would catch a lift or hitchhike with my friends to Boet Erasmus Stadium to watch my heroes play rugby for Eastern Province, or to St George's Park to watch Benson & Hedges one-day cricket. When we were older, my buddies and I went there on our motorbikes.

Everything important happened in Despatch, particularly in the hall next to the rugby club. When I think of that hall, I see many things – church bazaars, wrestling matches, judo and karate competitions, matric dances, sokkies, functions after every Despatch rugby match – if you were lucky enough to be able to sneak in. For a lot of people in Despatch, their lives revolved around that hall.

2

AT SCHOOL, I HAD A GROUP OF SIX FRIENDS and we called ourselves 'The Boys'. During break time, we played hard contact rugby in the quad, ending up all sweaty and with shirts torn. The teachers complained and insisted we stop 10 minutes before break time ended to shower before going back to class. The headmaster loved rugby so much that he allowed us to play on and get to class a little late.

All of us could have had girlfriends, but there was no time for that. All we were interested in was rugby and being boys. There were social events with the girls, like roller-skating evenings where you paid R10 and skated around the school quad holding a girl's hand.

I remember I wasn't interested in going to my matric dance, but my mother persuaded me to ask Liesl van Eeden, the girl across the road. I walked over to her house and said, 'If no one else's asked you, do you want to go to the dance?' And she said, 'Ja, sure.'

That's the way we did it in Despatch. Simple and innocent. We didn't plan our outfits, there were no pre-drinks nor huge after-party. Not like my kids today. It's crazy. You hire cars. It's like the grandest wedding ever.

Despatch people don't pronounce rugby properly. They say 'ruppy', never 'rugby'. We don't talk about *wasgoedpennetjies* or washing pegs. We say 'pecks'. If you put a Despatch person in a room with 10 other people speaking Afrikaans, I'll tell you which one is from Despatch.

There was a side to my father that understood what was really going on in Despatch, and in South Africa, beyond our whites-only borders. He told me about his work at Bantu Administration issuing dompasse. I remember how upset he became talking about issuing these documents so hated by black people. I sometimes wonder if this work played a part in his drinking. He told us the system was wrong, but I couldn't understand it because I would play with black and coloured children on my grandparents' farm. I slept alongside them. I didn't understand that in the towns and cities black people had to leave the white area by nightfall, and that only those with the correct dompas got to stay. The pass law system messed with his mind.

He hadn't started drinking that day, but he got quite emotional about an incident when a group of people had gathered outside his office building in Port Elizabeth, expecting to receive money that had been promised to them. I've kept a newspaper article about the incident, which ended violently after police fired rubber bullets to disperse the crowd. My father said the people were very calm and weren't trying to cause any trouble. He had told the people they would get their money and they'd accepted his word, so there was no need for aggression from the police. He was very angry at the way the whole incident was handled.

I was so naïve politically. Only later in my life did I realise how we were kept away from the harsh realities of life outside our little whites-only town in the 1970s and 1980s. The township of Khayamnandi was only a few kilometres outside of Uitenhage, but it might as well have been in another country because I never went there and knew nothing about what happened there. We had three domestic workers at different stages of my childhood. First there was Maina, followed later by Dorothy and then Gladys, who worked in the house and looked after me when my parents were at work. They lived in the township, but I never thought to find out what life was like there.

The language we used to refer to black people was incredibly derogatory. When I was growing up, the terms were so common that it seemed

normal. I don't for one second suggest this justified its use. I'm just pointing out the realities of growing up in a town like Despatch and the racism
that was part of society in those days. I didn't know how demeaning it was
to call a black adult a 'boy' or 'girl'. Or, even worse, to use the k-word.

The first time I realised the hurt caused by the k-word I was 10 years
old and used it to address an elderly black man. I was riding my bike and
the chain came off. I saw the man across the road and recognised him from
occasions when he had helped in the garden. I didn't know his name, so
I did what I had heard so many adults do – I called him by the k-word.
I will never forget his face. It haunts me to this day. It was almost like he
said, 'Fuck you, little white boy.' But he still came over, helped me put the
chain on and left. I felt terrible. I realised I had said something wrong, but I
didn't know why. He didn't have to say, 'Hey, don't call me that.' I just knew.

I went home and told my parents what had happened. They were
horrified. I said, '*Maar almal praat so*' (But everybody talks like that). My
mother was very stern with me and told me it was the ugliest of words. My
father was angry – '*Moet dit nie weer doen nie!*' (Don't do it again!)

I was upset that I had insulted and embarrassed that man. I could see
it in his eyes. I've never forgotten that moment when I realised how my
words could cause so much harm. Maybe because I knew what it was like
to feel terrible as a result of someone else's words – my father's words had
hurt me many times. But this was far worse, and I was the cause of this
man feeling shit. I never wanted anyone to feel embarrassed. It was a massive wake-up call.

A few kilometres away from Despatch is the township of KwaNobuhle,
where black people who worked in Uitenhage lived because they were
not allowed to live in the whites-only areas in the apartheid days. I was
12 years old in Standard 5 (Grade 7) and completely clueless about what
was going on outside of the white area of Despatch. The 1980s were a time
of huge political protest and violence in the Eastern Cape. All the black
townships were affected, including KwaNobuhle. I vaguely remember

hearing adults talking about '*die onluste*' (the unrest), but it meant nothing to me.

Living in white Despatch, I was protected from the political violence in the black townships. It might seem strange to an outsider that these incidents didn't affect me, but there was a lot of censorship of the media during the state of emergency imposed in 1985, and the SABC, our only source of TV news, gave a very biased picture of what was going on. It was easy to live in a bubble, especially when your world was Despatch, Kirkwood, Baviaanskloof, and not much else.

One day in 1985 my father came home from work very upset by a horrific incident that had occurred in KwaNobuhle. I will never forget it because of the unusual name of the man involved: Benjamin Kinikini. He and members of his family had been murdered in the street. I remember how appalled my father was because people were joking that you could get steak-and-Kinikini pies in KwaNobuhle. He was upset and angry that people could joke about something so terrible.

Benjamin Kinikini was the first victim of a particularly brutal form of killing known as necklacing, where a tyre was put over the head of a victim, filled with petrol and set alight. Our domestic worker at the time, Dorothy, told me '*O, hierdie necklace is lelik*' (Oh, this necklace is ugly). I didn't understand – '*Hoe bedoel jy die necklace is lelik?*' (What do you mean the necklace is ugly?) She said, '*Dis lelik, jong. As daai tyre so aan is, dan wriemel daai mense nog so*' (It's ugly, young man. When that tyre is on, then those people squirm like this).

As the memory of the Benjamin Kinikini incident came back to me, I decided to find out more. I met a journalist, Ken Vernon, who ran the *Argus* newspaper's Port Elizabeth bureau. He told me the remarkable story of the Kinikini murder.

On Thursday the 21st of March 1985, I was on the phone to the police media-liaison officer Gerrie van Rooyen when he suddenly said, 'I have to go, something is happening in Uitenhage' and slammed down the phone. My gut feeling said get there. I found the township of Langa outside Uitenhage was sealed off. There had been strikes the previous weekend where several activists had been shot dead, and people were now marching to the funerals. The police closed off the area, preventing people from marching any further. Rocks were thrown and the police opened fire on the crowd, killing 19 people. This became known as the Langa Massacre, and it happened on the exact day of the 25th anniversary of the Sharpeville Massacre. That was the trigger for further political violence. In the nearby township of KwaNobuhle, all the councillors belonging to the Black Local Authority were told to resign. They were seen as collaborators with the apartheid state. One of them was Benjamin Kinikini, and I interviewed him the following day. He refused to resign, saying he wouldn't give in to what he called 'these thugs and vandals'. Famous last words because he was attacked the next morning, the 23rd of March. He was stabbed with a shovel and forced to drink petrol, after which a tyre was put around his neck and he was set alight. He is thought to be the very first victim of the notorious 'necklace'.

I hurried back to Langa with my photographer Willie de Klerk to find the area was still sealed off. You could only get in with an official police permit. Willie happened to have a permit for access to Langa township outside Cape Town. We tried our luck. Willie showed the Langa Cape Town permit to the police. They presumed it was for Langa Uitenhage and allowed us in. We used that permit for a couple of days before the police figured out it wasn't valid. Langa and KwaNobuhle were very tense, with a lot of police and army patrols and activists roaming the streets. Willie suggested I get out of there because a white face would attract problems. He ran off to take photographs while I quickly made my way to the outskirts of Langa. I nearly drove into a crowd of about three or four thousand hostile people walking up the street. I parked *up on a hill and watched what was going on through a big 600mm lens. Willie soon reappeared with the photograph of Benjamin Kinikini's charred remains in the street and people in the background giving black power salutes. In the distance, you could see the burnt remains of four of his sons and nephews who had also been attacked and set alight.*

Willie was lucky not to have the film confiscated, but he was highly experienced in operating in the townships. Once he got the photograph, he quickly removed the film, shoved it into his sock and put a new film into the camera. As expected, he was stopped by the police and told to remove the film from his camera, which he did, and they let him go with the incriminating film carefully hidden away. Willie's photograph of Kinikini's body was published around the world, bringing the horror of the situation to the attention of a global audience.

Only recently I learnt that two men were sentenced to death and hanged for their role in the Kinikini murders. At the time, I didn't know what to make of my father's anguish. I remember the gruesome photograph taken by Willie de Klerk. When you are 12 years old, you remember these images. It made me realise there was a lot going on that I didn't understand.

My parents saw through the conservative world of Despatch and the prejudice that was so normal. My father was an enlightened man, and he knew what was going on in the townships. I think he was terribly torn about the situation.

I matriculated in 1990 with a university-entrance matric and was named Despatch High's Rugby Player of the Year. I decided to go to the army the following year. In those days, all white males over the age of 18 were conscripted to do compulsory service in the South African Defence Force for a year. It had previously been a two-year call-up but had now been reduced.

I wanted to follow the family tradition and become a teacher, specialising in Physical Education. But we didn't have the money for university, and I couldn't get a sports bursary, even though I had played Craven Week rugby. The only option I had was to do my national service or go to jail, but no one in Despatch ever defied their call-up.

I was called up to the 6 South African Infantry battalion in Grahamstown, where I could be selected for the Junior Leader training programme (JLs) at the Infantry School in Oudtshoorn. I was very nervous about going – not because of the unit's fearsome reputation, but because I just didn't know Oudtshoorn.

But then Gysie Pienaar, legendary fullback for Free State and the Springboks, who had seen me play in that school match, phoned me out of the blue and said he had organised me a transfer to the Pantserskool (the School of Armour) in Bloemfontein.

None of my friends – The Boys – went to the army. Some studied, one joined the police, another became a mechanic. I was the only one who was conscripted into the military.

When I got to the army base, I thought, 'Fuck, how am I going to survive this?' I had been spoilt at home. I had never ironed my clothes, never made food for myself; I couldn't fry an egg or make a cup of coffee. Either my mom or Dorothy had done that for me. I had done cadets at school, so I understood a little bit about marching, but that was about it.

My parents drove me, but in separate cars because they were now living apart. I was thrown in among a lot of intimidating people I had never encountered before. There were guys with long hair, guys with beards, guys with degrees, guys who smoked weed. And me. The first thing that happened was that our heads were shaved. Once we had our hair cut, we all looked the same; no one was intimidating any more, and I felt, 'Okay, I'll be fine.'

We were handed brown overalls and takkies and then the punishing physical training began. I was fit, but only school-rugby fit, certainly not opfok fit, which is in another league altogether. The physical side of things was tough on everybody. The political stuff they tried to feed us meant

29

nothing to me. I didn't know what they were talking about. I didn't know the wider world and I didn't care about it. I didn't know that troops were patrolling the townships and that this was a big deal for the residents because it meant they were living in a war zone. Even though we trained for urban warfare, I was never sent to the townships, nor did I do any army duty related to the unrest.

Many times, all we had to eat was fruit, so I just went hungry because here's a weird thing about me – I have a phobia about fruit. *Ek gril my dood vir vrugte* (I shudder with revulsion at just the thought of fruit). I can't look at fruit, I can't touch fruit, I can't be around fruit, and I can't watch or listen to anyone eating fruit. I can't even pick up a piece of fruit and throw it in the rubbish bin. Going hungry was better than eating fruit.

After two weeks, I was placed on the Junior Leadership programme to become a lieutenant. I was determined to be successful and become a commissioned officer. I worked hard to make sure I did well in the course and got my rank, first lieutenant. When I was in Despatch, although I knew how to drive, I didn't even know how to open a car bonnet. But now I knew everything there was to know about the engines in military vehicles. I could change a Rooikat armoured vehicle's tyre and got a licence to drive four different types of vehicle, even a bus, which I can still do to this day.

As part of our training, we did war games out in the bush at De Brug, 35 kilometres from Bloemfontein, using live ammunition. When I was still a troep with no rank, I got myself into serious trouble during one of those exercises. We were on patrol and I started shooting the Browning machine gun mounted on top of our Rooikat. The crew chief in the Rooikat in front of me had his head out of his vehicle with the hatch open behind him. Luckily, the bullets hit the hatch, otherwise I would have shot him in the head and killed him. It was an extremely serious mistake, and as punishment I had to do hard physical exercise for the next three weeks, day and night. I was a target for anyone who wanted to punish me. The normal troops left me alone, but the officers made sure that I suffered. I had to stand aside for everyone else in the mess queue, which meant the food was gone by the time I got to the front.

I hardly slept or ate. The opfoks were terrible and I battled to get through them. I survived, of course, but I know of some troeps who went through a similar experience and were later discharged from the army on medical grounds. I'd rather go through that punishment than live with myself for having killed a fellow soldier.

That wasn't my only mistake. The following year, when I was a lieutenant, we were doing night-driving from 8pm to 8am. We were simulating a chemical war, and I was in charge of 16 Rooikat armoured vehicles, riding in the second vehicle in the convoy. We were right behind one another, about five metres apart, with all engines on low revolution in the quietest gear. We were all sealed inside our vehicles, with the hatches closed, looking out through night sights. It was a long night of boredom as we drove, so I made myself comfortable with a bottle of Old Brown Sherry and started to doze.

My driver woke me up to tell me he had come across an obstacle. He couldn't see what it was but the vehicle had become sluggish. I told him to push through. We had no lights on and each vehicle would follow the small orange convoy lights on the rear of the vehicle in front. My driver couldn't see the lights of the front vehicle through his night sights. I left my sleeping position and got into my seat. I immediately realised something was wrong because the Rooikat was barely moving even though the driver had his foot on the accelerator. I called up my superior officer, a major who was coordinating the operation from a remote venue, who told me to open my hatch and fire off a couple of flares to light up the area.

Immediately, I could see the problem. The Rooikat in front had driven into a dam and we had followed it in. The barrel of the lead vehicle was sticking out above the water, with the rest of it underwater. The vehicles were perfectly sealed so no water got in and no one realised we had driven straight into the dam. Looking out of the hatch on the top of the Rooikat, I

31

could touch the water around me. The water then started to seep through the seals, and the troops scrambled out, otherwise they would have drowned. The vehicle behind me was also submerged and the next one back had its nose underwater.

On the horizon I could see the major approaching and knew I was in for another opfok. A bigger armoured vehicle pulled us out of the dam with a heavy steel towbar, which was humiliating in itself, but the worst wasn't over. My whole crew was ordered to carry that huge towbar back to camp on foot. It took us seven hours, and we were shattered when we got back to base. This time the opfok was longer than three weeks, but I survived because I was very fit. On weekends, I had to stay on my own at De Brug out in the veld, while my fellow officers were free to take time out in Bloemfontein. The punishment felt so much longer because I wasn't allowed to play sport for three months.

Despite having played first-team rugby at school and Craven Week for Eastern Province, initially I hardly played any rugby in the army other than a bit of social rugby between the squadrons, and that was it. When teams were picked shortly after we arrived, they said, 'Hands up those who played for Grey College or Paul Roos Gymnasium.' About 30 guys put up their hands. Then, 'Who's played for SA Schools?' Seven or eight hands went up. 'Who played Craven Week?' A further eight hands went up. By the time they came to me, they had enough players.

I decided not to complain, and my form in the inter-squadron league soon got me noticed. I started playing rugby properly in my second year in the army. Although legally I only had to do one year of military service, I volunteered for a second year so that I could save some money for my university education. I was concerned about what I was going to do with my life. I still had this dream to play for Despatch, not Eastern Province and certainly not the Springboks. My ambition stretched only as far as Despatch, and I was worried about having to earn a salary because Despatch rugby was an amateur game. So I decided to give the army a go for another year. After all, accommodation, food and clothing were free, and I could afford to buy a little car.

In my first year in the army, I wasn't focused on rugby but rather on being successful in the military. Another reason rugby took a back seat was that I was going through a rough time emotionally. My parents got divorced soon after I left home, and that had a devastating impact on me. Then my friend Murto died suddenly, which was another terrible shock. Around the same time, my father sobered up and my parents were able to put their problems aside and reconcile, but then my father fell ill.

My parents were living apart when my dad picked me up from the railway station on my first pass home in April 1991. He told me he had a bit of a stomach ache, but otherwise he was fine. But it was much more serious than that. It was liver cancer, which was probably brought on by cirrhosis of the liver because of all the alcohol. By the time I came home on my second pass in August, my parents were back together again but my father was bedridden. He was yellow from the liver cancer.

My memory of this time is very blurry, like I'm trying to forget it. I went to visit my father in hospital, but somehow things went badly wrong between us. I can't recall what happened, but I remember walking out of his hospital room in tears. I wasn't crying because he was ill; I was crying because of something he had said to me. I've buried what that was. I remember my dad's friend saying, 'Ek kan nie glo hy's so siek en hy praat so met jou nie' (I can't believe he's so sick yet he talks like that to you). I couldn't take my father's comments any longer and decided to leave. I was also grieving Murto's death and went to my friend Henri Hurter's house on a smallholding just outside Despatch to distract myself for a few days of riding motorbikes.

There were no cellphones and I remember Henri's mother calling me a few days later to say my sister had phoned. She wanted me to come back to the hospital urgently.

In the ward, my family stood around my dad's bed. His eyes were closed and I thought he was dead. Then he stirred and looked up at me. He said one word: 'Kwedin', acknowledging I was there. Then he closed his eyes and passed away. My brother-in-law later told me that they urged him to hang on. '*Wag, Johan is nog nie hier nie*' (Wait, Johan isn't here yet). I think he waited to see me one last time before letting go.

When I think about that moment now, I get incredibly sad. But at the time I didn't know what I felt. There was relief that he had died because he was so ill. But there was also guilt that I didn't have a better understanding of alcoholism and why he used to hit himself. If only I had been wiser and knew more about the world. When I look back, I know he wasn't a bad person. He provided for the family; he never missed work. Hell, he allowed me to drive the car when I was just a laaitie!

I think of how he was able to kick the drink in the last months of his life. If only we had done something sooner – a lot sooner. What this taught me is never to keep quiet when something is wrong. I couldn't live with myself knowing something is wrong and not acting on it. If I'm convinced something is not okay, I can't keep my mouth shut. It's not because I'm brave; it's because I know what the repercussions are of just keeping quiet. Maybe that's why I take on the referees.

I don't remember much about my dad's funeral. I was a pallbearer but have no memory of that. Afterwards, I went straight back to my army base and life went on. The older guys in my unit were concerned about me and offered to get me counselling. They would get together on a Sunday night, sing songs, and urge me to open up about my dad. These men, who with their long hair and university degrees had intimidated me when I first arrived in the army, just wanted to help me. They were really there for me, not like the dominee and the headmaster promising to help when my father's drinking was at its worst. Every night someone came and sat with me, and we'd talk through things. I remember one guy, Reinecke Oosthuizen, saying, '*Iemand moet jou help om die boek toe te maak*' (Somebody must help you close the book). My attitude was '*Moenie worry nie, die boek is toe*' (Don't worry, the book is closed). But it wasn't, and their warmth, care and comfort helped me to heal.

Except to my mother and friends in Despatch, I was no longer Hannie. I was now Rassie. I don't remember who gave me the nickname, but it came from someone in the army. All people with the surname Erasmus were immediately nicknamed Rassie. When I went to the army, I was called Troep Rassie. I also had a girlfriend, whom I had met while I was in my first year in the army. Her name was Nikki Myburgh and she was studying at the School of Nursing at the University of the Free State. Her cousin was in the same bungalow as me and he took me to meet his family one Sunday afternoon. Nikki and I became friends, and gradually it grew into something more serious.

3

IN MY SECOND YEAR IN THE ARMY, when I was 19, I started
playing rugby for the South African Army (Free State) senior team
in the Bloemfontein club league against good teams like Old Greys
and the University of the Free State team, Shimlas. From there, things
started happening for me. I made the South African Forces under-20
team (which included players from the Police and Prisons) and the army
under-20 national team. I also started playing for the Free State under-20
team, where I met Werner Swanepoel. Werner went on to have a solid
international career, winning 20 caps for the Springboks, and we played
together at the 1999 Rugby World Cup.

I played good rugby in 1992 and was named Free State Defence Force
Rugby Player of the Year. The dream of playing for Despatch started to
fade. It was still something I wanted to do, but it was no longer important.
I knew I didn't want to live in Despatch.

In December 1992, I was discharged from the army after doing the
extra year of service. The following year, using the money I had saved,
I enrolled at the University of the Free State to study Human Movement
Science. I rented a room in a house a block away from the university with
six or seven other students.

I was becoming known in Bloemfontein rugby circles because I had
played Free State under-21 and Defence Force under-20. I had also played
for the Defence Force team in the local club league that beat Shimlas for

the first time in years. As a student, I was selected for Shimlas. We had a good team, which included two players who became 1995 Rugby World Cup winners: captain Naka Drotské and Os du Randt (who also won the Rugby World Cup in 2007). Through rugby I started expanding my world. I travelled to Cape Town for the first time to play an inter-varsity match against Maties, the Stellenbosch University team, which we won. I was so naïve that I didn't even know there was a team called Maties.

In the middle of my first year of studying, my funds started running low and I wasn't successful in my application for a bursary. I couldn't ask my mother for help either, as she had retired and was living on my father's pension. I moved out of the university accommodation and into a pre-fab building close to the Shimla Park rugby ground. Naka stayed nearby in a converted storeroom next to the Shimla Park change rooms. The pre-fab was a better option than the university house because the electricity was free, but it was incredibly cold because there was no ceiling. It was a very simple set-up, but I liked it and ended up living there for two and a half years. A few other rugby players joined me and we started fixing the place up, putting in a ceiling, building a bar, and installing a Jacuzzi. It's now called Bosbok and students stay there to this day.

I was doing well academically but in my second year of study, in 1994, my financial situation was desperate. I hoped to play for Free State where, because it was an amateur game, I could get R800 in an envelope after each match and a further R800 if we won. R1 600 a weekend was good money, but I just wasn't making the provincial team. I decided to travel to Pretoria with two friends, Rampie Harmse and Tokkie Kasselman, to see if the University of Pretoria (UP) wanted us, because they knew us from the inter-varsity matches.

UP said they would take me based on my army experience but said I would have to work for university security. I was not interested. Rampie, Tokkie and I then drove to Durban and met the late Ian McIntosh, the legendary coach who had taken Natal to their first-ever Currie Cup triumph

– over Northern Transvaal, at Loftus in 1990. We stayed in the army bar-
racks close to the stadium and played a trial match for Durban Collegians.
The next day we received a call from Free State coach, Nelie Smith, who
told us to come home. We never heard from McIntosh again, but he probably knew we were back in Bloemfontein.

With my finances at an all-time low, I finally had to abandon my university studies. One of my teammates at Shimlas, Ryno Opperman, was a
sales manager at Minolta, the office-technology company, and I asked him
if there were any openings. He introduced me to his boss John Matthyssen,
who gave me a job as a salesman, selling office equipment. I teamed up
with colleague Blake Summers, and, with our very first sale, we made
enough on commission to fund another year at university. I'll never forget
the amount. It was the biggest sum of money I had made so far in my
life: R76 000. I never made that much commission again. I thought about
starting my studies again, but I couldn't face John and tell him I was leaving Minolta after only one month, so I stayed.

In 1994, at the age of 21, I made my debut for Free State in a midweek
game against Border. My mother and my sister Gerda drove from Despatch
to watch me play. It was memorable for all the wrong reasons because I
was sent off for head-butting an opposition player.

I still fought to get into the main Free State team. I was one of *die vurke*
(the forks), as the extra players were known. I went on a Super 10 tour
to New Zealand in 1995 as part of the expanded squad of 28 players, but
I didn't get a start in a great game where we beat the powerful Crusaders
at Lancaster Park 42–35. Players such as André Venter, Joe Beukes, Jaco
Coetzee and Luther Bakkes kept me out of the team.

I kept knocking on the door, playing for Shimlas, and training with
the Free State team. I don't think Nelie Smith rated me at first, but then
I started making more and more appearances, and by the following year
I was a regular in the Free State team and playing for Free State Sevens.
The highlight for Free State that year was making the semifinals of the

Currie Cup, but we lost to Natal 20–35.

We were a close-knit group at Free State, enjoying our rugby and sharing a lot of laughs. One of my favourite stories was when we were practising our lineouts. We were using a basic system of calls, using the letters B, O and K. If the call started with the letter B, the hooker threw the ball to the front of the lineout, O was to the middle, and K to the back. We all got into position, steadied ourselves for the throw from Naka Drotské, and our lock Braam Els called, 'Auckland!' Everyone stood up and looked at each other. Naka shouted from the sideline, '*Wat was die call?*' (What was the call?) 'Auckland!' repeated Braam. We were all confused. '*Wat bedoel jy Auckland?*' (What do you mean by Auckland?) Braam said the word slowly: '*Orkland, met 'n "O"*' (Orkland, with an 'O').

I'm not proud of the fact that I was given a red card – in front of my mother. I think it was in 1997, when the Cheetahs were playing Border in East London. My mom and some friends drove through from Despatch to watch the game. The referee, Tappe Henning, was staying at our hotel and at breakfast I teased him, '*Ja, vandag gaan ek jou baie kak gee*' (Yes, today I'm going to give you a lot of shit). He said, '*As ek vir jou 'n kaart gee, is dit net een kleur – rooi*' (If I give you a card, it'll be only one colour – red). During the game a fight broke out, and one of the Border players held my arms down. The Border flyhalf, Greg Miller, charged at me and I head-butted him. I deserved the red card.

I was totally committed to my job at Minolta, going to the gym early in the morning, then to the office to make some deals, then to evening rugby practice. I enjoyed negotiating deals at Minolta, but I hated the cold-calling. I preferred to find a lead and work out a package for a prospective client. I wasn't well known enough to simply call someone out of the blue and expect them to meet me because they knew me from rugby.

By this time, South Africa was back in the international game after several years of isolation following the sports boycott against apartheid. Teammates like Os du Randt and Naka Drotské were regulars in the Springbok team and had won World Cup medals. Os is a super-talented freak, who was always going to make it. I was very good friends with Naka and went on holiday with him and his girlfriend one December, sleeping in a two-man tent. I thought to myself, if Naka and Os can make it, then so can I.

I needed a change, and that came in 1996 when I met well-known South African businessman Bill Troskie. Bill and his brother Boet ran a successful movie company, Mimosa Films, and had a worldwide hit with *The Gods Must Be Crazy* in 1980. Bill gave me R10 000 for the year and asked me to leave Shimlas – which was an open club, so not just for students – to join Old Greys.

Then came a lucky break. The Springboks came to train against Free State in Bloemfontein. This gave all the youngsters, including me, a chance to play against the Boks. Of course, we went all out and fucked them up. We didn't play an actual game. It was *koppestamp-rugby* (bashing-heads rugby) and tackle drills with forwards against forwards, backs against backs. I tackled my heart out, trying to prove a point. Springbok coach Andre Markgraaff came up to me afterwards and asked me my name. I had obviously caught his eye. Later that year, he watched me play for Old Greys in the club rugby championships where we lost in the final to Pretoria Police.

Before club champs, I had developed a rather bizarre medical problem. It started as a sore hamstring, which my doctor treated with an injection of the anti-inflammatory Voltaren. That allowed me to train, but when I got home the pain would come back. Nikki, who was now a trained nurse, would give me another Voltaren injection. This went on for a few weeks. Nikki was very careful not to hit the same place with the needle and always checked where the doctor had injected – left or right bum cheek. I didn't tell the doctor that my girlfriend was also treating me. As luck would have it, eventually the doctor and Nikki hit the same pinprick, which was a disaster because I got cellulitis. A painful abscess formed on my right cheek, and I could barely walk. I felt I couldn't go to the club champs for Old Greys.

Bill Troskie was, however, adamant that I should go, as he had paid me R10 000, but I was feverish and in pain. I had to have an operation in which they cut out the abscess, leaving a hole as deep as the length of my little finger and the width of two fingers. The doctor cauterised the blood vessels so that the wound didn't ooze, but it could still get infected.

I was roommates with the wonderful Dennis van Zyl, who was coming to the end of his career. He was 10 years older than me, a diesel mechanic by trade, scared of nothing, and had seen it all. During the club champs, Dennis took a tampon, cut it to the right length, soaked it in antiseptic, shoved it into the hole in my bum and covered it with plasters. Then he made me a pair of rubber underpants from a car's inner tube, which I wore as protection for my shorts. When someone touched that area, it was very sore. Dennis said he'd never seen me run so fast on the field. When somebody wanted to tackle me from behind, I accelerated. That's the way I played in the club champs, where Andre Markgraaff noticed me for the second time.

My performances for Old Greys and Free State earned me a call-up for the South Africa A side to tour England and Wales. The Springboks were on tour in France at the same time and preparing for a match against the French Barbarians in Brive when the eighthman Schutte Bekker was injured during training.

I was preparing for a match against London Counties at Twickenham and had gone out for a training run with teammate Ricardo Loubscher. When I got back to the hotel, someone shoved a cellphone in my hand and said it was Andre Markgraaff on the line. I remember him asking, 'Do you want to play for the Springboks?' I had to fly to Paris and then make my way 500 kilometres south to Brive to meet up with the Springbok team.

My world was still very small back then. I had been on a tour to the UK with Shimlas in 1994, and to New Zealand and Australia with Free

State in the Super 10 competition in 1995. But now I would be on my own, flying to Paris and then somehow getting to Brive. I was simply given a plane ticket and sent on my way. I didn't have a cellphone and I had no idea what I was going to do when I arrived in Paris because I couldn't speak French. I couldn't even speak English properly!

When I landed, there was no one to meet me, so I phoned the French Rugby Federation, Fédération Française de Rugby (FFR), for help. They sent a bloke to meet me whose breath smelt like polony and who spoke broken English. At first, I couldn't find him because he didn't have a sign with my name at international arrivals. I had to ask around, but with my bad English, people weren't keen to help.

We eventually found each other and went to the Federation's offices where I explained that I had to get to Brive. But there was a problem. There was a truck drivers' strike, some of the main roads were blocked, and there was nothing they could do. It was Friday, and my game against the French Barbarians was the following afternoon. I was getting desperate.

By pure chance I bumped into a student outside the FFR offices who could speak English. We started chatting and I told him my problem and that I would probably miss the game. He said his mother stayed in Brive and he was going home for the weekend. I probably offered him some match tickets, and he agreed to give me a lift. I couldn't believe my luck. I hope one day I can meet this man to thank him once again.

I threw my bags on top of a pile of dirty laundry on the back seat of his car, and off we went. We headed out past tankers and trucks on the side of the road and drove through the night, stopping only for a short break or to fill up with fuel. I got to the hotel on Saturday morning in time for the game. I think I ended up giving the young student money because I couldn't organise tickets. It was my first time in the Springbok set-up, and I didn't know who to ask. I didn't even have any kit. I was so nervous.

The first time I saw the other players, they were doing their lineout drills, which happened on a Saturday morning. I started feeling even more uncomfortable when I realised I didn't know the lineout codes. Markgraaff wasn't there, but I met Nick Mallett, the assistant coach, who did his best to calm me down, saying, 'Don't worry, you just play like you always do.' The morning passed in a blur and the next thing I was running out at the Municipal Stadium in Brive to play my first match in a Springbok jersey, as eighthman on 23 November 1996. I didn't have time to process the moment. I had made it my goal to play for the Springboks and even though this wasn't a Test match, I was finally wearing the famous jersey. I couldn't appreciate it at the time.

At the first breakdown, as the ball came out, I saw it was an old leather ball. I remember thinking, 'Why are we playing with leather balls?' The next thing All Black flanker Josh Kronfeld hit me hard, tackling the shit out of me. As I lay on the ground, I heard Mallett shouting, 'Erasmus, you second-hand useless piece of $&^%!!' Nick denies this, but that memory is very clear. I've heard Nick shouting things from the side of the field many times when he was coaching Boland. That's just the way he spoke. We lost the match 22–30.

Even though I was new to the team, that didn't stop me from pulling some pranks. We were travelling by bus from Brive to Bordeaux when Dick Muir, Jeremy Thomson and I decided to catch Nick out. The team doctor, Dr Frans Verster, had given us some sleeping tablets to help us recover from jet lag, and we decided it would be a laugh to give him a couple during lunch, one in his fish and one in his cooldrink.

I was one of the youngsters who, according to hierarchy, sat at the front of the bus, so I was near Nick and could see the tablets kicking in. He said, 'Fuck, this jet lag! This is the first time it's caught up with me.' He was so sleepy, but being the guy that he is, he pushed on. He got off the bus to meet a group of French journalists and stepped straight into a puddle of water. But he didn't let that put him off and did his interviews in fluent French as if nothing had happened. He trained us for the whole session, spoke to us on the bus on the way back to the hotel, and then had dinner.

He went through the whole day on those tablets and only once remarked that he was struggling. I was impressed.

One of my childhood dreams was to win the Currie Cup, and in October 1997 I was in the Free State team to play Western Province in the final at Newlands. We had finished third on the log behind Province and defending champions Natal, and we weren't expected to beat Natal in the semifinal in Durban. But we won 40–22 and headed off to Cape Town the following week. We were evenly matched teams, both playing great rugby, although Province had beaten us 31–22 in Bloemfontein earlier in the season. As Province had home ground advantage, they were the favourites.

Free State hadn't won the Currie Cup since 1976 and had lost in the final four times since then. We were used to coming second. But that was Free State's problem – always second. We were everyone's second-favourite rugby team. That drove me mad. I thought we were better than Province. We had a very good team loaded with Springboks like Werner Swanepoel, Jannie de Beer, Os du Randt, Naka Drotské, Brendan Venter, AJ Venter, Willie Meyer, and our captain Helgard Müller. But we had that Afrikaans boerseun syndrome where we were simply too respectful – 'ja, Oom, nee, Oom' (yes, Uncle, no, Uncle). We just didn't believe in ourselves enough.

A group of us went for a jog the morning of the game and bumped into some Free State supporters who had driven down from Bloemfontein for the game. They had a flat tyre and we helped them push their car. It was a strange way to start one of the biggest days for Free State rugby.

About four minutes into the game, Province had a quick 22-metre kick-off and, as I caught the ball, I was hit hard by their lock Fritz van Heerden, which broke one of my ribs. I knew immediately it was fractured, but I wasn't going off so early in my very first Currie Cup final. Lots of people play with broken ribs; it wasn't a big deal. It just meant I wasn't tackling as hard as I usually would, wasn't running into players, and was just playing a linking game, catching and passing and managing what I could do. I couldn't avoid the scrums, rucks, mauls and breakdowns, but my adrenalin was so high that I didn't feel the pain.

Fourteen minutes from the end, with Province leading 14–9, I had a great chance to score a try. Jannie de Beer made a brilliant break for the line and was brought down two metres short. From the ruck, Werner threw me a long, low pass, which I ran on to with two Province players right in my face. I was stepping before I got the ball, and I knocked it on. The ball bounced forward, and the opportunity was lost.

I don't think I would have scored. If I hadn't stepped as I took the ball, they would have tackled the shit out of me and I might have lost the ball anyway. But I had to take a chance and step on the pass, which is difficult when the opposition are on top of you.

I wasn't feeling bad about the knock-on because we still had time and were dominating both territory and possession. Then Jannie kicked a long penalty in swirling conditions to bring us to within two points of the lead and 10 minutes to play.

We all started believing we could do this. In the final minute of the match, with Province leading 14–12, the ball came down the Free State line from a ruck 30 metres out. Helgard made a break and passed to winger Jan-Harm van Wyk who scored in the corner. But before he had even dotted the ball down, referee André Watson blew for a forward pass. I have no problems with that – it was clearly forward – but I know that die-hard Free State fans will dispute it to this day. I was named Man of the Match despite being on the losing side, but that did nothing to make up for the disappointment of defeat. We could have won that game.

On 10 January 1998, Nikki and I were married at the Bloemfontein Hotel, which was a posh place in those days. WJ Visagie, a Cheetahs teammate who stayed with me in Shimla Park, was my best man. It was quite a big wedding, with family and friends and a lot of rugby people. We went on honeymoon on a cruise ship to Bazaruto Island in Mozambique.

Later that year, I met Dr Louis Luyt, who was president of the Golden Lions. He had been the president of the South African Rugby Football Union (SARFU) when the Springboks won the Rugby World Cup in 1995. Luyt had a formidable, no-nonsense reputation and was a powerful figure in South African rugby. I had a lot of respect for him because of the way he had organised the World Cup and ensured that the Springboks' semifinal against France on the waterlogged pitch at Kings Park Stadium in Durban went ahead.

The meeting wasn't planned but came about when a group of us, including my Free State teammates, Werner Swanepoel, AJ Venter and Willie Meyer, told our wives we were going to Johannesburg for a fundraiser, but was actually a boys' golfing trip. We were playing the 14th hole at the Wanderers Golf Club when my phone rang. It was one of Doc Luyt's staff, who said he wanted to talk to me. The next thing, Doc Luyt was on the line, telling me to come and see him right away. At first, I thought it was well-known prankster Leon Schuster trying to wind me up. Leon was a regular at our clubhouse in Bloemfontein, so we were familiar with his nonsense.

When we got to the clubhouse, a man approached me and asked, 'Are you Rassie Erasmus?' I said yes and he said, 'Get in the car. Dr Luyt is waiting for you.' There were drinks in the car, so I helped myself to some champagne. When we got there I was shown into a big house with high walls. I was feeling a bit nervous because I knew Doc Luyt was an intimidating person. He walked into the room and the first thing he said was, 'Do you have a mandate to be here?' I didn't want to say yes because I didn't know what a mandate was, so I said no. The conversation then became a bit confusing because he asked, 'What does it help if you're here without a mandate?' I got flustered and said, 'No, no, you phoned me, on the golf course – I didn't just come to see you.' Then he asked if my wife knew I was with him. I told him she didn't and he said, 'Then you obviously don't have a mandate.'

He asked if I was happy at Free State. I was very happy, earning R360 000 a year, running a few businesses. Then he asked how much I wanted. I thought I would blow him out of the water with an outrageous demand, so I said I wanted R860 000 a year. He looked at me and said, 'You've got it.' I thought, 'Fuck, what now? I don't want to leave Free State.' Then he said, 'Phone your wife. Get the mandate.' Now I finally understood what mandate meant. I phoned Nikki and told her I was with Doc Luyt and he wanted me to play for the Golden Lions. She immediately said, 'Oh, you guys are kuiering again … Don't talk kak, man.'

When she realised I was serious, she said she couldn't move to Johannesburg because she had just started a new nursing job at the hospital. Doc Luyt said, 'Tell her how much you're getting.' I told her I'd be earning R860 000. She said, 'No, no we can make a plan.'

I thought of Werner (who we called Smiley because he's always got a smile on his face) and Willie, who were back at the Wanderers Golf Club. I told Doc Luyt we needed a scrumhalf and that I would try to get Smiley. He said, 'Phone him now.' When Smiley answered, I first had to convince him that I was doing salary negotiations with Louis Luyt. I asked him if he wanted to play for the Lions. He wasn't keen because his wife had a good job as a dietician in Bloemfontein. I asked him to name his price. He was earning R280 000 a year, so he decided to shoot high and ask for R400 000. Doc Luyt couldn't hear our conversation, so I turned to him and said, 'Smiley wants R800 000.' Doc Luyt said, 'He's got it.' I told Smiley, 'I'll talk to you later, but you've got your money.'

But now I felt bad that AJ Venter and Willie Meyer, who were also back at the clubhouse but weren't part of the discussions, so I told Doc Luyt that we needed a flank and a prop. AJ and Willie were promptly signed as well, and that's how we all moved to the Lions.

By this time, I was enjoying analysing players' performances on the field using VHS recordings of the match and decided to step up my game. I bought myself an expensive computer that had a software program called Rugbystat, which allowed me to analyse rugby matches in a more sophisticated way than rewinding, fast-forwarding and playing the VHS tapes. I had heard about it from the Council for Scientific and Industrial Research (CSIR), and was the first private person in South Africa to own one. I actually had to take out a bank loan to buy it from a company in Israel, with help from the CSIR, for R125 000. That's over R400 000 today. I knew a guy by the name of Willie Maree, now the technical-support manager for the South African Rugby Union (SARU), who was a Human Movement Science student at the time and, in his spare time, was learning how to code for other sports at the CSIR. After his lectures, I would sit with him, and he would teach me what he had learnt.

Analysing games was incredibly time-consuming because I had to go through the video footage over and over again to capture the information of each individual player: how many clean-outs he did, how many tackles he made, how many runs he had. I wasn't a computer expert and learnt through a lot of trial and error. Now there are big companies that employ up to 60 coders on one game to give you the information within eight hours of a match. Some teams have four technical analysts who then go through the data and filter the information through to the coaches. It's so sophisticated and a long way from VHS recorders. The Cheetahs eventually bought that computer from me for R15 000 when I left them in 2007. These days, laptops can do the same job.

I didn't play many games for the Golden Lions, about seven in total, and we won them all. I didn't play in the 1999 Currie Cup semifinal or the final when the Lions beat the Sharks 32–9, because by then I was preparing for the Rugby World Cup with the Springboks.

I had played for Free State in the Super 12 in 1997, and we hadn't been part of the inaugural Super 12 in 1996, but qualified the following year in the place of Western Province, who had failed to finish in the top four in the 1996 Currie Cup. We managed to finish 7th on the log and enjoyed a memorable 49–18 win against the Highlanders in Invercargill and a 35–23 win against Northern Transvaal in Pretoria. But the Brumbies and the Hurricanes put us in our place, running 50 points or more past us in both away games.

Whether I stayed with Free State or moved to the Golden Lions, it made no difference to me in the Super 12 because 1998 saw the birth of the Cats, a team made up of players from the Golden Lions, Free State, Griquas, Leopards, Pumas and Griffons. We trained in four different places – Kimberley, Welkom, Bloemfontein and Johannesburg – and played our home games in Joburg or Bloem. It didn't work; nobody can travel like that and still perform.

Andre Markgraaff, who had been sacked one year earlier as Springbok coach, was the Cats coach.

We had a terrible season, winning two games out of 11 and finishing bottom of the log. The simple fact is that we were a kak team. We weren't bad up front, but the backline lacked the punch.

One of my memories from that time is that, after yet another loss, Andre didn't want to do a TV interview and sent me out because I was captain. I didn't know what to say. With my Afrikaans accent, I said, 'We're very close to clicking.' The interviewer asked what I meant. I was on a roll and there was no stopping me. I said, 'Next week I'm pretty sure, 100% sure, 99% sure we're going to click. But if we don't click next week, we'll definitely click the week after that.' It goes down as one of my most embarrassing TV interviews and I've never forgotten it.

The following year was also forgettable as we finished second from the bottom, just above the Bulls, winning four out of the 11 games. We got some local pride, though, by putting 50 points past the Bulls and beating Western Province at Newlands.

In 2000, Laurie Mains was appointed the Golden Lions and Cats coach. Laurie, a former All Black fullback who coached New Zealand for the 1995 Rugby World Cup and claimed his team had been poisoned before the final by a hotel waitress, managed to turn the Cats' fortunes around very quickly. From finishing last and second last the previous two years, the Cats reached the Super 12 semifinals two years in a row.

We had a good team in 2000 but lost four of our first six games, including an embarrassing 64–0 defeat to the Brumbies in Canberra. I was the captain in that game, and at one stage we had two yellow cards and I had to play inside centre next to Japie Mulder. The Brumbies ran unbelievable lines. As we stood behind the poles for one conversion, we looked at the big screen to see who missed a tackle. Eventually I said, 'Listen here, we know we're going to stand behind these poles again in the next few minutes, then everybody must just say which fucking player they hit or did not hit.' It got so bad at one stage that I asked the referee if the Brumbies had more than 15 players on the field. I was only half joking.

But the rest of the season went well and we managed to win all our remaining games and finished fourth on the log. We had to travel back to Canberra to play the Brumbies in the semifinal and lost again, this time 28–5.

During the 2001 season, my relationship with Laurie deteriorated fast. This was at a time when SARFU started introducing quotas to bring more black players into the game and, even though Laurie's wife is South African, I felt he didn't properly understand South Africa and its people. He didn't appreciate the political sensitivities in South Africa, the inequalities people faced, and what transformation meant. He was stubborn and blundered when he tried to make quotas work.

He preferred Dean Hall to Conrad Jantjes, who was a hugely talented player. Conrad played international football at under-17, international cricket at under-19 and 24 Tests for the Springboks. He had gone to a private school in Boksburg, where he had thrived. To be considered 'a quota player' came as a huge surprise to him. Dean was a big, hard winger from Springs, who should have played more than the 13 times he appeared for the Springboks.

Conrad was selected to start a game, but Laurie told him to fake an injury after seven minutes so that Dean could come on. I went to Conrad and asked, 'What the fuck's going on here?' I was very angry because I felt this was a huge embarrassment for Conrad, and unfair on Dean. I said to Laurie, 'Don't do this – let's make another plan, but don't make a person fake an injury.'

You can't build a team and get the players to believe in each other when this is going on. How do you have a team talk with a guy who knows he's only going to play seven minutes and then has to fake an injury?

But because my credibility wasn't great, Laurie didn't take me seriously. I had started behaving badly and was becoming more and more self-centred. It was all about Rassie Erasmus. I was on top of the world, the captain of the Cats, and earning over R1 million a year (compared to the other guys earning R700 000).

Nikki and I had been married for two years, but she was living in Bloemfontein, working at Universitas Hospital, while I was living the high life in Joburg, jolling in rave clubs, indulging and partying too much. The Free State boys – me, Smiley Swanepoel, Naka Drotské and Willie Meyer – would train on Monday, Tuesday and Wednesday, hop in the car on Wednesday afternoon, stay over in Bloem on Thursday and drive back for captain's practice on Friday. I was playing well, so I thought, 'Why not?' The only way I can describe this is: *Die liggies het my gevang* (I got caught up by the bright lights).

With that lifestyle of excess, partying and drinking too much, how could I be the guy to tell Laurie what to do? He regarded me as a windgat and a dronkgat. He wasn't prepared to change his ways, so before we played the next game I phoned my old Free State coach Peet Kleynhans and told him what would happen with Conrad and Dean. Peet tipped off a rugby journalist who then wrote the story, and a storm broke around Laurie.

Another problem was that Laurie didn't know how to treat us and talk to us, particularly the black players. Maybe he knew how to talk to a Maori player, but you can't talk the same way to South Africans, with their mix of home languages, different cultures and different backgrounds. Conrad was often picked on the bench, knowing full well that Laurie would never give him a run. Chester Williams and I, as the senior players, went to Doc Luyt and told him we couldn't play under Laurie. Doc listened to us and started to work Laurie out of the job.

I felt Laurie's coaching methods were outdated as he didn't do a proper analysis on his own players and the opposition. He preferred the old-school way of coaching. I was doing a lot of technical analysis for the team, and Laurie would fall asleep while I was going through the stats on my computer. He didn't care to learn the modern approach to coaching.

Our relationship became particularly toxic on our trip to New Zealand and Australia. Despite the problems, I was playing good rugby (I was later named SANZAR's Players' Player of the Year), and we beat the Blues and the Crusaders, who are always tough to beat at home.

Laurie told us the danger men in the Blues team were Matua Parkinson and Carlos Spencer. But because he didn't believe in studying the opposition properly, he didn't know that neither of them were playing. During the game, Laurie accused me of changing the game plan. He didn't understand that André Venter and I were alternating our roles on the field, and the game plan was unchanged. I was struggling with a stomach bug and wanted to go off at halftime, but Laurie refused to let me. After the match, I didn't hang around for the post-match function and took a taxi back to the hotel.

Things blew up when we got to Brisbane to play the Reds. Laurie and I had a blazing row in the team room at the hotel, which some of the players witnessed. He accused me of being disruptive and unstable, and said I needed counselling for depression. That was the final straw. I called the players together and told them I would fake a muscle injury and fly home. Looking back, that was the wrong decision. As captain, I should have had it out with Laurie and resolved the problem.

I had a lot of support from the black players in the team. I gave them encouragement where Laurie would tear into them. He gave Conrad hell for the way he tackled Trevor Halstead during a game against the Sharks. I thought Conrad had done incredibly well to stop Trevor, who was three centimetres taller and 18 kilograms heavier than Conrad, and told him so.

Then, just before our final game of the season against the Bulls, Laurie tried to get the players to choose between him or me. They went with me.

We narrowly lost our final two games to the Reds and the Bulls – which I didn't play – and managed to finish third on the log, qualifying for the semifinals. I then rejoined the team for the game against the Sharks in Durban, losing 12–30.

I take a lot of blame for what happened. I should have had a proper discussion with Laurie about the issues that troubled me, rather than allowing them to simmer and eventually boil over. But I learnt from the mistakes both of us made. I won't have players who behave as badly as I did, feeling entitled just because they are playing well. How Laurie coached and analysed is exactly how I don't want to be as a coach. But, more importantly, I learnt to have proper communication with the players, to address grievances properly and not allow ill feelings to fester and affect the whole team.

As 2001 progressed, I finally realised I needed to get a grip on my own life, which was getting out of control with all the rave clubs, the excessive behaviour and partying. I was away from Nikki a lot, and nothing stops you from living the high life when you have money and no family responsibilities. I was basically a bachelor who was married.

My health was also starting to suffer. I had tests done on my metabolism and the results showed that my metabolism while sleeping was the same as that of a person who was walking slowly, I was burning up so much energy. I weighed 92 kilograms and they put me on a diet where I was given food three times overnight – at 6pm and 11pm and at 3am.

Sometimes I would put on my heart-rate monitor for training and the fitness coach would tell me to take another one because the one I was wearing had to be faulty. My heart rate would be 180 beats per minute during the warm-up and peak around 192, yet I didn't even feel it – all because of so little sleep and a lot of raving. Sometimes I wouldn't sleep on the Friday at all, then play a match on the Saturday, win Man of the Match, go out partying and not sleep on Saturday night or Sunday night. On Monday morning I would be back at training.

So when I was pointing a finger at Laurie Mains, there were three fingers pointing right back at me. To be fair, I can't complain about anything. Laurie may not have been up to date or cutting edge, but I wasn't a cutting-edge professional player either.

I had been dropped from the Springboks because of my partying, so I faked a hamstring injury and left the Springbok team ahead of the Test match against Italy in Port Elizabeth. It was time to go back to Bloemfontein. I went to Louis Luyt and told him I had to leave the Golden Lions. He didn't argue and just tore up my contract and released me.

I didn't even ask the Free State rugby guys if I could come back. I then phoned Harold Verster, the managing director of the Cheetahs, and told him I was back. He said, 'Lekker,' and gave me a new contract. My salary dropped substantially, but that didn't bother me in the least.

I settled down in Bloemfontein and bought a house on a smallholding. It was called The Ark because it had two eland, two zebra, two cows, two sheep, two pigs, two donkeys … you get the picture. It had seven dams with swans and ducks. The Free State team used to come for a braai.

It was like life had stood still for three years and then it just picked up again where I had left off in Bloem. Oom Peet Kleynhans was still the coach, my wife still had a job there. People already knew me. It was lekker.

4

I MADE MY TEST DEBUT FOR THE SPRINGBOKS in the third Test against the British and Irish Lions on 5 July 1997 at Ellis Park. It wasn't a great time because the Lions had already won the series after beating the Boks in the first two Tests of the three-Test series, and there was huge disappointment that these great rivals had won a second series in South Africa after their win in 1974.

I had been on the fringes of the Bok team ever since I had been called up to play the game in Brive against the French Barbarians the previous year. I had even been initiated into the team, which involved singing a song or telling a joke. But there was also a very painful part of the initiation. A senior Springbok – in my case, it was André Joubert – hit you on your backside with a whip named Bliksem after Danie Craven's dog. As you got hit, you had to shout out, '*Bliksem!*' It was an old tradition in the Bok team, so I didn't really mind, even if it was fucking sore. I got three shots from André, shook everybody's hand and had a few beers. That made me feel, okay, I'm part of this team now. I was part of the extended squad and training with the Boks.

Carel du Plessis became the new Springbok coach in June 1997, taking over from Andre Markgraaff. He inherited a loose trio of Gary Teichmann, André Venter and Ruben Kruger, who were all very settled in the team and understood each other well. Carel stuck with those three for a one-off Test against Tonga and the first two Tests against the Lions.

I felt I was close to getting picked, but I was competing against some big names with impressive reputations. André was my friend and teammate from Free State, playing for Technikon when I played for Shimlas or Old Greys. We trained and went for runs together. Ruben was also a Free State boykie. He came from Vrede, went to Grey College and was on the team that had won the Rugby World Cup in 1995, but he was now playing for Northern Transvaal. He was something of a hero of mine and initially I was a bit scared of him. Gary, the captain from Natal, was a quiet leader and an extremely good eighthman. I had a lot of respect for him.

I got my chance when Ruben Kruger was injured in the second Test at Kings Park in Durban, and I was selected for the following weekend's game at Ellis Park. I honestly didn't know the Lions were such a big deal, with a long history of rivalry against the Springboks and that they only toured South Africa once every 12 years. It didn't occur to me at the time that I would probably only have one shot at playing a Test against them because the next tour was a long way off in 2009.

What was lekker for me was making my international debut in the same game as two of my Free State teammates, my good friend Smiley and Jannie de Beer. We had played a midweek game for Free State against the Lions between the first and second Tests, where their centre Will Greenwood cut us to pieces. He sidestepped me with ease and I realised they would be a problem. Their ball skills were amazing, and even though the Free State team could run the ball, we were no match for them. With players like Helgard Müller, Brendan Venter, Jannie de Beer, André Venter and me, we had pace in our team, but they just outran us in Bloemfontein on a dry pitch, winning 52–30.

I was told on the Tuesday before the game that I would make my debut but it didn't feel like a big moment. Lions centre Jeremy Guscott kicked a drop goal four minutes from the final whistle in the second Test in Durban to clinch the series, so instead of a big hype around the game, there was a kak feeling in the camp because the third Test was meaningless, a dead rubber. The vibe was more about getting some respect with a win. Not a great week to make my debut.

Our Springbok jerseys were waiting for us in the change room on the day of the Test, unlike these days when they're handed out the day before. They had long sleeves, and the tradition was to take a pair of scissors and cut the sleeves off. But you had to get it just right so it didn't look like you'd hacked at them. I was a bit nervous cutting away at my jersey because I actually wanted to play with long sleeves.

Even if the series was won and lost, making my debut was obviously a big deal personally, although I didn't get goosebumps when we were singing the anthems. I was just looking forward to the match.

The Lions' handling was unbelievably superior to ours. Our guys couldn't pass both left and right with the same accuracy and we lacked their core skills. They could throw two passes and cover the width of the field. Guscott and Scott Gibbs glided past us.

But we had something they lacked – strength. That's not something you can teach. We gave them some good old-fashioned South African power up front, and then those passing skills weren't as effective. With big guys like Os du Randt, Dawie Theron, Hannes Strydom and Krynauw Otto next to me, when we were in their faces, their running and passing skills faded away. We dominated the game and beat the Lions 35–16, scoring four tries to one.

Ruben recovered from injury and came back into the Springbok side for the Tri Nations, so I was in the stands and watched as we lost 32–35 to New Zealand at Ellis Park before we headed off to Australia and New Zealand for the away leg of the competition.

Carel was under pressure because the British and Irish Lions had just won a series for only the second time in South Africa since 1896. He couldn't afford to lose the Tri Nations as well. The problem was that he just couldn't explain his rugby vision to us. When Carel told us his game plan, big English words came out of his mouth. He was a brilliant player and was highly intelligent in his understanding of the game, but we simply couldn't see what he saw. The way he explained spaces on the field was almost scientific. We didn't have time to adapt to his style of play and I think he got frustrated.

I didn't play in any of the away games, all of which ended in defeat for the Boks. We were very sluggish in losing 20–32 to Australia in Brisbane, but started well against New Zealand at Eden Park in Auckland. We had a 10-point lead early in the match and were still in the game at halftime, trailing by just two points, 21–23. But then the wheels fell off when André Venter got a red card for stamping on Sean Fitzpatrick, James Small got a yellow card for attempting to trip Christian Cullen, and Ruben Kruger broke his ankle. We faded badly, and the All Blacks scored seven tries to put 55 points past us for the first time in a Test match.

We weren't going to win the Tri Nations now. There was a bad atmosphere in the team, and we felt the writing was on the wall for Carel. We came home and I was selected for my second Test, replacing the suspended André at number 7, while Warren Brosnihan made his debut replacing Ruben on the other side of the scrum against Australia in Pretoria.

I scored my debut international try in the first five minutes of the game. Joost van der Westhuizen created the try by kicking a loose ball ahead when Aussie scrumhalf George Gregan couldn't gather. He passed to me on his inside just as he was tackled, and I sprinted for the line. Flanker David Wilson was right on my ass, and tried to ankle-tap me, but I got away and scored just as centre James Holbeck dived on top of me. But it was all Joost; I simply took the pass and ran the last few metres.

That first try was lekker, but strangely I would have preferred Joost to have made that try. I like out-thinking the opposition, out-passing and out-planning them. There was a game later in my career against New Zealand where I created two tries for Robbie Fleck – now *that* gave me satisfaction. (In the same way, a guy like Willie le Roux is happy to score a try, but his satisfaction is greater when he's made a try and few people realise it. He makes the most tries and it's much more fulfilling for him.)

We scored eight tries that day and won 61–22, the first time the Wallabies had conceded more than 50 points in a Test match. We finally realised what Carel had been trying to teach us all this time. I might not have understood what he was saying, but I now understood what he wanted. But it came too late, as this turned out to be his last match as Bok coach and he was sacked a week later.

I felt so bad. I hated that the fans and the media were taking out this ex-Springbok hero, a calm, reserved family man. I believe you need to give a guy a chance and then, if he's not successful, let people who know rugby decide on his future. Instead, I saw people who weren't at all involved in rugby breaking him down. I didn't have a special relationship with Carel, but that's when I saw the cruelty of rugby.

By now, I was starting to feel more confident as an international player. I was getting used to travelling, even enjoying it, and while I had only played two Tests, I felt comfortable in the team. But I couldn't afford to relax because other players, such as Warren Brosnihan, Bobby Skinstad, André Vos, Corné Krige, Wayne Fyvie and Andrew Aitken, were biting my ass for a place in the team.

I didn't appreciate Bobby at first (although, later, I really did). He had a great sidestep and could be very physical.

Corné Krige was this well-spoken guy from Paarl Boys' High who had an aura about him. He was great at stealing the ball. Wayne was tough and Warren was fast, while André was great at linking. They all had attributes to keep me on my toes.

I felt that, for my size (I weighed 92 kilograms at the time), my defence was consistently more accurate and aggressive than a lot of those players. I wasn't afraid of tackling and did it well. I could steal a ball, jump in the lineout, catch a high ball, chip-kick and, on attack, I could sidestep. I could even kick a drop goal. Perhaps I wasn't necessarily the fastest of all the flankers, but I could hold my own. Over 100 metres,

Bobby would beat me by 10 metres. I knew that on the physical side I could mix it, because I was a bit of a streetfighter from Despatch so I wasn't afraid of a fight. My whole life growing up I just played touch rugby, so I knew how to take short cuts to get to the action. My vision and understanding of the different types of games and where to find the space came naturally to me.

Even though I was young and a newcomer, I wasn't nervous to talk to my teammates and remind them of the game plan. '*André, onthou, jy moet hierdie lyn hardloop*' (André, remember you must run this line), or '*Smiley, ek gaan op jou skouer wees*' (Smiley, I'll be on your shoulder), or '*Hoor julle, boys, watch vir Kronfeld*' (Listen, guys, watch out for Kronfeld).

I loved watching the same player in 10 different games before I faced him in a game. I would work him out and show the others what to do at training sessions. I'd remind a teammate of his running line and of his defence. The players accepted this, though sometimes they would get impatient and say, '*Ja, fok, ek weet, man*' (Yes, fuck, I know, man). That's where my style of coaching started. I knew exactly what I had to do, and I could get the players around me to do what I had shown them. That was lekker for me.

On 25 September 1997, Nick Mallett – who had lost out to Carel for the Springbok head coach position six months earlier – was finally given the job. He was coaching Boland at the time but knew the Bok players and wasn't about to make any major changes. He brought Dick Muir and Breyton Paulse into the backs and Adrian Garvey into the forwards, but the rest of the team remained virtually the same.

I didn't know Nick well back then. I had played against his team when he coached Boland, and I encountered him in that one-off game I played for the Bok team against the French Barbarians the previous year, when he was the Boks' assistant coach. I knew he was a direct guy and very sure of himself. I also knew he wasn't afraid of strong language. When Free State played Boland in Bloemfontein, we gave them a hiding and I – standing in the pavilion rather than at the side of the field – could hear Nick swearing at his players.

As I got to know him, I realised he had great rugby knowledge, a good heart and was very passionate. The shouting was just his personality. He's brutally honest and he's not going to let a swear word stop him. He was into rugby for all the right reasons. When my mom met him at the World Cup in 1999, he gave her a hug and she said he was the nicest man she'd ever met.

I wasn't sure, though, if my place in Nick Mallett's team was secure. Skinstad, Aitken and Krige were right there and biting me hard. Ruben Kruger was recovering from injury and André Venter was already well established. I felt that I had the qualities that Nick wanted, but I never felt completely comfortable that my place was guaranteed.

If only I had known that I was Nick's first choice for the openside flanker's position. This is what he said about me:

Rassie was a guy I never, ever considered dropping because I admired all the aspects of his game and all the things he added to our team. He tackled incredibly well and was very physical. But his strong point was his ability to read what the opposition was going to do, and disrupt them by getting in the way, or tackling the right guy, or intercepting a pass. He had amazing intuition. He had different qualities to someone like Corné Krige, who was an absolute workhorse and would make count- less tackles and turnovers in a game. They weren't often the qualities I was looking for. I was loyal to the players, provided we won. When I was coaching the Springboks, Rassie was playing well for the Cheetahs and there was no reason to pick a guy like Corné or Andrew Aitken ahead of him unless he was injured. He was always my first choice and there was never a case when I thought I would change my selection. In my recol- lection, I never dropped Rassie. He was only excluded from one of my Test teams because he was injured.

Rassie was outstanding. He wasn't a big, strong guy, nor was he particularly fast, but he was fast enough and had an unbelievable understanding of the game with brilliant anticipation. He was a player like Rob Louw or the Frenchman Laurent Cabannes, who could play flank and centre. He had the ability to hold the ball up, to take it into contact, to pass at the right time, to see space. He knew exactly where the ball was going so he could take the direct line to where it was headed. Other players chase the ball. They can run twice as fast, but they've also run twice as far. Rassie had superb ball skills and an understanding of what an opposition player is going to do; he can see the set-up and anticipates the next move. He could look at the field, make an analysis of what he thought was going to happen even before he had packed down in the scrum. He wasn't really a fetcher, but he could steal the ball through an interception or by applying pressure to force the opposition to knock-on. I particularly loved his attacking skills. With a flanker like him, we had a third centre in the team and sometimes he passed better than the centres.

Nick had a sense for picking the right players who would gel quickly. In those days there were no alignment camps and roadmaps, nobody spoke to the provincial and franchise coaches, and no one shared video clips with the players. It was impossible for Nick to coach new skills or give a player a new vision because there just wasn't enough time.

Nick believed you had to pick some hard fucking Afrikaans guys in your pack, one or two English guys in your loose forwards, some hard men in the backline, and some with flair.

We arrived in Bologna, Italy, for the start of the Boks' end-of-year tour. I wasn't nervous going into that game against Italy, not because I underestimated them but because we knew we had better players and were better organised. Italy's entry into the Six Nations was still three years away, so we didn't get much chance to watch or follow them, and I didn't know half their players. Italy were full of confidence because they had beaten Ireland in Dublin at the start of the year, and held Argentina to a draw in the Latin Cup in France the previous month, and, in the first half, they were holding their own. We only had a two-point lead at halftime. Nick had said he wanted four tries per game, but we gave him nine, scoring 40 points in the second half and winning 62–31.

After the break, I scored two tries but I barely remember the first, which was started by Joost. In the first minute, he kicked ahead and the ball bounced off Justin Swart's leg in the in-goal area. All I had to do was fall on the ball. Ten minutes later, Joost got the ball from Henry Honiball – who had drawn the defence and slipped past a potential tackler and passed to me as I came up on his inside. I was hard to stop at full pace.

Victory against Italy was never in any doubt, but we still had work to do to become a great team, though we'd had a confident start to the tour.

We travelled from Bologna to Lyon for the first of two Tests against France, who had been crowned Five Nations Grand Slam winners earlier that year. They had quality players in their backline, including their captain Philippe Saint-André, Christophe Lamaison, Thierry Lacroix and Fabien Galthié, and some beasts up front, among them Christian Califano, Olivier Merle, Olivier Brouzet, Laurent Cabannes and the massive Abdelatif Benazzi.

It was a hell of a tough encounter, but things started to come together for us in that match. We had a 25-point lead at one stage, then leaked three tries in the last 20 minutes for a final score of 36–32.

On the Wednesday before the game I hurt my back and was battling to walk because of the pain. Somehow, I had managed to tweak my back in a weird way and it just locked up. While the training continued, two of my teammates carried me onto the bus, and I lay in the aisle with my feet up on a seat.

Back at the hotel, Doc Verster injected me with painkillers and anti-inflammatories to get me ready for the game. Smiley was my roommate and we made space so that I could sleep on the floor with my legs on the bed because I'd heard that this helps with spasms or pinched nerves. We didn't go for scans in those days. My back was still extremely stiff when we finally ran out at Stade de Gerland in Lyon, which was still in the process of being expanded.

During the first half, Benazzi came charging towards me at speed, the ball tucked under his arm. Six foot six and weighing 115 kilograms. I thought, 'Fuck, I'm going to tackle the shit out of him.' I ran into him and then woke up in the change room to find Doc Verster busy stitching up my eye. I was obviously concussed. Doc asked me, 'How's the pain in your back?' and I said, 'What pain?' He looked at me closely and said, 'Your back was buggered before the game – how is it now?' Benazzi hit me so hard that my back was just fine.

I got stitches and went back onto the field. After the game I asked Benazzi if I had at least managed to bring him down. 'No,' he said, 'I just ran over you.'

Whatever had been wrong with my back, Benazzi was able to fix by crashing into me, cutting my eye, but realigning my back. I was fine after that.

There was a huge build-up to the second Test in Paris, which was billed as the last rugby international to be played at the famous Parc des Princes before the home of French rugby moved to Stade de France. Cabannes, Merle, Lacroix and Saint-André – all legends of French rugby – were playing their final Tests so emotions were high among the French crowd.

The game was tight in the beginning, and the French were already starting to get in our faces. In about the 20th minute, with the Boks leading 7–3, I made an intercept on our 22-metre line and had a clear run for their line. Lacroix was coming up fast and would have caught me, but I flicked the ball inside to Pieter Rossouw who scored the first of his four tries under the posts.

Nick Mallett remembers that move:

Rassie was a broken-field specialist. In an instant, he would sum up a turnover situation or an interception situation. In that match against France at Parc des Princes, we were leading by four points when France went on the blindside. Rassie saw the move coming, grabbed the intercept and sprinted for the French line before passing to Pieter Rossouw who scored. It was a game-changer as it broke the French spirit. It was the kind of thing that other players couldn't do. None of the players read the game the same way Rassie did.

That move opened the floodgates for us and we scored five more tries after that. It was one of the best performances by a Springbok team, but I couldn't remember half of it because I got concussed. In the second half, Smiley broke from a scrum, threw an overhead pass to Henry Honiball at flyhalf, who tried to flick the ball inside to me as I looped around him. But I couldn't gather it and the ball went loose. I instinctively dived onto the ball at the same time as Laurent Leflamand ran in to kick it clear. I slid into his leg as he swung at the ball, cracking my head against his shin. He seemed to feel no pain and simply carried on, chasing after the ball. I was rolling on the ground, blood gushing from a cut on my head. Os came over to see if I was okay, but I could only clutch my head in pain.

Doc Verster crouched next to me, examining the wound and asking me questions to assess if I was concussed. As I stood up, I was very wobbly on my feet and he had to grab hold of my jersey to stop me falling over. Andrew Aitken ran on to replace me as the medics arrived with a stretcher. By now I was a mess, with blood on both my hands and Doc pressing an icepack on the cut to my head.

I went off to get stitched up. Doc asked me more questions as he worked, such as 'What's the score?' I couldn't remember. I couldn't remember anything. I was in no state to carry on, particularly after taking the big hit from Benazzi the week before.

When I look back at the game, I realise why Gary Teichmann described it as the finest 80 minutes of rugby he had ever seen the Springboks play. I sat on the side of the field and watched the rest of the match. Nick came down from the stands and enjoyed those fine minutes as the crowd applauded him. He had tears in his eyes and I can understand why he was emotional. He had had a long road with the Boks, from being a player in 1984, then assistant coach, and now head coach. He was under a lot of pressure to turn the team around after those losses to the British and Irish Lions and in the Tri Nations. And now his team was destroying the Five Nations champions. Those last 10 minutes of that game were special for him; he could relax and know we were buggering them up.

In the last few minutes, Henry scored a try that rounded off a move in which the ball went through 10 pairs of Springbok hands as we ran the ball from our 22-metre line. Commentator Hugh Bladen said we were 'playing' with the French. He was spot on.

After the match we did a lap of honour, with some of the Bok players wearing French jerseys. We received a standing ovation from the usually partisan French crowd, who were obviously fed up with their own team's performance but were still able to appreciate the running rugby we'd laid on.

The English media made out that the next game, against England at Twickenham, would be a revenge match after the Lions defeat, but we didn't see it like that. For us, it was just another Test match.

I tried everything to persuade Doc Verster to clear me to play, but he refused. I was gutted. There were no protocols in those days saying I couldn't play. Doc just refused on medical grounds. He wasn't the kind of guy who would keep you off the field for nothing. He was a tough man himself, a former soldier with the South African Special Forces (also known as the Recces), the toughest unit in the Defence Force. He was a very calm man, probably because he had treated wounded soldiers in his previous life. He always had a plan. Whether you came to him with a cold, a dislocated shoulder, a broken bone, or concussion, he would quietly say, 'O ja, ek sien' (Oh yes, I see) and work out a solution. For him to say I wasn't fit to play meant my concussion was serious.

And so I watched from the stands as Andrew Aitken took my place and the Springboks handed England their biggest defeat (at the time) at Twickenham, winning 29–11. England led 11–0, but after their flyhalf and my old Eastern Province Craven Week teammate Mike Catt was stretchered off, we dominated the game.

I marked my return to the side the next week with an easy try against Scotland as we ran up another huge score, winning 68–10 at Murrayfield. Jannie de Beer made a break and threw a low pass slightly behind me. I reached back, gathered the ball and dotted it down. It was a simple run-in without having to beat anyone, but I loved listening to the legendary Scottish commentator Bill McLaren admiring my try: 'Did you see the pass gathered in by this laddie, Johan Erasmus of the Orange Free State, in only his sixth international? He took a ball behind him with probably three fingers.' McLaren was a great broadcaster, and it was always a pleasure when I was doing the video analysis, rewinding and fast-forwarding footage where he was the commentator, listening to his voice.

Nick remembers another incident from that game where I made a try for Pieter Rossouw:

In that game against Scotland, our strategy from their kick-off was for Krynauw Otto to catch the ball and for our forwards to start a driving maul from which we'd either win a penalty or play off our centres. Rassie looked up and saw that the Scottish forwards had all joined the maul and the backs had stayed deep. So he said to Krynauw to take the ball but just throw it off the top down to him. I'm watching this from the stands and it looks like basketball. Krynauw gets the ball, throws it down to Rassie, who gives a little sidestep to beat their flyhalf Gregor

Townsend, and he was through. Rassie was quick over 20 metres, but not as quick over 70 metres. He looks up and sees Pieter Rossouw out on the wing 35 metres away, so he kicks a long grubber up the left. The ball bounces perfectly for Pieter and he scores under the poles. We never practised that move. It was an idea that came to him on the field. That's the genius of Rassie Erasmus.

In that game James Small scored two tries to break the Springbok try-scoring record. The second try showed the spirit in the team and the bonds that had formed between the players. Percy Montgomery could have scored the try because he had a clear run-in, but he passed the ball to James on his outside so that he could get the record-breaking 20th try. James immediately ran off the field, job done, giving the sign for a replacement to come on. He retired after that match.

James was something of a hero for me. He was quite emotional on the bus back to the hotel. He had a hell of a lot of passion for the game. I know he was considered the bad boy of rugby because he was a rebel, but I had a lot of respect for him. The right player in a team doesn't have to be a person who just says yes, no or maybe. You want people who will challenge what they're told if they believe there's a better way. James would do that. Sometimes he was otherwise just for the sake of it, but he always came from left field and did things differently. I was his captain at the Cats and I always made sure I heard him out. If he had a kak idea, I would tell him straight and he accepted it. But I realised it was a mistake to ignore him. I saw in myself some of that fun-loving rebel and my strong desire to be heard when I felt things were wrong and could be done differently.

Nick had an interesting approach to keep James in line. He made James handle team discipline by appointing him the fines master. This was the guy who would dish out fines if, for example, someone was late for the bus. After a match, we'd have a fines meeting, known as a kontiki, and James dealt out the punishment – usually a down-down of beer.

We had some great characters in that side, and few come bigger in stature than Krynauw Otto. We were once at a sponsor's function where popular TV presenter Candice Hillebrand was doing interviews. She wanted to talk to a Springbok player. The Afrikaans guys were a bit shy about talking to Candice in English, but Krynauw was always keen on a challenge, so he stepped up. We gathered close by to listen as Candice asked Krynauw how he felt when he sang the national anthem before a Test match. Krynauw thought about this for a second. He wanted to say he got goosebumps, and quickly translated from Afrikaans to English in his head. The Afrikaans word for goosebumps is *hoendervleis* (chicken flesh). Confidently, Krynauw spoke up, 'Ja, it's quite emotional. I get chicken pox all over.' The English players burst out laughing, but the Afrikaans guys were impressed and gave Krynauw a big thumbs-up, '*Kolskoot!*' (Bull's eye!)

At Free State, the players were often reluctant to be named Man of the Match because that meant they had to do an interview in English on TV. When I was a player, we would push the guys who were more comfortable speaking English forward to accept the award and do the dreaded TV interview, and spare the rest of us any potential embarrassment. When I became coach of the Free State Vodacom Cup team, we had a similar issue. Fortunately, we had signed English-speaker Rory Duncan, and he solved the problem. For something like seven successive games, to the surprise of the commentators, Rory stepped up to be interviewed as the Man of the Match – even when he hadn't played a great game.

Another incident of a conversation lost in translation took place when the Cheetahs were in Hamilton, New Zealand, preparing for a game against the Chiefs. A group of us decided to have a beer after a meeting in our team room at the hotel. A beautiful woman sitting at the bar started chatting to our lock Corniel van Zyl. He was a very tall, slow-talking guy with a great sense of humour. She asked him what he did, and he told her he was a rugby player. Union or league? Union, he replied. When are you playing? Saturday, said Corniel. We were all straining to hear the conversation, slightly jealous that she chose him to talk to. Then she asked, 'So where are you guys from?' Corniel thought about this for a few seconds and replied, 'Well, we're from the team room.'

Smiley and I were always up to mischief. On a long flight home from Australia, he was fast asleep. I found a copy of the Sunday newspaper and wrapped him from head to foot in the pages. He looked like an Egyptian mummy. Then I pushed his button to call the flight attendant and went back to my seat to watch the surprised flight attendant dealing with a bewildered Smiley. On another occasion, in New Zealand, just as he was getting used to the time difference, I set his watch forward by an hour while he was sleeping. Then I woke him up, pretending we were late for the bus to the airport and watched while he frantically started packing his bags.

At the start of the 1998 international season, we played in white Springbok jerseys against Ireland in two home Tests. The first one in front of my home crowd in Bloemfontein was very special and my family came to watch. Dion O'Cuinneagain, the schoolboy who made the SA Schools team ahead of me in our Craven Week, made his debut for Ireland.

It was a vicious game, with their captain Paddy Johns and hooker Keith Wood getting stuck in with their fists. Our flyhalf Gaffie du Toit, in his debut game, suffered broken ribs and a cut head after being hit by Johns. I knew that Wood was a tough character, having come across him when South Africa A played Ireland A two years earlier in Dublin, which we lost 25–28. Wood was probably one of the hardest players I ever encountered, but he was up against James Dalton who wasn't afraid of a fight, and the same went for Ollie le Roux at prop. Then we had Krynauw Otto and Mark Andrews who were beasts in terms of physicality and hitting rucks. Although he would never start a fight, our captain Gary Teichmann wasn't someone to stand back either. André Venter was as strong as you can get and Joost was a hard-nosed guy. So we were ready for any physical intimidation.

We led by three points at halftime, but then blew them away in the second half to win 37–13, with Stefan Terblanche scoring four tries on debut.

The second Test at Loftus a week later was the dirtiest game I ever played in. I'd never seen so many punches thrown in a rugby match. Some of the forwards punched each other square in the face, while others were kicked in the head. Looking back on that game, I think most of us who were involved, from both sides, would be embarrassed at the way we behaved. If that game was played today, the ref would have handed out at least seven red cards. Years later, when I joined Munster, I met their head coach Anthony Foley, who was in that Irish squad but didn't play the Tests. He called that game The Battle of Pretoria.

The fight might have been a draw, but in rugby we destroyed Ireland. We won 33–0 and I scored one of our five tries. That was our eighth win in a row, but we weren't thinking about breaking any records for successive Test victories just yet. We were starting to feel very comfortable and confident about the starting line-up. Our loose trio was settled with me, André Venter and captain Gary Teichmann. The locks were Krynauw Otto and Mark Andrews; Os, Ollie or Adrian Garvey were the props; James Dalton or Naka were at hooker. When you know who 99% of the team will be, you know what you have to do on the field to win.

We annihilated a third-string Wales side at Loftus 96–13, scoring 15 tries. Hugh Bladen was the commentator and he complained that he was running out of paper to record the score. I scored one of the tries after throwing a dummy.

England sent a B team and we beat them 18–0 in the mud at Newlands. The drainage wasn't working and the field was still churned up from a game a couple of weeks earlier. All I remember from that match is that I didn't want the ball to be passed to me because you couldn't handle it. Everyone was covered in mud and we couldn't tell the difference between the jerseys. If a player didn't clean the mud off his face or talk to you, you wouldn't know if it was an Englishman or a Springbok right next to you. Nick didn't bother with a video session after the game because it was just knock-on after knock-on after knock-on.

We were now 10 games unbeaten and the media was starting to speculate about the chances of us breaking the record for most Test wins in a row, which stood at 17. We weren't thinking about that and were more focused on getting our first away win in the Tri Nations.

We nearly came unstuck in the rain at Subiaco Oval in Perth, had it not been for Aussie fullback Matt Burke missing a penalty in front of the posts in the final minutes. We scraped home 14–13 in our worst performance under Nick Mallett. Behind the scenes, some of the senior players were complaining about how little we were being paid, which would have distracted them. I was from Free State and whatever the contract said or the Test match fee was, I was happy. I wasn't part of any complaint to management; I didn't know about it and I didn't vote or do anything about it. What I do remember, though, is Nick ripping us apart in the post-match video session because of our kak performance.

While we were in Perth a cut on my leg became infected, probably due to fertiliser on the grass. The wound started swelling up and formed an abscess. Doc Verster gave me some potent antibiotics, so I was still hopeful I'd be able to play in the next match, against New Zealand at Athletic Park in Wellington. I knew the game against Australia had just been a glitch, and we had a great chance of beating the All Blacks at one of their fortress grounds. I was desperate to be on the field.

The problem with my leg wasn't the pain, but rather the fevers caused by the infection. The abscess didn't go away and I had to have an operation to remove it. Andrew Aitken replaced me and had a great game, though I wasn't worried yet that he'd take my place going forward. The team was settled and, while it wasn't great to miss the Wellington Test, it was lekker for me to watch us beat the All Blacks, even if I had to sit on the side of the field with my leg raised, resting on top of the advertising boards. I didn't feel, ag, I'm not on the fucking field! I just enjoyed the game.

Nick was in tears again after the match, and for good reason. It was a resounding victory as we returned to our dominant ways and won the match 13–3. All Black flyhalf Carlos Spencer had a shocker, missing five penalties.

I was on crutches as we celebrated in the change room after the game. It was a special time, but I was still feeling ill. That was the one night I didn't party and enjoy the victory as much as I normally would.

The return game against New Zealand at Kings Park in Durban was one of the most famous comebacks in Test history, and again I wasn't on the field to be part of it. Going into the final 15 minutes, we were down 5–23, and Nick decided to replace me with Andrew Aitken. I felt, 'Fuck, it's not nice being replaced.' I couldn't understand why I was being pulled off because I wasn't having a bad game. It wasn't a tactical substitution as we didn't have the 'Bomb Squad' system that we have today, where players go all out for the time they're on the field, knowing they'll be replaced by one of the Bomb Squad reserves later in the game.

That pissed-off feeling stayed with me and when I became Bok coach, I made sure my players always understood who would start the game and who would finish, and the reasons why. I ask them, do you want to be on the field at the start of the match or do you want to be on the field when the final whistle goes? I didn't want anyone to feel bad that they were being replaced.

In those days, you were replaced if you played badly, or if you were tired or injured. I was feeling good and felt I could still make a difference. That's when I knew, okay, there's somebody starting to bite at my ass now, because we had Aitken, Bobby Skinstad, Corné Krige and André Vos in the wings.

We won the Test in dramatic style, remarkably scoring three tries in the final 15 minutes to win 24–23. Time was up on the clock when we got a lineout on their five-metre line. We drove them back, and as the pack fell in a heap over the line, referee Peter Marshall awarded a try to James Dalton. After the match Andrew Aitken was quoted as saying, 'We just about scored it.'

We were really happy with back-to-back wins against the mighty All Blacks, but I was pissed off about being replaced, and Nick was furious that we had only started playing properly right at the end and gave us shit for it after the game.

I was feeling sorry for myself, but had to admit Andrew Aitken had had a fantastic game and made a difference when it counted. I couldn't be a dikbek and gatvol about it. I had to be a good team guy who understood what was important for us and be happy with the result.

Next we faced Australia at Ellis Park for what was a straight shoot-out for the Tri Nations title. For me personally, it was tougher playing against the likes of George Gregan, Stephen Larkham, Toutai Kefu and John Eales than it was against the All Blacks.

The Wallabies had beaten the All Blacks at Lancaster Park in Christchurch, so we expected a tough match. They had these calm guys like Gregan who was always chirping you. They could demoralise you with sledging, like the Aussie cricket players. It wasn't bad sledging but just enough to make you feel like an asshole. We won 29–15 and the result was never in danger. Bobby came on as a replacement and scored a brilliant try.

The victory was a relief, but I'm not proud of the way I celebrated winning the Tri Nations. This was the start of my wild partying. I took the Tri Nations trophy to a nightclub where we all drank booze out of it. I think that's where I started upsetting the balance of respect for the game and fun for myself. I started enjoying the partying too much. A normal player would have said, 'Guys, let's put the cup down, be humble and be good ambassadors.' I certainly wasn't one of those guys and I'm ashamed of it today.

By the time the end-of-year tour rolled round, I was feeling entitled and assured of my place in the team. But there was also a sense that things weren't as tight as they were before. There had always been some provincialism in the Springbok team, but it seemed to have worsened. Gary Teichmann picked up an injury in the Tri Nations and his form had slumped. Media speculation started growing about whether he would captain the Springboks at the 1999 Rugby World Cup.

Five months after we had destroyed Wales by 83 points at Loftus, we faced them again, this time at London's Wembley Stadium because the Millennium Stadium in Cardiff was still being built. This was a different Wales team, with only three players from the Loftus match and a new coach in New Zealander Graham Henry.

We struggled against their pack, and I didn't have a great game. I got some shit from Nick about that afterwards. We were trailing 17–20 with three minutes to go. But Franco Smith kicked two penalties and, with time up on the clock, Joost broke for Corné and offloaded to me in the tackle. I couldn't gather the ball, but André Venter was right behind me to control it and score. It was our 15th successive victory, only two off the record of 17 in a row.

Bobby Skinstad was now making a strong claim to actually start a Test match rather than coming on as a substitute as he had in all seven of the Tests he had played so far, each time making a significant difference and having scored three tries. He never failed to make an impact, on and off the field. Bobby was an incredible rugby player. He could tackle superbly, he could steal a ball, he could sidestep and pass on both sides, and he could run. I knew he should be in the starting team.

Sometimes we misunderstood him as a windgat laaitie, but he was just outspoken. He should have had a career of 100 Test matches instead of 42, but he didn't always get his chance in the beginning, and he also got injured.

We weren't ready for the Bobby Skinstad era. When we had time off on Wednesdays and Thursdays and went to a nightclub, Bobby would go to SuperSport and do extra classes on how to communicate. He could be a stoutgat and have a few drinks, but if Bobby went to a function, he would remember every single person's name. I was terrible at that. Bobby was the guy behind the Stormers' image of 'the men in black' with their black kit. The guys might have thought he was windgat, but we were a bit *agter die klip* (behind the times) – Bobby was ahead of the game.

At this point, rugby league tactics and defence systems were starting to make their way into rugby union, which meant defences were more organised and solid. André, with his power, could run over the opposition. I couldn't because I weighed just 92 kilograms. It was also difficult to sidestep the opposition in the face of a wall of defenders who knew how to do their jobs.

I started developing skills like stealing the ball, securing the turnover ball, and hitting and spinning, which kept me in the team. My strength was that I could read the game. Also, I analysed the hell out of the opposition on my computer. As a result, I thought that if they wanted Bobby in the starting line-up, it wouldn't be in the place of André or me. André was as solid as a rock at openside flanker. My job was at close quarters, while Bobby thrived as a more open player. I was playing well, and I thought Gary might be the one who wouldn't make the team if Bobby had to start.

Bobby was an eighthman who could play openside flanker as well, while I was the blindside flanker who could also play eighthman. According to my thinking purely on rugby grounds, Bobby would be a natural replacement for Gary.

While we expected Bobby to get his chance, it was still a shock when Nick made the call to put André on the bench as a replacement lock for the Scotland Test at Murrayfield, with Bobby taking his place on the side of the scrum. I felt so bad for André because we were good mates and he was my Free State teammate. He was very upset and close to tears about the decision.

We were nervous about how this change would affect the team. We had been a settled team for 15 Tests and now felt we were starting to unravel. We also started to hear rumblings that the relationship between Gary and Nick wasn't great and that Gary might not be captain at the World Cup the following year. And so a few of us informally decided that whoever was offered the captaincy after Gary would say no. We could see things were going pear-shaped.

One of the problems was that we weren't properly briefed. We were simply expected to understand what the coaches were saying and why they were saying it. Instead, we only heard rumours; it was never out in the open. In those days, rugby worked like that – there was very little transparency. Nick didn't have one-on-ones every day telling people what was going on, and so of course there was bound to be uncertainty in the team.

The problems in the camp affected all of us and we put in a sluggish performance against Scotland, even though we won 35–10. Bobby justified his selection with a great try. We now had 16 wins in a row and I hadn't yet lost a match as a Springbok.

I learnt a hell of a lot from this experience. Coaches and players need to communicate properly. Players need to ask the coach what is going on if they're unsure. They shouldn't make assumptions and make pacts like we did. When we heard stories of André or Gary being replaced, we should have spoken to Nick. I don't think we were mature enough to handle professional sport. This team was so comfortable playing and winning together that we were nervous about change. Maybe we were just too naïve to ask the right questions about the captaincy issue. We acted in a stupid players' way of 'Fuck that! If they want to work Gary out, we're not going to take the captaincy.' Even at training sessions, it was us against them. When I think back, it was so fucking stupid.

A coach has to have a proper, open communication system with his players. Whatever is going on, or decided in the boardroom and at selection meetings, if the coach isn't consistently giving players information, then all they get are rumours and misinformation through other means like social media. I've had situations where we've had a team talk in the morning, a player leaves full of confidence, and the next day he comes back a broken man because of things his friends or parents have told him were said on Twitter. Whatever rumours are going around, they eventually get to the players. Transparency is vital.

We, however, were now one match away from equalling the All Blacks' record of 17 wins in a row. Still, the record wasn't an issue for the team, even if the media and the fans were making a big deal out of it. I didn't even know that a win against Ireland at Lansdowne Road in Dublin equalled the record. We just wanted to beat Ireland after the brutal Tests earlier in the year. The match was as tough as we expected and three yellow cards were handed out: Keith Wood once again in trouble, along with Peter Clohessy, and Adrian Garvey for the Boks. We were constantly penalised – there were something like 25 penalties against us. But it was nothing like those Tests in Bloemfontein and Pretoria.

We won 27–13 and so equalled the record. I was very happy with the way I played, and I scored one of my better Test tries, picking up a loose ball after Mark Andrews wasn't able to gather a pass from Pieter Rossouw. The ball was rolling behind me, but I controlled it and, as the defence came up, I dummied a pass to Bobby, spotted a gap and ran 30 metres to score next to the upright.

And so we went on to Twickenham where we were overwhelming favourites to beat England the following weekend and break the Test victory record. But this wasn't the confident team of seven Tests ago. There have been stories that we were distracted because the wives and girlfriends joined us. That's bullshit. Their presence actually helps you to focus on the game if you're mature about it.

We blew it, losing 7–13, though we had our chances. Monty missed a sitter in front of the poles. In the final move of the match, we had an opportunity to score but, as we surged towards their line, their winger Dan Luger managed to interfere with the final pass, which would have sent Stefan Terblanche clear. That's how close the margins are in international rugby. Had Luger not swatted the ball away, Stefan would have scored and we would have won 14–13, broken the record and returned home as heroes.

Instead, we were justifiably criticised as being tired, unfocused and lacking motivation. Nick said we partied too much. A group of players did go out earlier in the week before the Test match, but I wasn't interested in partying before the game. By this stage of the tour, breaking that record had become a big deal for some of the guys, including me. All I remember was that I fought like mad. I really wanted to win that match. There were a number of reasons why we lost, including the fact that expectations of breaking the record lay heavily on some of the players – the pressure became too much and they couldn't perform because of it.

We didn't realise it then, but it was the end of an era. We were about to go through a difficult time in the build-up to the World Cup just 10 months away.

5

THE RUGBY WORLD CUP WAS THE FOCUS of the 1999 international season. We started with two home Tests against Italy in June, before a one-off Test against Wales in Cardiff, then the Tri Nations in July and August, and finally the Rugby World Cup in October and November. The Wales match fell outside the Test calendar, which meant clubs weren't obliged to release their players. It was played to mark the opening of the new Millennium Stadium which replaced Cardiff Arms Park, and to generate money for SARFU and the Welsh Rugby Union.

Italy weren't slouches and could perform well against the traditional rugby nations. The previous year, they had beaten both Argentina and Scotland and came close to an upset against Wales in Llanelli. Their 1999 season started with defeats away to Scotland and Ireland, although they had given the Irish a fright by leading at halftime. But they were no match for the Springboks and we ran up cricket scores against them: 74–3 in Port Elizabeth, and 101–0 in Durban.

Despite these easy victories, we remained unsettled, with growing rumours about the fate of Gary Teichmann not only as captain but also as a member of the World Cup squad. He was battling with a neck injury and had missed some big Super Rugby matches. Nick also started experimenting and gave 11 players their international debuts, including André Vos and Corné Krige, which added to the pressure I felt to keep my place. Bobby Skinstad was out because of injury, having seriously damaged his knee in a car accident the previous month.

In the Kings Park Test against Italy, Gary was ruled out with a hamstring injury and Nick asked me to be the captain. My memory is that he asked me twice, the first time quite casually in the week before the game. He just said, 'Would you consider being the captain?' I was 26 years old and wasn't keen, so I turned it down. Later he was a lot more serious when he called me in and started the conversation with, 'Now listen here ...'

It wasn't a difficult decision to say no for a second time. I was partying quite hard in those days and wasn't a particularly good role model. My view is the captain has to be near-perfect and, with my bad behaviour away from rugby, I was far from it. Frankly, I was a bit surprised Nick asked me because I never thought the captaincy would come my way. I know he was very disappointed because he thought I had the leadership potential. But I understood what was required of a captain, having done the job at school, for Free State and for the Cats. The Bok captaincy came at the wrong time for me.

Nick was surprised that I turned him down:

I knew about his partying behaviour. But I could never, ever understand his reluctance to be the captain. He had been captain of his team from his school days. I can only put it down to his own insecurities. I don't think he likes being head coach either. He doesn't like to sit in front of media and explain himself. For him, that part of the job is the most painful because he gets embarrassed.

I was aware that he was partying hard. The game wasn't 100% pro-fessional and we were all partying hard. When we beat France 52–10, I was out with Gary Teichmann at a nightclub until 6am. We celebrated victories like that. We didn't go to bed at 9pm. It bonded the team and made us better. I never worried about the partying on a Saturday night. What would have angered me is if I had known they were partying on the Wednesday or Thursday. I left the responsibility with the players. I told them early on that I wasn't going to be a policeman, but if I found out they were drinking on weekdays, they'd get dropped. I wasn't going to knock on their doors at 11pm to see if they were in bed. They were adults. They were letting their team down if they didn't prepare properly for the game. They had to respect their teammates.

There was an occasion in 1998 when I was told [Rassie] had gone out with a few of the other players before the England Test, but I couldn't verify it and they denied it, so what could I do? He was pissed off that Gary Teichmann wasn't going to the World Cup but he did his best to motivate the team. He and Smiley decided not to drink alcohol, but after we beat England in the quarterfinal and there was so much pressure on us because we hadn't played well in the group stage, Rassie broke his fast. We were back in London and Rassie said to the players, we've got nine days to the semifinal. Let's have a proper party, not with the coaching staff, just with ourselves. He got the gees going; he was good at that.

Apart from my behaviour, I also didn't want to be the captain at a time when things were changing and the players were so unsure of themselves. Being the captain under those circumstances wasn't something I wanted because I wasn't keen to be the centre of attention. I also didn't want people to think I desperately wanted to be captain and was stabbing Gary in the back. He was such a role model as captain.

Corné came into the side as captain on debut and took my openside flanker place. I moved to the other side of the scrum with André Vos at eighthman and André Venter on the bench.

We had a crazy schedule after the Italy series, flying to Wales for the Test match to open the Millennium Stadium, back to South Africa and then off to New Zealand for the Tri Nations. I didn't mind all the travelling. I was enjoying seeing the world and meeting people from different cultures.

The Wales Test will be remembered for being the first time Wales beat

South Africa in a rugby international, and for being the last time South Africa started a Test match with an all-white team (Breyton Paulse was on the bench).

Before the game, there was some distraction about money, with the senior players arguing with management about a fair share of the profits being earned from this one-off game. I wasn't involved. Coming from Despatch and Free State, I just wanted to play. I didn't want to fight about the money.

We lost the match 19–29. All I remember is missing a tackle on the Welsh centre Mark Taylor, which resulted in a try. I was shitting myself for the video session afterwards because it was such an easy tackle. That might have been the reason I was dropped for the next Test match.

We then flew to Dunedin to play the All Blacks at Carisbrook in the Tri Nations, which I watched from the stands while Corné played in my place. The match – played, appropriately, at the stadium nicknamed The House of Pain – was a disaster, with Corné shattering his knee in a collision between himself and Os du Randt and All Black winger Christian Cullen, which ended Corné's hopes of playing in the Rugby World Cup. We couldn't even get on the scoreboard and lost 0–28. As it turned out, this was Gary's last Test match. He took a knock on the leg and suffered a haematoma, which ruled him out of the next match, against Australia in Brisbane. He was starting to be isolated and knew his place in the team was in danger. When we got back to South Africa, Nick sacked him.

With Gary and André Vos injured and Corné having already flown home, there simply wasn't anyone else with experience to captain the side. We didn't even have a loose forward on the bench. This time Nick didn't ask me if I wanted to be captain. He was a lot more blunt about it, saying, 'Fuck you, now you won't say no, you *will* be captain.' And that's how I became the Springbok captain. For one game only.

Gary could have gone home, but he chose to stay with the team and give me support and advice in the days leading up to the game. It should have been a big moment for me, but with the drama in the team regarding the issue of the captaincy and uncertainty over who would be in the World Cup squad, I didn't feel a sense of occasion. I wasn't this charismatic guy with the ability to pull the team together in a World Cup year. I knew my limitations.

We lost 6–32, at the time the second-biggest defeat in Springbok history and worst-ever against Australia. With the likes of Gregan and Larkham in their ranks, I knew we didn't have a team able to beat the Wallabies. I had a good game, but I was devastated by the result.

We'd had three captains in three Tests, but I didn't have the maturity or emotional intelligence to discuss the captaincy issue with Nick. I didn't feel it was my place to challenge him. I was this Afrikaans-speaking guy who hadn't won anything at Free State. I didn't have an inferiority complex – I just thought I knew my place.

The team was starting to break up into factions. Provincialism is always an issue, but this was intense. Coming from Free State, I couldn't get the Stormers, Bulls and Sharks guys to pull themselves together in these uncertain times. Competition for places was also hotting up, with Ruben Kruger (now back from injury), Skinstad (returning from injury), Aitken, Vos, Venter, Teichmann and me – seven guys vying for three places (Corné's terrible knee injury had ruled him out). We were all in survival mode.

It wasn't just the loose forwards – everyone was feeling the pressure to play in the World Cup. Players plan their whole careers around it, and will play another year even when they're too old. Youngsters will be pushed in because of public opinion. In a World Cup year, you must have a core of players, and if the team changes, it should change only when someone shows such great form that they just kick down the door. If somebody becomes entitled, you drop him. If someone loses form badly, you drop him. So, naturally, groups start to form. Things become chaotic and the media starts jumping on the bandwagon, selecting teams with dark horses that few people have considered. Sometimes coaches give in to that.

The coaches are also under enormous pressure because they don't know if they're about to become unemployed. Seldom in a World Cup year does the Springbok coach know if he has a job next year, nor do the assistant coaches and analysts.

With Gary having been dropped, we came back home to face the All Blacks at Loftus Versfeld, with Joost van der Westhuizen as our new captain. I took Gary's place at the back of the scrum for my first international appearance as eighthman. If there wasn't already pressure on this team, we were now heading to the fourth defeat in a row. There were also issues of transformation as Nick had chosen another all-white starting XV. I wasn't aware of this at the time, but Rian Oberholzer, chief executive of SARFU, had told him to change the team, which meant Deon Kayser now started, with Stefan on the bench. Looking back, I see that this was unfair on both players, because Deon was made to feel that his selection was based only on his skin colour, while Stefan knew he had lost his starting place for reasons other than rugby. We didn't make a big issue about it, and I don't recall it being a distraction.

We lost the All Blacks Test 18–34, the fourth loss in a row and our worst run of defeats since 1974. How quickly our fortunes had changed in nine months when we enjoyed our best run of victories. We sneaked a 10–9 victory against Australia at Newlands in terrible weather conditions to end a miserable Tri Nations, but at least avoiding a winless tournament. We were now heading off to the World Cup having lost four out of our last five Tests.

6

DETERMINED TO BE IN PEAK CONDITION for the tournament, Smiley and I went on a beer fast for over 50 days in the build-up to the 1999 World Cup, marking each day off on a calendar. The weeks leading up to the squad announcement were very tense. I started thinking, 'Ag, if I don't make it, I'll get another chance in 2003.' But I was working my ass off to get selected.

Nick didn't tell us we were in the World Cup squad but dropped hints by asking players to apply for visas for the UK. The big giveaway was that the selected players received an invitation to what turned out to be a bizarre function at SuperSport where the team was officially announced to the media and the public. The organisers of the announcement made us wear ridiculous space suits with helmets that covered our faces. We were called out one by one and then took off our helmets to reveal our identity. It was very cheesy and definitely not my thing.

Once the team was selected, we started training together, adjusting to Joost as captain, and trying to get over the fact that some guys, like Gary Teichmann, hadn't been picked.

A big problem was that I was experiencing a lot of pain and swelling around my groin area. I first felt it at the beginning of the year, and the pain would come and go. It turned out to be osteitis pubis, where the joint between the left and right pubic bones becomes inflamed. It's a common problem among footballers. For a long time the injury wasn't properly diagnosed, but with the help of treatment from Doc Verster, I was able to play through the pain. There's a seam between the pubic bones just above the groin and Doc injected me with cortisone, right into that seam. Fuck, it was sore. I couldn't lift the blanket up off the bed with my foot without pain. Even moving my foot from the accelerator to the brake was sore. In 2000, I eventually had an operation performed by Dr Mark Ferguson, a specialist orthopaedic surgeon at Rosebank Clinic, who fixed the problem. But in the build-up to the World Cup there wasn't time for surgery. I wasn't particularly worried because I knew that once I had warmed up I would be okay, and I could also have an anti-inflammatory injection at halftime if the pain was really bad. I also had issues with my shoulders and often had one of them strapped for a game. It would take major surgery – like a knee ligament operation – to keep me out of the World Cup. Lots of players carried injuries. Os played with a knee injury and wore a knee-guard.

Doc Verster understood how much pain we could play through. He had pulled me out of the game against England the previous year after I was concussed playing France. He would know if a player was so sore that he couldn't play. I made sure he didn't hear me complain about my injuries. If I said it wasn't sore and Doc could get me past the injury to play, then I'd play.

The World Cup was hosted by Wales, but we were based in Edinburgh, Scotland. I couldn't care where we were, because I didn't pay attention to these things. Instead, I was focused on how we were being coached, who we were going to play and what our tactics were.

Our opening match was against Scotland in front of a passionate crowd at Murrayfield. Scotland was always the kind of team that could disappoint and play kak when you least expected it, but when it came to a World Cup they were real contenders. They were also the Five Nations champions, losing only to England (by three points) in that tournament and beating France in Paris. With their great lead-up to the tournament, especially compared with our disastrous run, they were fancied to pull off an upset against us.

We suffered an immediate blow when Henry Honiball injured his hamstring in training, and Nick had to change his tactics to accommodate my Free State teammate Jannie de Beer at flyhalf. We started slowly against Scotland and trailed at halftime before a second-half burst gave us a 46–29 victory, including a try by another Free State teammate, Ollie le Roux, a prop who ran like a back.

We followed that up with two big wins, against Spain (47–3) and Uruguay (39–3), but because they were such minnows and we were the defending World Cup champions, we were expected to beat them by much higher margins. The Uruguay players even celebrated after the match, having expected a much bigger drubbing. Brendan Venter got a red card for stamping – although it really should have been a yellow card – so now we had a mark on our disciplinary record which would have been a deciding factor if a game ended in a draw or a washout.

As a team, we were still picking up momentum, but suddenly, because we had failed to destroy Spain and Uruguay, the media started to write us off, despite the fact that we had scored an average of 44 points per game in the tournament.

We met England in the quarterfinals. They were so confident about beating us that they didn't bother checking out of their hotel in London ahead of the game. They thought they'd be back there that evening, through to the semifinals. I was very confident about our chances, though, because mentally we didn't have a barrier against England. Sure, we had lost to them at critical times, but I had never gone into a game against England believing we would lose.

The game was Jannie de Beer's finest moment, scoring 34 points (a Springbok record), including five drop goals (a world record). I've heard lots of people claim that they had the idea of the drop goals, but it was actually Jannie's plan. I knew from playing with him at Free State that he

Where it all began – the under-9A team at Despatch Voorbereidingskool. I am in the middle row on the extreme left. Frikkie Meyer, a Despatch legend, is the coach, with his son (also Frikkie) in the front row on the left. PERSONAL COLLECTION

The under-13 team at Susannah Fourie Primary School. I am in the middle of the front row with the ball. The coaches are Blits Fourie (on my left) and Theo Strydom (on my right). PERSONAL COLLECTION

On the South Africa A tour in England in November 1996 and seeing snow for the first time.
PERSONAL COLLECTION

In action for Free State against Natal. My teammates behind me are Naka Drotské and the late Dougie Heymans. The Sharks player is French legend Thierry Lacroix. PERSONAL COLLECTION

On the 1996 South Africa A tour with Cheetahs teammates Ryno Opperman (who became my boss at Minolta), Naka Drotské, Willie Meyer (who lived on my street in Despatch) and Edrich Lubbe.
PERSONAL COLLECTION

In action for the Cheetahs, showing that forwards can also sprint like backs.
PERSONAL COLLECTION

With fellow Free Stater Franco Smith, coach Nick Mallett and Transvaal's Hannes Strydom on the 1996 South Africa A tour of the UK. PERSONAL COLLECTION

With Cheetahs teammates Willie Meyer and Naka Drotské before the South Africa A team's opening match against the University of Cambridge at Grange Road in November 1996. We won 57–11.
PERSONAL COLLECTION

Celebrating Free State's first Currie Cup victory in 29 years at Loftus Versfeld with assistant coach Helgard Müller on 22 October 2005.
PERSONAL COLLECTION

In action against Australia during the 1999 World Cup semifinal at Twickenham on 30 October 1999. Behind me is my Cheetahs teammate and one of the toughest people I know, on and off the field, André Venter.
PROFESSIONAL SPORT/GETTY IMAGES

Hanging on to Australia's flyhalf Stephen Larkham in the 1999 World Cup semifinal. Krynauw Otto comes in to assist with Deon Kayser (far right). Behind me is Aussie eighthman Toutai Kefu, with Michael Foley on the left.
POPPERFOTO/GETTY IMAGES

At Adidas in Herzogenaurach, Germany, with Frikkie Erasmus in 2003, trying to solve the problem of my broken foot. PERSONAL COLLECTION

The official Free State team photo with the Currie Cup, back at Free State Stadium for the first time since 1976 after beating the Blue Bulls 29–25 at Loftus in 2005. PERSONAL COLLECTION

Coaching at the Stormers in 2008 with Gary Gold (right). The players are AJ Venter (left) and Schalk Brits. I worked again with Gary when he was assistant Springbok coach at the 2011 World Cup. GARY GOLD

A great honour when the main pavilion at Hoërskool Despatch was named after me in March 2016. Next to me is headmaster Colin Bartle, and alongside him is Springbok legend Danie Gerber, after whom the sports complex was named. HOËRSKOOL DESPATCH

Enjoying ice cream with my daughters, Carli, Nikki and Jani, on a family outing to Dingle, a small holiday town on the southwest coast of Ireland in 2016.
PERSONAL COLLECTION

A minute's silence in memory of the late Munster Rugby head coach Anthony 'Axel' Foley before a match between Munster and Glasgow Warriors at Thomond Park in Limerick on 22 October 2016. Munster won 38–17.
DIARMUID GREENE/SPORTSFILE

When in Ireland, do as the Irish do. Jacques Nienaber acquires a taste for Guinness at our favourite pub, The Black Swan, just outside Castleconnell in 2017. PERSONAL COLLECTION

The end of our Munster adventure. Jacques at the bus stop on our way to the airport to fly home in November 2017. Our families had left for South Africa a few weeks earlier.
PERSONAL COLLECTION

could kick a drop goal from anywhere on the field. He raised the idea during training, so we practised a few moves on how to set up the opportunities. We called a drop goal 'a Naas', after Naas Botha, the master of the drop goal in the 1980s, with 18 drop goals in his 28 Tests and having famously dropkicked Northern Transvaal to victory in the 1987 Currie Cup final against Transvaal at Ellis Park in the mud and rain.

Nick has a different recollection of the dropgoal strategy:

I was sitting on a golf cart with Brendan Venter on the Wednesday before the game. I was worried about England because they didn't give penalties away easily and had a good pack of forwards that could perhaps match us. Henry Honiball was injured, so Jannie would play flyhalf. He couldn't attack the gain line in the same way Henry could, so our backs weren't getting across the advantage line. Brendan, who knew Jannie from Free State, said, 'Why don't you ask Jannie to kick drop goals?' Jannie was also playing golf and I went over to ask him about Brendan's idea. I asked him, if he could drop goals, why hadn't he kicked any so far? He said because I made him play flat like Henry. I said this was a vital game and, if he wanted to kick drop goals, how should we set him up? He said, 'From in front of the poles,' and looked at me as if I was mad. In practice the next day we worked out a strategy where the forwards took the ball up, passed to the backs, who took the ball into the middle of the field and passed back to Jannie for the drop. Jannie kicked 10 out of 10, and the longest was 45 metres. I couldn't believe it. In the game he kicked two or three from those scenarios we practised, but a few of them were from general play.

After Jannie slotted his first 'Naas' just after halftime, he thought, 'Why not go again?' and repeated the feat two minutes later. It had the effect of keeping the scoreboard ticking over steadily and the points margin widening. Joost at scrumhalf had a great understanding with Jannie and made sure he had plenty of opportunities.

Jannie was probably the best flyhalf I've ever played with in my whole career. I played with him from university days at Shimlas. He was very much like Henry Honiball – quiet and hard working. Jannie was naturally talented, could tackle and could kick. Few people knew how good this guy really was. But I think sometimes he didn't back himself as much as he should have.

We won 44–21 and were in the World Cup semifinals. The victory erased all the shit that we had gone through with Gary and the captaincy. We had to wait for the England players to check out of The Petersham Hotel in Richmond so that we could move in.

Now we faced Australia, a team we often struggled to beat, in our semifinal at Twickenham. I had a mental barrier when it came to playing the Wallabies. We were without Brendan Venter after a disciplinary committee gave him a 21-day suspension for the red card against Uruguay, which meant he was only available the day before the World Cup final. Henry Honiball was fit, but Jannie's heroics six days earlier made him the first-choice flyhalf and Henry was on the bench.

What followed was the most intense Test match, very tense and physical. No tries were scored, but Jannie and Australia's Matt Burke kept the scoreboard moving with penalties, and one drop goal from Jannie. The pressure was relentless as the Aussies launched wave after wave of attacks, and we tackled them back every time.

It was a hell of a game to watch, with both teams playing incredible rugby, attacking each other's line despite the difficult playing conditions in rain and a swirling wind. Throughout the 80 minutes of normal time, we were never in the lead. Every time Burke kicked a penalty or two to increase the points deficit, Jannie would chip away at it with a couple of penalties or a drop goal. We were never more than six points behind.

The second half never seemed to end as referee Derek Bevan played eight minutes of added time. We weren't complaining because we were down 15–18. We had the momentum and were on the attack when Bevan penalised the Wallabies for playing the ball on the ground, with seconds left on the clock. I had always believed in Jannie's abilities, but this was a tricky kick wide on the right-hand side, midway between the halfway line and the Aussies' 22-metre line. I didn't want to think about the pressure Jannie must have been feeling, knowing that this kick would keep our chances alive in the tournament. A number of players had started cramping, and I wondered how Jannie's legs were feeling. He seemed completely calm and took his time to position the ball. Because of the gusting wind, he asked Robbie Fleck to hold it steady while he lined up for the kick. I stood on the halfway line, barely able to watch. After what seemed ages, he finally kicked it ... sweetly between the uprights. The scores were tied at 18–all and Bevan immediately blew the full-time whistle to take the match into 20 minutes of extra time.

Burke and Jannie traded penalties, and then came the sucker-punch. In the second period of extra time, the Wallabies flyhalf Stephen Larkham decided to borrow from Jannie's playbook and went for a drop kick. We were hardly expecting it because Larkham didn't kick drop goals, and he was also a long way out, 48 metres from the poles. I was bearing down on him and instinctively threw my hands in the air to block the kick. It didn't even look like a drop kick. I thought he was kicking for the corner, but then I realised he was going for poles. I swear the damn ball flew between my outstretched thumbs.

People remember that drop kick being the winner for Australia, but there were still seven minutes left to play, enough time for us to draw level again. The problem was that we needed a try to win the match. If the game ended level on points, Australia would go through to the final because they had a better disciplinary record, with Brendan Venter's red card counting against us.

Everyone started cramping badly, and we couldn't run any more. None of us had played extra time in a rugby international before, and we never looked like scoring a try. It started pissing with rain and we had to run from everywhere to try to get that try. Matt Burke kicked another penalty with three minutes left on the clock. We tried one final attack, but the Wallabies' defence was solid and they held out for a 27–21 victory.

I knew we had played in a rugby match that would be remembered for a very long time. We had battled our hearts out, so there was no disgrace being beaten. I was quoted as saying, 'The heart stays a little more sore than the body after losing a game like that.' I don't actually remember saying that, but it's an accurate reflection of how I felt.

It was so disappointing for me personally. I thought, 'Fuck man, we've worked so hard, against all the odds. Why couldn't that drop kick just hit my hand and deflect?' It was one of the most disappointing things to have happened to me on a rugby field.

We now had to face either France or New Zealand in the third-place playoff match. We fully expected to play France, and Nick gave us three days off. Our wives had joined us, so Nikki and I, and Smiley and his wife, Corne, hopped over to visit Amsterdam. We decided to take a break from rugby and didn't bother to watch the France–New Zealand semifinal, so we missed the dramatic French fightback and the incredible upset as they beat the mighty All Blacks 43–31. We came in from sightseeing and Smiley suggested we check on the score.

We couldn't believe it. We were playing New Zealand for third place. I didn't think we were allowed to go to Amsterdam. I didn't think Nick even knew we were there as we weren't supposed to go off and have fun in another country. We had to rush to change our flights and get back. We had only been there for a day and now we had to start training again.

It turns out Nick knew exactly where we were:

I was well aware of that trip to Amsterdam, and it didn't bother me at all. We had worked so hard for the past three months preparing for that World Cup, and it was desperately disappointing to lose and then have

to play New Zealand in the third-place playoff. I didn't think that prac-
tising on the Monday night before the game on Thursday was going to
help at all. So I told the players I wanted them all back by Wednesday.
We'd have a captain's run on Wednesday night, and play the game the
next day. I told them we were prepared enough, so go and have fun, go
to Spain, go wherever, I don't care.

It was hard to get motivated for what seemed like a meaningless game. No
one wants to win third place at the World Cup. But it was our old enemy,
so there was some satisfaction in beating them. We led throughout the
match and eventually won 22–18. The only thing that stood out for me
there, apart from winning, was that I'd never faced a haka in which the All
Blacks looked so unmotivated. I remember looking at their captain, Taine
Randell, and seeing how, mentally, he wasn't in the game. I have faced the
All Black haka five times in my career, and that was the only time I looked
at them and thought, 'Fuck, they are not up for this game.'

When the Springboks' 2000 international season resumed in June with
a one-off Test against Canada and two Tests against England, Nick was
still the coach, though under pressure for having lost the World Cup. I
was living the high life in Johannesburg, playing for the Cats, nursing my
various injuries with frequent injections, but still playing good rugby. The
Cats, now coached by Laurie Mains, had finished fourth on the Super
12 log, and lost to the Brumbies in the semifinals in Canberra. The Cats'
loose trio was André Venter, André Vos and me – the same three who
played for the Springboks in our final game of the 1999 World Cup. Nick
opted to keep this successful trio for the new Springbok season, and the
captaincy was given to Vossie rather than Joost van der Westhuizen, who
was returning from injury and had missed most of the Super 12.

Nick was taking a new approach – as happens with every coach
when he's trying to hang onto his job. He can so easily fall into the trap

of listening to too many people just to keep the media and those who play political games happy. I remember the attempt at a whole mind-shift change but it was never going to work for us. Previously, we had relied a lot on the physical strength and hard tackling of the forwards. We would do the grunt work up front, while the backs made magic out wide. With the change, the forwards were now expected to play a running game, which didn't suit many of the big locks. We had to develop a fast, attacking mindset with a circus trick or two, which not everybody had. It suited me because I tackled hard but I could also run with the ball, spot the gap and sidestep my opponent. I was finding it more difficult to run over the opposition because of the rugby league-style defence system that was gaining popularity in rugby union, so I was quite excited about the new game plan.

As expected, we beat Canada in East London, 51–18, trying out Nick's new 'ball-in-hand' tactics, but were lucky to scrape a victory against England the following weekend at Loftus after the video ref ruled out an England try.

Then we went on another four-game losing streak, which just added to Nick's pressure to keep his job. England squared the two-Test series with a victory in Bloemfontein before we flew to Melbourne for a money-maker Test match played under the roof at the Docklands Stadium. It was our fourth attempt at Nick's new running-rugby tactic, against a team that had already perfected it. No surprise that we came unstuck, losing 23–44. We also lost our two Tri Nations matches, against New Zealand in Christchurch, and then Australia in Sydney, before salvaging some pride by beating the All Blacks at Ellis Park 46–40, scoring six tries – the most points and the most tries the All Blacks had ever conceded in a Test match. Nick's game plan seemed to be coming together and I played a slightly unusual role of auxiliary flyhalf, which allowed me to run more and set up the backline.

7

A S GREAT AS IT WAS TO SCORE SIX TRIES against the All Blacks, we had also leaked four tries, which was a concern. The Wallabies were ranked number one in the world and we had to face them next. I was always worried about Australia. For me they were always much trickier to play than New Zealand. The win against the All Blacks, our biggest rivals, did nothing to take the pressure off Nick. We had now lost four out of five matches, and SARFU was looking for a reason to get rid of him. But we thought they couldn't just sack him if we had successive victories over Tri Nations teams.

We gave one of our best performances at Kings Park against a very tough Australian side. Before the match, I had shown Nick a move that the Aussies used from a lineout. I suggested a strategy to counter the move, which involved me going for an interception rather than defending against their eighthman Toutai Kefu. I had noticed that Kefu was merely a dummy runner in that move, so if I went for the interception instead of guarding Kefu, it might lead to us scoring a try. Nick was initially sceptical but when he saw that the idea had potential, he agreed to us trying it on the field. We saw the move coming, put our plan in place and it worked perfectly. I burst away and went over the line for a try. But the referee Paul Honiss ruled that he couldn't be certain that I had grounded the ball and so disallowed the try.

Nick Mallett also remembered the incident:

On the Wednesday before the game Rassie came to me with his computer and said, 'Have a look at this.' In their 22, they have a move from defensive lineout that they use every single time. It was very effective. They do a dummy jump, and John Eales takes the ball coming forward and palms it down to Michael Foley at hooker. He gives it to George Gregan, who passes behind Toutai Kefu to Stirling Mortlock who clears. I said, 'It's no problem, we've blocked them up. You tackle Kefu, André Venter tackles Gregan, and Henry Honiball tackles Mortlock.' But he pointed out that Kefu never gets the ball – he just does a dummy run. He said, 'Let me go for the interception. If they do give the ball to Kefu, our scrumhalf is there to defend.' They got a lineout in their 22, and there was the move – Eales to Foley, Foley to Gregan, Gregan to … Rassie Erasmus, who had intercepted the ball. He ran 20 metres and dived over the line. But two players tackled him as he went over.

It was the very first time they went upstairs to the TMO [television match official]. The referee didn't say, 'Is there any reason I can't award the try?' They've changed the instruction since then. He asked, 'Can you see the ball being grounded?' The TMO said, 'Unfortunately, there are two Australian players on Rassie's back, so I can't see the ball being grounded,' so the ref said, 'Well, I can't award the try.' It was ridiculous. Rassie was lying on top of the ball, pressed firmly into the ground, with the other players on top of him. That cost us seven points, we lost the game 18–19, and I was subsequently fired.

That summed up Rassie's ability as a flanker, working out the opposition and understanding what he had to do. It was a massive blow for me to stop coaching the Springboks at that stage, having a player who could exploit weak points in the opposition's game. I'm not sure why Rassie didn't come to me earlier in his career with this kind of analysis. Maybe he thought I wouldn't take it well, and that I would see it as a criticism of the coach. I certainly didn't take it like that. I thought it was fantastic. Rassie was quite self-deprecating about it, playing it down, saying it was just something he spotted, not really wanting to attract attention to himself. I wish more players could analyse like that.

Braam van Straaten kept us in the game with six penalties, the last one from inside our half to give us an 18–16 lead with the final whistle looming. That would have been enough for us to salvage a lot of pride and make it difficult for Nick to be fired. But we gave away a penalty in the dying seconds of the match, which Stirling Mortlock converted, and so we lost 18–19.

Once again, the tight margins of international rugby were clear. If Mortlock had missed that penalty, we would have won and Nick may well have survived. SARFU was looking for something to use against him. Their opportunity came when, earlier in the week, Nick agreed with a woman – who had asked him to sign some rugby balls – that ticket prices were too high. She was, in fact, a journalist for the *Independent on Sunday* and Nick's comments made the front page on the day of the Test. That made it easy for SARFU. They accused him of damaging SARFU and started disciplinary procedures against him a month later.

We all felt that if we had won, the ticket price issue wouldn't have had such an impact. SARFU issued a statement that said the matter had been resolved before the disciplinary hearing was held and that Nick would no longer be the coach, but we suspected he had effectively been fired.

Harry Viljoen, the former Transvaal scrumhalf, took over from Nick. Harry had coached Transvaal (and got them into two Currie Cup finals), Natal (one Currie Cup final) and Western Province (where he finally won the Currie Cup in 1997). He was also a very successful businessman, having made his money in insurance.

He knew about my reputation as a bad boy, with all the drinking and partying I was doing at the time, and didn't select me for the end-of-year tour to Argentina, Ireland, Wales and England. Instead, Harry went for Corné Krige, André Venter and André Vos as his loose trio, with AJ Venter coming off the bench in the England game, which was the only defeat of the tour. Even though I was playing well, I deserved to be dropped. My discipline was terrible and I needed a wake-up call. That's when I went to Doc Luyt and told him I wanted to go back to Free State, and he tore up my contract.

I was briefly back in favour for two Tests of the 2001 international season, against France at Ellis Park and Kings Park in June, but I soon realised there were aspects of Harry's approach to rugby that I found a bit strange. As we prepared for the first Test at a training base in Plettenberg Bay, Harry started talking about us being the best-dressed team. We already had good clothing sponsors, but Harry wanted us wearing much fancier brands. That wasn't my style. I couldn't be bothered if I was wearing Armani or Gucci. All I needed was a good-quality tracksuit and I was fine. He then asked us how many tries we would score against France, and we were realistic about it, suggesting we would aim for three or four. He said we should score seven per Test match, which was hugely ambitious. In the end, we scored one try in each of the Tests. Harry also wanted me to be like Australia's Owen Finegan, who could play flank and lock. But Finegan weighed 120 kilograms and was six foot five. I was three inches shorter and weighed 92 kilograms at the time. There was no way I could play the same game. I found it all a bit weird.

We lost 23–32 at Ellis Park to an inexperienced French team that included four debutants. The side also included Pieter de Villiers, the South African-born prop, playing for the first time against the Springboks. He was a man I later respected as a forwards coach. We came from behind to win the return Test at Kings Park 20–15. I didn't know it then, but that was the last time I played for the Springboks.

The following Saturday, we were in Port Elizabeth to face Italy. This is where the shit hit the fan. My whole family was coming to the match – I think I must have organised about 25 tickets. But I suspected Harry wouldn't pick me because he thought I was too light. He wanted someone bigger and heavier. Bobby Skinstad was being eased back into the side after being injured for most of the previous season. He had played off the bench in both French Tests and was now ready to start. Corné was also back from injury and André Venter was establishing himself as a versatile loose forward/lock. I was feeling uncomfortable in this team.

I didn't expect to be named in the starting XV, but to my amazement, Harry picked me on the bench as the reserve lock. It made no sense. I went to Andre Markgraaff, my very first Springbok coach when I had played for the midweek team four years earlier and now one of the selectors, and said to him, 'If I'm too light for loose forward, how the fuck can I be on the bench for reserve lock, especially when our locks are Johan Ackermann, who weighs 110 kilograms, and Mark Andrews, who weighs 115 kilograms?'

I was being set up for failure and that's when I decided to fake a hamstring injury to get out of the game. I told Markgraaff about my plan and he told me I would be the first player to sacrifice himself like that. I wasn't expecting to be selected for the Tri Nations series in three weeks' time and felt I would probably be sent home after the Italy game anyway. I went over to Victor Matfield, who hadn't been picked for the Springbok team. He was a promising newcomer at that stage, waiting for his break, and I was the person who was going to give it to him. I said, 'Victor, listen here, you must fucking get up and start running. I'm going to withdraw. I'm going to say my hamstring is sore. Will you be able to play?'

Victor couldn't believe his ears. 'Ja, fok, fok!' and he jumped up to join the rest of the squad in training. I went to Harry and told him I had pulled my hamstring, and that I was sure it was gone because I knew the feeling. I didn't want him ordering scans, which would expose my lie. I told him I wanted to go home to Bloemfontein. I felt embarrassed because 25 friends and family were coming to the game. I didn't want to sit in Port Elizabeth and watch the game knowing that I could have played and that my hamstring wasn't buggered. I felt very hartseer. Victor took my place on the bench, and that was the slightly bizarre start to his remarkable 127-Test career, which included a World Cup victory.

At the airport, as I was about to fly home, one of the Springbok support staff asked me to hand back my playing manual. I asked him why he wanted it because we would soon be getting together for the Tri Nations. He said he didn't know and was just doing what he had been told. That's when I realised for sure that Harry wasn't selecting me for the tournament. I just said, 'Okay, you can have it.' That was my last contact with the Springbok team as a player, and I handed the manual over without any emotion.

I phoned Andre Markgraaff and told him that I wasn't in Harry's plans for the Tri Nations, that my last Test match had been against France and that my international career was over. I needed to make peace with that. I told him I wasn't going to train any further with the Springboks and my focus would now be with Free State Cheetahs and winning the Currie Cup.

Markgraaff said, 'If you are not picked for this Tri Nations, I will resign as a selector.' I was surprised and told him he didn't have to do that. I appreciated his gesture and told him so, and that he had always been very good to me when we were at the Cats.

The following Tuesday I got a call from Markgraaff. He told me he was resigning later that morning because, as I had expected, I wasn't in the squad for the Tri Nations. He was true to his word and quit the selection panel later that day.

I could feel when people were working me out of a team. I just knew in my heart what Harry was doing. I wish he could have just come to me and told me what the problem was – you're too entitled, you party too much, you don't fit into our culture, you're not a team player, whatever. It wouldn't have been nice to hear and I wouldn't have been able to cry about it because it was my own doing. I was the one who chose to lead this partying lifestyle and now it had resulted in me losing my place in the Springbok team. But I didn't think it was the end. I thought I could play myself back into the team by getting away from Johannesburg, stopping the partying and the drinking, focusing on doing well with Free State and realising my big ambition to win the Currie Cup. There was no sense of disappointment because I promised myself I would have another bite at this. I told myself that this wasn't the end.

At the start of the 2002 season, I was back at Free State doing pre-season training with the Cheetahs. We were at the municipal grounds just outside the city, next to the golf course, for our second training session. I wasn't doing anything dangerous or reckless when I jumped over a player who was on the ground, in my way. As I landed, I felt a burning sensation on the inside of my left foot as the bridge of the foot collapsed. I immediately went for X-rays and consulted with some of the best foot doctors in the country, but because of the way the bone was broken, no one picked up a fracture. I spent most of 2002 hobbling around.

I was used to being injured and managing pain. I dealt with the abscess in my backside. I have dislocated both my shoulders many times. I can' t lift my left arm above my shoulder. I really need to have all the scar tissue cleaned up. My fingers have been broken so often in games to the point I can't grip a golf club properly. I've broken my jaw three times, the first time in 1993 playing for Shimlas against Old Greys when my Cheetahs roommate Dennis van Zyl, who was playing for Old Greys, accidently caught my jaw with his elbow. My jaw was wired closed and I had to sip custard and eat mash and gravy for 12 weeks. I ended up weighing only 84 kilograms after that.

Then, in 1997, I broke my jaw again in a game against the Waratahs at the Sydney Football Stadium when Tiaan Strauss ran into me and our heads collided. The doctor gave me some painkillers, but when I tried to drink, the water just ran straight out of my mouth and we realised my jaw was broken. I was taken to a Sydney hospital for surgery to fix the break. When I came round in the ward, our match was being replayed on the TV above my bed. The first thing I saw when I opened my eyes was a replay of Tiaan and I colliding. The doctor, Dr Hook (I couldn't forget that name), told me my jaw had been shattered and that I would probably not play rugby again.

Two years later we played the Waratahs – again at the Sydney Football Stadium – and I broke my jaw again. This time Os du Randt and I ran into each other. I went back to the same hospital for more surgery by Dr Hook. When I came round, he was there and said, 'But didn't I say you can't play rugby ever again?'

My nose has been broken so many times that I've got a piece of plastic to replace my septum. I had an operation to fix my pubic bones. I've had an operation to fix a dislocated elbow. I've had three operations for piles, one of which was on the Sunday before a Test match six days later. I've had my knee cleaned of scar tissue. When I count it all up, I've had 38 operations. But my most serious medical battle was still to come and is ongoing.

I flew to Germany to visit the experts at Adidas to see if they could make a special boot to help with the pain in my left foot. I went with my friend Frikkie Erasmus, who is a huge influence in my life. I met Frikkie when I was 26 and the captain of the Cats. He was a lawyer friend of Markgraaff. The two of us just clicked, despite a big age difference of almost 30 years. He became a sounding board for me, rather like a father figure, and gave me a lot of invaluable advice and assistance. We live very different lives, but we are very good friends, and our families go on holiday together. Frikkie helps me out with legal issues, but he has never charged me a cent. I have never had an agent to represent me and prefer to do business myself, but Frikkie checks my contracts and makes changes if necessary. He has always looked out for me, on personal matters and in business. He was the right person to help me.

We went to Adidas in Herzogenaurach in Germany where artisans made rugby boots, smart shoes and golf shoes for me in the shape of my foot. There weren't inner soles but rather used a mould for my foot. They made four pairs of rugby boots that would help make life a bit more normal. They certainly helped, but I was still in pain every time I put pressure on the bridge of my foot.

We then went to the Ludwig Maximilian University in Munich where a professor examined my foot. He prescribed cortisone and I could play again. I didn't train during the week, and I was only available for captain's practice on the Friday (I was the captain) when I'd had my cortisone injection, so my foot was dead. Oom Peet knew I was injured but he kept selecting me because I was still playing better than the other guy who wasn't injured. I would get my injection before a game and the following week we repeated the procedure.

It went on like that for 18 months: injections, play, injections, play. I got away with it because I was in good form, and Oom Peet and my teammates didn't mind. It was a very strange set-up and certainly not one I would allow as a coach today. The whole team must train on a Monday otherwise you become what we call 'a purple member', where you think you're a little god. As I look back on it, I wasn't a good team member even though I had stopped my wild behaviour and was no longer a virus in my team.

By 2003 my foot was fucked after all the cortisone injections and playing rugby at full pace. I went to an orthopaedic surgeon in Pretoria by the name of Dr Fief Ferreira, and he picked up an undiagnosed horizontal fracture of one of the bones in my foot. After surgery to repair the damage, I was in a cast for six weeks, and then physiotherapist Elmarie Nienaber, the wife of the current Springbok coach, Jacques Nienaber, did intensive rehabilitation. I couldn't play for a year, but I was on a player's contract, so I coached the Free State Vodacom Cup team.

This was the first time I was doing formal coaching. Behind the scenes with the Springboks, with Nick Mallett's blessing, I had been analysing the opposition and discussing moves and running lines with the other players. I had also done analysis for Laurie Mains and was becoming more involved in the coaching, and because I had the confidence of the players, they listened to me. I used the same style of coaching with the Vodacom Cup team, with the approval of Oom Peet and Harold Verster. We had a successful season, losing just two games and reaching the semifinals of the competition. I played in only one game because of the injury in a warm-up match in Pacaltsdorp, the township outside George, but I first had to check with the ref if he'd allow the coach to play.

8

EVENTUALLY, IN 2003, I was invited back to play for the Springboks ahead of the World Cup later that year. Rudolf Straeuli was the coach, and he asked me to come to a training session. I was playing very well for the Free State Cheetahs in the Currie Cup and the media was putting pressure on Rudolf to pick me for the Springbok team. The problem was that I was still battling with my foot injury and there was no way I could play at an international level. I knew I couldn't have a cortisone injection and then run with the intensity of Bobby Skinstad or André Venter. They were supreme athletes, and I wasn't up to it. I could still inject my foot and play Currie Cup games because of the way I played and analysed the game, but Test rugby was a bridge too far. I didn't officially resign from Test rugby – I just told Rudolf I wasn't available so that the media would back off. And that was the end of my international career.

I could now focus on my career at Free State and achieve that goal of winning the Currie Cup. In 2004, Free State had mixed fortunes in the competition, but luckily so did some of the other teams. When the group stage of the competition was over, Free State finished in third place on the log, ahead of the Golden Lions on points difference, and qualified for the semifinal against Western Province at Newlands. I'd been in this position before, in 1997 when we beat the Sharks against all expectations 40–22 in Durban to reach the final, which we then lost to Western Province after Helgard Müller's forward pass in the dying minutes.

My foot was still not coming right, however, and the constant pain was affecting my game. I faced the sad inevitability that I would have to retire from competitive rugby as a player. My career would end as soon as Free State's run in the Currie Cup came to an end. We had beaten Western Province 26–20 earlier in the season at Newlands, and they evened the score by winning in Bloemfontein 29–25. But conditions for the semi-final were cold, with lots of rain, which suited Province and they were widely expected to win again. If that happened, I would end my career at Newlands.

During the match, I tried to grab hold of Robbie Fleck's shorts with my right hand, and one of my fingers somehow got caught in his waistband. As he pulled himself free, my finger broke. I realised immediately that it was serious, but as I was tucking my shirt into my shorts, I was horrified to see the bone sticking out through the skin. I knew that referee Mark Lawrence would tell me to go off and get medical attention and, because there was no blood bin in those days, that would be the end of my game. But Mark also knew that this was my last chance at winning the Currie Cup. I am eternally grateful to him for checking with the Province captain, and allowing the doctor to strap me up on the field so that I could carry on playing. Both teams scored a try, but our trusty flyhalf Willem de Waal was outstanding and his boot made the difference because we won 17–11. My career would now end in the Currie Cup final the following Saturday.

We were up against the defending champions, the Blue Bulls, at Loftus Versfeld, and my finger was infected. I had to have injections for the pain and slept with my hand suspended above my head because it was too sore. My foot was also painful, even after the surgery. I was feeling very emotional because, unlike in my international career, I knew this would be my final game of rugby. I tried to fight back the tears, but couldn't help it and wept as I ran out onto the field, with a big bandage on my broken finger. The TV cameras focused on me wiping away the tears as I got ready for the kick-off. I'm not a guy who usually cries on the field, but I remember thinking, 'Okay, it's done, rugby's finished.'

I was playing eighthman and, in the seventh minute of the game, I joined a backline move out on the left wing. I took an overhead pass from AJ Venter, cut inside to avoid a tackle from Blue Bulls centre Etienne Botha and, as one of the Bulls defenders tip-tackled me, I tried to dot the ball down over the tryline with three teammates falling on top of me.

Thank goodness for the TMO, Mark Lawrence, because match referee André Watson thought I had knocked the ball on and was about to call for a scrum but decided to send the decision upstairs. After what seemed ages, Mark ruled that I had dropped the ball straight down and our winger, Anton Pitout, who was following up, scored the try. It was an early breakthrough, but the Blue Bulls came back at us hard and dominated the match. They scored six tries and led 42–19 with 13 minutes left in the match.

As we were trying to close the gap, I got a breakaway, but the touch judge ruled that I had knocked the ball on in the move. I went to André Watson and said, 'I promise you, I didn't knock it on.' He believed me, but the decision had been made and he couldn't go back on it. It wouldn't have affected the outcome. André later wrote a column in which he said he reviewed the match and saw that the Bulls' JP Nel had touched the ball, not me. One decision went for me, another against me. That's rugby for you.

We managed to score two more tries, but the gap was too big and the Bulls won 42–33. It was the most disappointing end to a rugby match in my playing career, including the 1999 World Cup semifinal against Australia. What added to the emotion was that I had no idea at that stage if I would ever be involved in rugby again. Even though I had coached the Vodacom Cup side, Free State had said nothing up until then about me carrying on in a coaching role.

Because I was something of an entrepreneur, I didn't have any financial worries. I had worked at Minolta, but over the years I had been involved in at least 16 other businesses. I had a company called Edge Sport Consultants, which employed three cameramen to film rugby matches when there was no TV coverage. We gave the suite holders at Free State Stadium a free feed and sold on-air advertising. We also filmed weddings and other events.

I also ran a security company called DCT Security, which guarded and maintained properties repossessed by a bank. We made proper money for about three years, but after we lost the contract with the bank, we closed it down.

I co-owned a BP petrol station with Dennis van Zyl, while Naka Drotské sold vehicle silencers at the back. My brother-in-law helped me in that operation, which was very successful. We sold almost 400 000 litres of fuel a month before closing it down when it eventually became too much to manage, particularly when BP brought in their convenience store. Before then, we had our own shop, which sold everything from condoms to steak pies – our main customers were the students whose residences were on the same street. Naka and I also owned a couple of guesthouses. My mother ran one and Naka's family ran the other.

I got involved with cattle farming because it was a good tax break. I started with eight Simmentaler cattle and ended up with 64. The farm was about 10 kilometres outside Bloemfontein, and I hired someone to manage it for me.

For five months, I worked for Protea Coin as a general manager. I had to go to Joburg and experience what it feels like to pick up bags from a bank, or to be a driver, or to be a guard in the back of a cash-in-transit van. After the army, that was probably one of my scariest experiences, particularly because my foot was in plaster at the time. I didn't do that for long, though, because I wasn't good at managing such a big company. I felt out of my depth and would get nervous going into work. I could run my little things on the side, but I didn't have the experience to be a general manager for the whole of the Free State for Protea Coin Security.

Along with my teammate Barend Pieterse's father, I was also involved in a financial-services company, which provided bridging finance to customers.

After my exit from rugby, I now had to consider what to do with my life. My foot was still a problem because I hadn't given it enough time to heal, though the pain was substantially reduced after the surgery. But I knew that taking rugby out of my life would be much more painful than anything I had experienced from all of my injuries. Then Oom Peet announced he was retiring from coaching Free State. And so he, Harold Verster and the board of Free State Rugby Union threw me a lifeline and offered me the position of head coach of the Cheetahs starting on 1 January 2005.

I wasn't expecting to be offered the job and thought Gysie Pienaar, a Springbok legend who had been Kitch Christie's assistant at the 1995 Rugby World Cup, as well as the assistant coach of Free State, would be the natural successor. I knew Gysie to be a pure, honest, good guy while he coached me at Free State. He was the person who brought me to Free State in the first place by getting my army call-up papers changed from the 6 South African Infantry battalion in Grahamstown to the School of Armour in Bloemfontein. When he didn't get appointed into Oom Peet's place, I felt like I was backstabbing him, even though I hadn't done any-thing to get rid of him and work my way into his job. I know he was very upset, and shortly afterwards he became the Griquas coach in the place of Kobus van der Merwe who went to Western Province.

I started working with Jacques Nienaber, whose reputation as a rugby physiotherapist was growing. He and I first met in the army at Tempe Military Base in Bloemfontein, though we were in different units. After the army, Jacques went to the University of the Free State to study physiotherapy, and then he became the physio for Shimlas and later the Cheetahs' junior teams. I met him again when he helped out with the Cheetahs senior team on a few occasions, and our paths crossed in 1999 when I went to the Cats where Jacques was the full-time physio. In 2004 Jacques did a strength-and-conditioning (S&C) course and became the S&C coach at the Cheetahs, taking the place of Derek Coetzee who had joined Jake White's Springbok team.

When you lie on a physio bed for 45 minutes to an hour, you chat a lot. Jacques and I analysed rugby, and I was impressed by how much he knew. When I became the Cheetahs' head coach, Jacques was my S&C coach. He roamed alongside the field and could tell a player anything: how to tackle, where to tackle, when to tackle, who to tackle. He understood all the calls because he was with us in all our training sessions. He and I started working more closely together and he acted almost like an assistant coach.

In 2007, when I went to the Stormers, I brought him in as S&C coach. Around that time, the position of specialist defence coach – as they had in rugby league – was becoming more established. I wrote a manual for defence coaching and then brought Jacques into that position. He showed great interest in my computer analysis of the games, and I could see he was a natural coach.

Jacques stayed with the Stormers when I left to become the high-performance manager at SARU (which had changed its name from SARFU in 2005), but when I joined Bok coach Peter de Villiers as a technical adviser at the 2011 World Cup, Jacques joined us as defence coach. We worked together again as a team in 2012 on the MOBI unit, a programme that allowed us to move around the country doing training.

One of the first things I wanted to do as the new head coach of Free State Cheetahs was change the way people supported the team. We were always the fans' second-choice team, and I wanted to get the pride back into Free State and make us the number-one team for the fans. I knew that in order to get people back into the stadium, and to encourage people to invest in the corporate suites, we had to start winning regularly. And if we were going to start winning, we needed some new players, and that's where I faced immediate pushback from some members of the board who felt that would be too expensive.

We needed more money. Even though we had reached the Currie Cup final the previous year, which had the potential to earn us revenue, both the semifinal and final were away from home. We needed big matches to earn big bucks. A Currie Cup semifinal and final at Free State Stadium would mean millions of rand in the coffers.

I knew that if we started winning, people would start coming to watch. We had to go out and create some excitement around our games. I got the players involved, particularly well-known guys like Os du Randt and Naka Drotské; we stood at the traffic lights in town and handed out match tickets during the morning rush hour. There we were, at 7am, giving tickets to parents taking their children to school, asking them if they had friends or relatives who also wanted to come, and then giving them more tickets for those people. People felt, hell, if the players are coming to the streets to get us, they must really want us.

Some of the younger players were a little shy to hand out tickets because they weren't well known, but they soon warmed up when they were with one of the famous players. It was interesting to watch the reaction when people saw Os peering through their car window. If Os gave you two tickets for Saturday's game, you were definitely going. Sometimes I got a bit of shit from die-hard fans who complained that Gysie should be the coach and not me.

I took a whole lot of tickets and went to one of the army bases in Bloemfontein and handed them out. I then went to the university hostels with match tickets and cases of beer donated by a friend of mine who worked for South African Breweries. I gave the army guys tickets to sit behind the poles at one end of the ground, while the students filled up the stands at the opposite end of the stadium. We got a vibe going by encouraging them to chant 'Attack, attack!' and 'Defend, defend!' depending on what the Cheetahs were doing at their end of the ground. Sometimes the fans forgot that the teams had changed ends at halftime and mistakenly shouted encouragement to the opposition in the second half.

In 2005, the Currie Cup was made up of a qualifying round, with 14 teams divided into two groups of seven. We played six games, three of them at Free State Stadium. We were unbeaten in that preliminary competition, with a hugely satisfying win over Western Province and some big wins against the Pumas and the Leopards. As I had predicted, the fans started coming to watch us play and we had to put in more seats because we were filling the stadium. I remember the players and coaches getting involved, carrying in and even building those extra seats.

Because we could no longer rely on players coming through from the clubs like Shimlas, as they were being taken by the big unions who could offer more money, I also started buying new players. But instead of looking at the best players at other provinces, I focused on the second-best players or the players who were frustrated at a bigger union. There were players like Ryno van der Merwe from Western Province and Barend Pieterse from the Lions. We also snapped up Kabamba Floors and Bevin Fortuin from South Western Districts, and Willem de Waal from the Leopards. Kabamba was a former South Africa Sevens player, who became a big attraction with his short, blond dreadlocks and incredible pace for a flanker. He ended up playing over 150 games for Free State.

We also started training in different places, like the townships, to show off the game to a new target audience. We had fantastic players of colour like Kabamba Floors and Bevin Fortuin, Eddie Fredericks, Kennedy Tsimba and Ashwell Rafferty, who were great assets in getting a new demographic behind the Cheetahs.

I knew I had to get the right players in the team, not necessarily the best players. Take a guy like Willem de Waal at flyhalf. He might not have been the best flyhalf in the country, but he was the guy who would win you a Currie Cup, and he was a team man.

To build that team spirit, we constructed the 'Cheetah Den' outside my office in Free State Stadium's main pavilion next to the cricket stadium.

We put in a bar, a trophy cabinet for the Currie Cup, and computers so that players could relax and work there. I bought a big eight-seater Jacuzzi for about R12 000 and put it in the change room and, after the game, the boys would get in the Jacuzzi with a few beers. They loved it so much that sometimes they asked me for the change-room keys so they could use it during the week. Sometimes people like Leon Schuster and Steve Hofmeyr visited and entertained the team with some songs. The players socialised a lot, with the forwards coming to my house for a braai and the backs having drinks with assistant coach Helgard Müller after training on a Tuesday.

I also became famous for using disco lights during training. Here's how that initiative started ... During training we worked out various strategies and identified each of them using the name of a colour. We also had different players running different parts of the game. One person ran scrums, another was responsible for lineouts, another in charge of breakdowns. The person in charge would call out a colour and the players immediately knew what tactic to execute. For example, if the player shouted 'Yellow!' that meant maul, 'Red!' meant hit it up short, 'Blue!' meant go wide.

Then Ollie le Roux suggested I take over the responsibility of deciding which colour to call out. We planned everything together, with the players providing their input and challenging what the coaches were telling them. They signed off on everything. We then trained using those tactics for the whole week so that everyone knew what we were doing, and where and when we'd do it. I sat on the side of the field with Helgard and we decided what move the players should execute. We used four plastic coloured marker cones, which we normally used to mark out the field in training. For example, if we wanted the forwards to drive, I would hold up a green cone. Before every set piece, the players would stop and look at me for direction. I checked where we were on the field, consulted my play sheet and selected a cone.

On a couple of occasions, I mistakenly held up a cone that was obviously wrong. All the players would then stare at me, shaking their heads. Realising my mistake, I'd hold up the correct cone, and the players would nod at me. It must have looked rather strange to the opposition and the fans. But it was highly effective, and we scored try after try.

But there was a problem with the players seeing the cones clearly, especially if they were on the other side of the field or down near the poles. So we started using coloured paddles, which were bigger and more visible. We decided to make it tricky for the opposition to decipher what we were doing by putting big capital letters on the paddles that were completely meaningless – a red herring to make the opposition think the letter corresponded to something on the field. We also changed the tactics and colours around so that the opposition couldn't learn the moves. We also had colours that meant absolutely nothing. But the next week that same colour could mean 'kick for touch'.

To make the colours more visible to the players, I had disco lights installed on the roof of Free State Stadium, and that got us a lot of publicity. The media and the fans got very excited about the novelty of the disco lights. Quite a few people thought I was mad, but the players and I knew that the lights worked.

On one occasion, the Bulls were in Bloemfontein for a Currie Cup match against the Cheetahs. They were given access to the stadium for their Friday captain's practice and used this opportunity to pull a prank on us. They climbed up to the lights and swopped the bulbs around, so when I flicked the switch for the red light, a blue light came on. I could see that the Cheetahs players were just staring at me, waiting for the light, because I had made a totally incorrect call with the light that was on. Helgard came on the walkie-talkie from the side of the pitch and asked me what was going on. After about five minutes of confusion, we realised what had happened and swopped the bulbs back into their correct positions. We did see the funny side of it, though.

The Bulls got us again when we went to Loftus. We now had our own mobile lighting rig so we could take our operation to the away games. I was in the coaches' box and just as I was about to flick a switch for a light, the power to the box went off. Someone had switched it off at the main board. With no power, our lights didn't work. We tried to use the coloured paddles, but the players couldn't see them properly from the field and the whole system was a mess. For later away games, we had a box made with a battery back-up. I must admit that I would have done exactly the same thing if I was with the Bulls.

We got heart-rate monitors for the players and received data on their performance throughout the game. If we saw that the props' recovery rate wasn't great, we would use the appropriate coloured light to call for a move that involved the backs, which would give the forwards time to get their breath back. When we saw that the forwards were fresh again, we would call a move that involved a drive from them.

We were the first team to get a supplement sponsor, PVM (Protein, Vitamins and Minerals). Their scientists were nutritional experts and they started testing the players' blood sugar at halftime to work out who needed a boost. We saw an immediate difference in the players' performances.

Something else that made a difference is that we imported tackle machines from the USA. I had watched the Oliver Stone movie, *Any Given Sunday*, starring Al Pacino, Cameron Diaz and Jamie Foxx, about an American gridiron football team. I was fascinated by the tackle machines used in American football that contained a large spring. If a player hit the tackle bag at the wrong angle, the spring catapulted him backwards onto his arse. The player had to hit the machine perfectly to prevent the spring from recoiling and sending him flying. They were very different from the tackle bags we were using and I knew they would work for us. In 2005, we imported three of them, and they proved to be fantastic in improving our technique. I think World Rugby should consider using these machines to educate players and coaches about safer tackle techniques to prevent injury.

My main goal for Free State's 2005 season was to win the Currie Cup for the first time since 1976. We easily qualified for the Premier Division of the competition in the same group as Western Province, Griquas and Leopards. Although we suffered a few losses, we finished second in our group to earn a second, successive semifinal against Western Province at Newlands. It was another tense affair, which we won 16–11. We were through to the Currie Cup final where we would face the Blue Bulls at Loftus once again. We were up against a team that had finished third on the log in the Super 12 earlier in the year and lost in the semifinal to the Waratahs. They had players like Fourie du Preez, Victor Matfield, Bakkies Botha, Derick Hougaard and Morné Steyn.

But we could match them up front. We had Jannie du Plessis, CJ van der Linde, Os du Randt, Ollie le Roux and Wian du Preez. At hooker we had Naka Drotské. That's where the Bomb Squad started. It wasn't from the 2019 Rugby World Cup. I mixed up the props and had Os and Jannie starting, with Ollie and CJ coming off the bench, or Wian and CJ starting, with Jannie and Ollie on the bench. All of them were Springboks. Wian only played one Test but he had a great career with Munster and Lyon.

I always kept Naka on the field, but he had a fresh prop alongside him every 20 minutes. For the first few games the props were pissed off, demanding to start a match. But when they saw the tactic was working, they thought, 'Hey, this is lekker!'

At the start of the season, we knew the Bulls would be our toughest opposition. We lost both of our league matches to them, 16–26 at Loftus and 22–26 in Bloemfontein. We knew, too, that if we were to beat them in the final at Loftus, we had to be able to maul them. We put a particular focus on that aspect of the game. We also concentrated on the lineouts, which we lost badly earlier in the season. Everything was slotting into place: we knew how to maul them, how to disrupt the lineouts, we had our game plan, and we had our Bomb Squad, which included three props. We had our lights, our blood-sugar tests, our vitamins and minerals.

We had the big men who were not scared of anyone and anything. In one of the earlier Bulls games, Ollie le Roux punched their flanker Pedrie Wannenburg and was sent off. I didn't give him shit about it. I told the others I couldn't excuse his behaviour, but I wanted them to see how badly Ollie wanted to destroy those guys. That's how you play the Bulls.

There was another part of the Bulls experience that I wanted our players prepared for. Seven of the Cheetahs hadn't played in the final at Loftus the previous year and I wanted them to be able to handle the Loftus crowds and the music, which can be quite intimidating. Franco Smith, our assistant coach, suggested we train with Steve Hofmeyr's Blue Bulls song blaring in the background, just like it does at Loftus. I played it during training until they almost vomited. We practised shouting lineout calls with the music thumping away to recreate the Loftus experience.

The game was incredibly tight, with no tries scored in the first half. We allowed Akona Ndungane through for a soft try early in the second half and, with 10 minutes left on the clock, we were trailing 15–25. I felt the game slipping away from us. I looked down at the reserves' bench and the white scrumcap of Kabamba Floors caught my eye. I knew he was our last chance and so sent him on, along with scrumhalf Noël Oelschig and wing Meyer Bosman. We needed tries and immediately these guys made an impact, with Kabamba a vital part of creating a try for Bevin Fortuin.

Then came the best part of the match. We were still trailing 22–25 when the Bulls kicked off on us in the 74th minute. We took the ball just outside our 22-metre line and started to maul them, just like we had practised over and over again in training. We mauled them until we were close to the halfway line, and then Noël kicked a perfect box kick that came down over the Bulls' 22-metre line. Bulls scrumhalf Fourie du Preez appeared to have the ball covered, but fullback Johan Roets was also coming up to take the ball and the two of them collided. The ball bounced loose, and Meyer Bosman gathered and sprinted unchallenged to score under the poles.

117

There were still six minutes on the clock and that was very nerve-wracking, because they had players who could still turn the game around. We held on, though, and won 29–25, a huge upset win at Loftus. What gave me great satisfaction was that we beat the Bulls at their own game in their own backyard.

After I left Despatch and realised I was going to be a professional rugby player, my biggest dream was to become a Springbok. But after playing for the Cheetahs and never winning a Currie Cup, after playing in so many semifinals and finals, even playing for the Lions in a semifinal, and now finally tasting success as a coach, I would rate that victory right up there with playing for the Springboks.

Coming back to Bloemfontein was an incredible experience. We weren't prepared for the emotions from the people of Bloem. People hadn't seen their team with the trophy since 1976; they had waited 29 years for this. When we landed at the airport, we could see that the whole parking lot was full. While I drove to the smallholding near the airport where I was staying, people were standing outside their houses cheering. That was one of the best feelings of my life. Fuck it, that's a day I will never forget.

9

W̶E WERE FULL OF CONFIDENCE as the 2006 season started because the Cheetahs were now included in Super Rugby, which had been expanded from 12 teams to 14, with the addition of Western Force and the Cheetahs. We finished 10th on the log, ahead of the Stormers and the Cats, winning five of our 13 matches.

But we needed more money if we wanted to compete with the bigger franchises, so Harold Verster and I drove up to Johannesburg to meet with the CEO of SuperSport Imtiaz Patel to ask for one to two million rand to strengthen the union. Our budget at the time was seven million rand, not just for salaries, but for everything. We didn't fly because we simply didn't have the money. Imtiaz heard us out but was forthright in turning us down. He said for a city the size of Bloemfontein we would never be able to fill the stadium consistently. We proved him wrong by selling out six or seven times that season, with thousands upon thousands of people wearing shirts in the Free State colour of orange. But to earn some proper money, we realised that we needed to secure a home semifinal and a home final in the Currie Cup. If we were successful in doing this, we could earn up to R10 million.

The format of the competition changed and there was no longer a qualifying round. The five provincial teams directly affiliated with Super 14 franchises automatically qualified for the Premier Division. We picked up from where we left off in 2005, and after 14 rounds of the competition we topped the log, guaranteeing us the home-ground advantage in the knockouts.

In our final game of the season, we only needed to score four tries against the Blue Bulls at Loftus for a bonus point to guarantee the top spot on the log and a semifinal at Free State Stadium. We didn't care if we lost the game. We scored all four tries in the first half, with Philip Burger scoring twice. Everyone on the bench and in the coaches' box was jumping up and down when we got that fourth try as if we had won the game. Then we just took it easy, knowing we could throw this game away because we had done what we had set out to do. We put on all the reserves to save our top players for the semifinal and to ensure no key players picked up an injury. I remember the Bulls fans going at us, with 'Aah, lekker, you're losing,' but this was actually a victory for us. We lost the match 31–41 and we didn't care.

We beat the Sharks 30–14 in the semifinal and prepared to face the Blue Bulls once again in the final, but this time in our own backyard. Rugby fever hit Bloemfontein in a big way – people wore orange and created an incredible atmosphere at the stadium.

We led 14–8 at halftime after Philip Burger scored a try, and we extended the lead to 25–18 thanks to a try from Kabamba Floors, and the boot of Willem de Waal who kicked five penalties. With two minutes left on the clock, we were 25–18 ahead and, to my horror, we let Bulls centre JP Nel through for his second try. Morné Steyn kicked an easy conversion to level the scores at 25–all, and the match went into 20 minutes of extra time, a first in Currie Cup history. No points were scored and the match was heading for a draw. The hooter sounded as referee Jonathan Kaplan called for one more scrum, on the Bulls' 10-metre line. The Bulls won a penalty from the scrum, and now Morné Steyn was faced with a choice: does he go for poles (which I thought was in his range) and risk the Cheetahs getting the ball if he missed and launching another attack, or does he go for the draw and kick the ball out? He had a quick chat with his captain Gary Botha, and then punted the ball into touch: 25–all, and so we shared the Currie Cup with the Blue Bulls.

I was standing at the side of the field with Helgard Müller. As Kaplan blew the final whistle, we just shook hands quietly, not acting at all like coaches who had just won the Currie Cup for a successive year. Sharing it didn't feel like we had successfully defended it. It wasn't a lekker feeling. We still had the trophy, but the Bulls wanted it in their change room. We joked with their team manager Wynie Strydom that he could come and collect it at midnight. Leon Schuster joined us and we had a good party, despite feeling a bit deflated. The biggest win was that we got the money we wanted from the home semi and final, which made a huge difference to us.

In 2007, I got offered what I thought was an opportunity I couldn't afford to miss. It was another Rugby World Cup year, and Springbok coach Jake White asked me to come on board as the technical analyst. He wanted me to devise game plans and train the squad in the build-up to the tournament. I had to seriously consider my prospects at the Cheetahs. I had won the Currie Cup twice as coach, but I didn't think we had the financial muscle to build a squad that would be good enough to win Super Rugby. Since joining the Super 14 tournament in 2006, we had come 10th and 11th. While I knew we could win the Currie Cup again, I didn't feel we would be able to beat the likes of the Crusaders in New Zealand. Even in Bloem they scored 49 points against us, and we had lost all our matches in Australia and New Zealand in 2007. I decided it was time for a new challenge and resigned from the Cheetahs. I had to go for it, but it was tough to leave the team. I was hartseer when I went to tell Harold Verster, who was desperate for me to stay and kept asking me what he could do to keep me.

When I joined the Boks, Jake was off in Australia and New Zealand with a B team to compete in the away leg of the Tri Nations. Sports psychologist Dr Henning Gericke (who was also a fitness expert) and I worked with the Boks at SACS school in Cape Town to get them ready for the World Cup. I had been doing the job for about three weeks and was expecting to get some job security after the World Cup in the form of a contract with SA Rugby. But they turned around and said they couldn't promise me anything after the tournament. Suddenly, my future was up in the air. I wasn't happy with this financial uncertainty because my twin daughters, Carli and Nikki, were three years old.

The girls were born on 10 July 2004 in Bloemfontein. I was on the golf course when Nikki phoned me to tell me she was pregnant. A few weeks later, I was playing golf at the Hankey Golf Club near Patensie when she called again to say I'd better double my budget for the baby, because we were having twins. There are twins on Nikki's side of the family, but the news left me a little shocked because I really didn't have much money. I was absolutely thrilled, however, and even though I'm incredibly squeamish around blood, I was in the operating theatre when they were born by caesarean section. The babies were beautiful – but only once they had been cleaned up and were wrapped in blankets in my arms.

So I had big responsibilities and needed security.

10

IN JULY 2007, I WAS APPOINTED Senior Professional Coach at Western Province (WP) Rugby, which combined the roles of Western Province Director of Rugby and Stormers head coach. I decided to take the job because I knew I stood a good chance of winning a Super Rugby title with them. I had an initial meeting with the CEO of the Western Province Rugby Union, Rob Wagner, and Nick Mallett, who was then the Director of Rugby. Nick was about to leave to become the coach of Italy, and he recommended me for the position. I then had a formal interview in front of a panel – and the job was mine.

I had to go to Jake and tell him I wasn't going to the World Cup. Jake was annoyed because there was no one in South Africa who could do the same job as me. He wasn't angry, though, as he understood that the Province and Stormers job was a great opportunity, but my timing was terrible because the World Cup squad was set to be announced the following week. Luckily, Jake had invited Eddie Jones, the current Australia coach, to have a few sessions with the Springboks before taking up a full-time job at Saracens. He asked Eddie if he could stay on, and Eddie ended up playing a critical role in guiding the Springboks to victory in the World Cup final against England

Nikki was unbelievable in dealing with all the chopping and changing. After we got married in 1998, I had gone off to Johannesburg to play for the Cats while she stayed in Bloemfontein. I came back and worked for the Cheetahs, and then suddenly I was off to Cape Town to work for the Springboks. Four months later, I had chucked that job and had taken the Stormers job, and the whole family had to move to Cape Town. It takes a special kind of person to hang in there.

Going to the Stormers was a huge culture shock. Bloemfontein was so small that it was easy for newcomers to adapt to the way things were done there. There was no battle to find each other's culture. Although the players came from different races and different backgrounds, in Bloem there was only one cinema, one Spur restaurant and two golf courses, so we braaied together, went to movies together and played golf together. When I got to Cape Town, though, I was competing against kitesurfing and socialising at the J&B Met horse race. Dealing with the differences in cultures, language and even religion was much trickier in Cape Town, but this is something the current Stormers coach John Dobson has got right – and brilliantly so.

In Cape Town pressure came from many different places, which meant that the coach was regularly criticised about the way he coached, how he managed the team, and even how he lived his life. In Despatch and Bloemfontein, everybody knew everybody else. Although people worried about how the coach did his job and how the team played, they allowed the coach to live his life in peace. If he didn't make the grade and the team always lost, he got fired, but nobody interfered in his private life.

In Cape Town I learnt very quickly that you had to keep a lot of people happy before it actually got to coaching. The coaching part was easy for me, but the politics from outside took me by surprise. I wasn't a complete novice in Cape Town, though, having played four Super 12 games for the Stormers in 2003 on loan from the Cheetahs. Gert Smal, who was coach at the time, asked me to play for them because they were struggling with injuries. At that stage, my foot was buggered, but I still managed to play four games before I realised I just wasn't up to the standard for the competition.

When I got there and became the Stormers coach, I had no experience of how rugby operated in the Western Cape, so it was a case of learning, fucking it up, and working out what makes them tick. In Bloemfontein, things had been so much simpler. There were only five rugby clubs, but Province had something like 90 clubs, all of which wanted to ask me questions about the way the team was playing. That was new for me, sitting in front of all of these people and explaining what I was doing. I got to see how different the clubs were, from the University of Cape Town (UCT), one of the finest clubs, to Stellenbosch, one of the biggest and richest clubs, to Belhar, one of the poorer clubs. I started understanding the history of rugby in the Western Cape and meeting people who were still feeling aggrieved for not having had opportunities to represent their province. A lot of people opened my eyes about what they had been through as they told me their stories.

I decided to bring in Allister Coetzee as the backline coach. He had been the Springbok backline coach under Jake White since 2004, and was at the 2007 World Cup in France when Frikkie Erasmus and I flew over to sign him. I knew Coetzee didn't have a job lined up after the World Cup. He applied for the job as Springbok head coach when Jake's contract wasn't renewed after the World Cup, but lost out to Peter de Villiers. In 2008, I made him the coach of the Currie Cup team. He took over from Gary Gold, who became an assistant Springbok coach. Two years later, in 2010, I appointed Allister as the head coach of the Stormers and brought in Robbie Fleck, Matt Proudfoot and Jacques Nienaber as his assistants. I continued as Senior Professional Coach, responsible for strategy, tactics and the contracting of players.

A big learning experience for me in Cape Town was the way in which former players and administrators felt they still had a say about how things worked at Western Province even when they were no longer involved. I didn't understand the system. I didn't grow up in Cape Town, or go to a private school, or have this long CV. I didn't even speak English very well. I always thought former players just supported their province or their school, like former Free State players did. But in Cape Town, people wanted to be involved with the team and have a say, and I thought that was weird. People who I thought would simply be supporters and lovers of the game, and who I regarded as irrelevant to my job, were now trying to tell me what to do. Some of them were former players, former Springboks, players' fathers or even grandfathers, and sometimes businessmen who presumed their name and stature gave them the right to get involved in rugby. We didn't have that in Bloemfontein.

For the first time, I started thinking about other factors whenever I picked a player. It was not only about is he the right player, is he a good player, is he a team player? I started to consider a lot of different opinions and to think about the repercussions that could flow from my team selection. I could see in the faces of my colleagues at the Stormers that they were thinking: 'Are you sure you want to make this decision?' Sometimes the impact was too big for me to understand. The external pressures started to get to me, and occasionally I even felt nervous about my selections. If it was a purely rugby decision, then it was easy to pick the team, but I had to contend with strong opinions – some political, some religious, some financial, some historical – and they all played a role in influencing me.

I had a situation where I had three different players all vying for the same position, and several people outside the team and WP Rugby wanting to share their opinions on who should be selected. This was something new that I had to handle. It was like me playing for Despatch or the Cheetahs and one of my family members phoning the coach to discuss my selection.

I realised that if I was going to coach by listening to all the other voices, I wouldn't fall on my own sword, I would fall on *their* sword. I would go out knowing that I hadn't done it my way. And if I was wrong with my selection under those circumstances, then I didn't deserve to keep the job. That's when I learnt not to listen to outside forces. From that experience, I devised a system for team selection based on each player's roadmap, where we track their progress and abilities, and they have to fit in with the way we do things.

I got a big wake-up call at the Stormers. I found out that it's not just how you coach, it's how you pick a team, and how you get that team to believe in itself. The moment you start listening to other people outside the team and trying to please them, you're going to lose the team and you're going to lose on the scoreboard, and you'll get fired.

If I hadn't experienced that level of interference, I think I would have made big mistakes in my Springbok team selections where the pressure is ten times worse. Not that I haven't made mistakes as Bok coach, but I certainly learnt to deal with things differently.

In my first season at the Stormers in 2008, we finished fifth on the Super 14 log and missed out on the playoffs on a points difference after having the same win/loss record as the fourth-placed Hurricanes. The following year was a disappointing one, and we only won five of our 13 matches to end in 10th place. But we came back strongly in 2010 and finished second on the log behind the Bulls. The season included a very satisfying 42–14 win over the powerful Crusaders, the 2008 champions, in Cape Town.

It took me a while to sort out the politics in the first year, and even in the second year I was pandering to all those outside forces, but in the third year I had figured it out and could now apply myself to coaching the team properly, along with my assistants Brendan Venter, Allister Coetzee and Jacques Nienaber. I also brought in some key players like Jaque Fourie from the Lions and Bryan Habana from the Bulls.

We beat the third-placed Waratahs 25–6 at Newlands to secure a place in the Super 14 final against the Bulls, who had made history in their semifinal by playing at the Orlando Stadium, the first time a major rugby match had been played in Soweto. This had been a big hit with the locals who adopted the Bulls as their team. They beat the Crusaders 39–24 to set up an all-South African final, again played at Orlando Stadium because Loftus Versfeld was unavailable as it was being used for the 2010 FIFA World Cup. We couldn't use Ellis Park in Johannesburg for the same reason.

In keeping with World Cup fever, the fans arrived at Orlando with their vuvuzelas, bringing a unique South African football atmosphere to the game. I had never been to Soweto and loved the way the locals, particularly those who lived in the streets around the stadium, were partying with the travelling Bulls fans. It was a great example of how, despite our many differences, there is so much that brings us together. It's a pity the Bulls couldn't build on that spirit in the years that followed, but I understand the financial imperatives that make it important to keep their home games at Loftus.

We trailed throughout the Super 14 final, with the Bulls leading 16–3 at halftime before Bryan Habana scored a trademark intercept try to bring us back into the game. But Morné Steyn was as reliable as ever and his boot slowly took the game away from us. The Bulls won 25–17.

When the Stormers failed to win the Super Rugby title, I felt I'd pretty much done all I could with the team. But I had learnt valuable lessons on how to keep your focus purely on coaching, and to not allow yourself to be distracted by other voices.

In March 2010, Frikkie Erasmus, Andre Markgraaff and I developed the idea of a shortened format for rugby, based on the premise of T20 cricket, with each half lasting 20 minutes, with a two-minute halftime break. We envisaged a two-week tournament in January, before the major rugby competitions began, during which three games would be played back-to-back-to-back in one evening. In just over two hours, fans could watch some of the world's top players in action. We saw it as part of pre-season training and commissioned sports scientists to check if it would be too taxing for the players. We planned a televised event in London to auction the players and coaches, and obtained commitments from big-name sponsors and broadcasters.

We contracted more than 100 top international players. While we were talking to players from the Crusaders, including Richie McCaw and Dan Carter, after a Super Rugby match against the Stormers in Cape Town, we were spotted by the Crusaders coaching staff, who thought we were trying to sign their players to join the Stormers. They immediately reported the incident to New Zealand Rugby CEO Steve Tew, and he sent a formal complaint to the then-president of SA Rugby Regan Hoskins.

Hoskins knew what we were doing because we had briefed him in full about our plans. He asked Frikkie and South African rugby administrator Dr Jan Marais to fly to Sydney to explain the concept and the financial benefits to the CEOs of the Australian Rugby Union and New Zealand Rugby. Unfortunately, they weren't in favour of the competition and made it clear they wouldn't allow their players to take part. But because of the money they would receive, the players remained committed, so we said we would continue with our plans. Tew then complained to the International Rugby Board (IRB; the precursor to World Rugby), and we subsequently received a letter from the IRB notifying us that any player or coach who took part in the competition would be permanently banned from playing rugby. That brought an abrupt end to our idea.

I was honoured when I got a call from Peter de Villiers at the Springboks to join his team for the 2011 Rugby World Cup in New Zealand. He had previously asked me to work with him with the under-20s, which I couldn't do because we were in the Super Rugby final. But now I was available. The experience was incredibly enjoyable because Peter gave Jacques and me the freedom to do our own thing. He was amazing with people and enjoyed a very good relationship with the players. I wish I had that knack. Players really wanted to do their best for him.

It was great to work once again with Gary Gold after our collaboration at Western Province. He was now an assistant to De Villiers, along with an old adversary of mine from my playing days, Dick Muir.

From this experience with the Springboks, I learnt how a coach should trust his players, but also how not to let them take over and run the show. I also learnt you can't judge a player on leadership but rather on ownership. Leadership gets paired with age and experience, but ownership means the player understands his place in the team and that has nothing to do with experience. You have to measure a player by his talent and ask if he's the *right* person, not necessarily the *best* person, and does he take ownership of that? You actually don't need a lot of leaders, in my opinion. You need players who take ownership, who challenge themselves to be the most professional player, and to be the best Springbok in their position.

We had a squad of 30 players, but there were six or seven older players who had vast experience. What we gained from them was big-match temperament and good decision-making; they never got flustered. But what we lost was speed, agility and availability. That team was too old. There was a group of players who were almost considered 'special'. I could see that the older guys ran the show and were treated differently simply because they were older. In that situation, a young guy would struggle to take ownership and never achieve his full potential.

Peter did many things very well, which I definitely copy, such as communication skills and having a happy camp. He was a very good leader, but his leadership group in the team tended to be older players with a great deal of experience. I preferred to give younger players the opportunity to take ownership and lead. I prefer to treat everybody as the same. I'd been in that position before, being treated differently because of my experience, getting special treatment and being allowed to train with a buggered foot – and only at captain's practice. What is a young guy supposed to think about that?

In the build-up to the 2011 World Cup in New Zealand, I became a father for the third time. I was keen on a son, so Nikki and I had been trying for a third child. But when Jani was born on 4 May in Cape Town, I was thrilled to have another daughter. I was with Nikki at the birth, but because of my aversion to blood, I could only appreciate how beautiful my child was once she had been cleaned and was sleeping in my arms, wrapped in a blanket.

We came through the group stage at the World Cup with a narrow win against Wales, comfortable wins against Fiji and Namibia, and a typically tough victory over Samoa. When Frans Steyn was injured in that Samoa match, I got a hollow feeling in my stomach. I felt he was crucial for our chance of success. I didn't raise the issue with Peter or my fellow assistant coaches because I didn't want to cause any alarm. There wasn't a solution to the problem, and I didn't want my insecurity to make people feel nervous. But my gut told me this was not good.

In the quarterfinals in Wellington we were up against our old nemesis Australia, their flanker David Pocock frustrating us throughout the game. Morné Steyn kicked two penalties and a drop, and we led 9–8 with 20 minutes to play. Right up until the final whistle I kept thinking we would score again, but Pat Lambie had a try disallowed because of a forward pass in the build-up, and Fourie du Preez lost the ball in a tackle as he was going over the line. For me the worst was when Pat went for a drop goal and for a moment the ball appeared to be heading between the uprights, but then drifted wide. If that had been successful, I think we'd have won the match because Australia would have needed a try to overtake us. But we gave away a penalty at a lineout nine minutes from time, and James O'Connor kicked it to give them an 11–9 win and send us home early.

Sitting in the coaches' box, I couldn't believe what had happened. I just sat there thinking, 'Fuck, it's over. Did we really just lose?' That was the most disappointing and soul-ripped-out feeling I've ever had as a coach. One moment I was confident we would win because we were well coached, we had experienced players and we were thinking about our next hotel for the semifinal. We were heading for victory. And just like that it was over.

We had no time to reflect on the game as a team and get some closure, because suddenly everyone was going home in small groups at different times. Before a quarterfinal, nobody knows who will lose and fly home after the match. It's different after a semifinal because everyone stays on for the third- and fourth-place playoff and the final. But if you lose in the quarterfinal, you fly home straight away and there's a mad scramble to find seats on the different airlines. The next thing, we were all standing in the change room and Peter was saying something, but no one was listening properly because we were all so shocked, and our operations manager Charles Wessels started talking, saying, 'Okay, guys, these are the players who will fly out via Dubai tomorrow morning, and these are the guys who fly in the afternoon.' We broke up into five or six different groups and never got back together again. We'd been through so much together and now suddenly we were saying goodbye and flying home on different flights. It felt brutal because it was over so abruptly.

When I look back at that World Cup, one of the things that stands out is the way the players played flat out for Peter de Villiers. I know the public criticised him for the way he spoke and the eccentric things he said at news conferences, but the way he spoke to players and managed relationships was exceptional. He didn't suck up to players; he was upfront and straightforward with them. That's the main thing I learnt from him. But I also learnt that you can't give a player too much power. Even if the player respects you, he will find a short cut somewhere and not train as hard as he should. Peter had the players playing for him, and they enjoyed having him as head coach. There is no doubt in my mind; it's a fact. I saw it.

I went back to the Stormers for a short period, knowing that I wasn't in the running to become the next Springbok coach. Heyneke Meyer got the job – and rightly so, because he was a highly respected coach who had achieved so much with the Bulls, including a Super Rugby title in 2007 and four Currie Cup titles. I resigned from my position as Senior Professional Coach at Western Province Rugby and left at the end of January 2012.

11

AT THE BEGINNING OF 2012, I began a long association with SARU when I was appointed the high-performance manager with varied responsibilities, including setting up a programme to develop young players, with a particular emphasis on transformation.

In February 2012, Frikkie Erasmus and I were in France on business when my elbow swelled up alarmingly and I developed a terrible fever. I was in a bad way at Charles de Gaulle Airport in Paris waiting for a connecting flight to Perpignan, lying on a bench and shivering so much that the airport police suspected I was either blind drunk or having a drug-induced fit. When we arrived in Perpignan, our French host immediately called the Perpignan rugby team's doctor, who referred us to the local hospital. I had surgery that same evening to drain my elbow under a general anaesthetic, which involved a long cut in my arm. I stayed overnight, and the next morning Frikkie and our hosts fetched me from hospital and took me straight off to explore the region's wine farms.

I wasn't keen, but I didn't want to be rude and accepted the invitation. I was so drugged from the anaesthetic and pain medication that I forgot to spit out my wine after each tasting. Glass after glass of red wine coupled with the meds was a very bad idea, as I found out later. I recovered to a certain extent, but the swelling came and went until eventually a doctor in Cape Town diagnosed the problem. It turned out to be tuberculosis (TB) in my elbow, and I was put on TB medication for nine months.

In 2013, I started the Elite Player Development (EPD) Pathway, and brought in Jacques Nienaber to assist me. We had a group of EPD managers who assisted me by appointing scouts in the various provinces to help identify players at under-15 level. We knew we couldn't make a difference to rugby at under-19 or under-20 level, because a player who is 19 or 20 years old can't catch up what he has lost in the previous five or six years. So we started working with under-15s by getting promising youngsters from that age on our radar.

To make sure we were hitting transformation goals, we would pick three players for each position. If all three were white, we would keep picking until we had two black players. And if we then ended up with five players in one position, that's the number we would go with. Our final group varied from 75 to 100 players. If a promising black player missed out because he wasn't quite good enough, we would monitor him and follow his progress. We'd regularly check how his skills were developing, possibly get him placed at a better school, or find him a mentor, suggest a better diet, or help him at his school.

The programme is still running, and we now have managers of under-15, under-16 and under-17 groups. We're seeing the rewards with the Junior Springboks (the under-20s) winning all four games in the U20 Six Nations Summer Series in 2022, beating England, Ireland, France and Wales. They were also unbeaten in 2021, beating Argentina twice, and Uruguay and Georgia. There is a filtering system in place so that a player doesn't fall out along the way. We emphasised with the coaches that a black player must be exposed to things other than the skills he may have learnt kicking a ball in the street with his friends.

Some of the players who made a name for themselves in Super Rugby and the United Rugby Championship came through the EPD ranks, among them Aphelele Fassi, Jaden Hendrikse, Curwin Bosch, Sbu Nkosi, Canan Moodie, Damian Willemse, Salmaan Moerat and Sanele Nohamba, to name a few.

I first saw Makazole Mapimpi and Lukhanyo Am when Jacques Nienaber and I went to coach at Border while the union was under SARU administration. I phoned the agent, Craig Livingstone, and told him to move Lukhanyo to where we could see him more often. The Border coaches didn't really latch onto Mapimpi right away, and he was already 23 when we noticed him. I could see that he was exceptionally fast, but he couldn't catch a high ball.

In the High Performance department at SARU we set up the MOBI unit, which consisted of five coaches with different specialities who travelled around the country to provide skills to players and coaches from schools level to club level to Super Rugby. We went wherever we were wanted. Sometimes one of us might be required, other times all five of us would go to a far-flung place to help coach a team. I coached the breakdown, while Jacques coached defence. We brought in the former French prop Pieter de Villiers to take control of scrums. Louis Koen coached kicking and Chean Roux handled the lineouts. With this mobile unit we could go anywhere. We had been missing coaching, because we didn't have a team and we hadn't been involved in any selection panels.

We knew that most young kids in the township played touch rugby and were mainly exposed to fast, running rugby. That's why so many good black players coming through in the early days of transformation were wingers or centres. But these kids weren't being exposed to the physicality of the breakdown, how to do clean-outs, how to maul, how to jump in a lineout. So we took our mobile training unit and went to the rural areas to coach. We would also have a coaches' forum where we exposed players to aspects of the game they might not have experienced much of before. Not only did we go to the Kings in Port Elizabeth to help with the defence training, but Pieter and Jacques also worked with the Junior Boks and were familiar with some of the players because they had been part of the EPD Pathway. Eventually, when we got to 2019 and the Rugby World Cup, we knew all the players because we had either coached them somewhere along the way or had seen them as part of the EPD Pathway.

We travelled to rugby academies, funded by the National Lottery Distribution Trust Fund, which had been set up by SARU in Boland, South Western Districts, Eastern Province and Border to identify talented young players aged between 15 and 18. I put together the coaching manuals. Unfortunately, they came to a premature end when the lottery funding dried up.

In 2018 we also started a programme, which still runs today, to fast-track elite black coaches who have the potential and skills but lack the experience in handling media and the politics of sport at the higher level. We worked with industrial psychologists to develop programmes to provide them with the skills they needed to deal with issues away from the training field. Currently there isn't a single black head coach in charge at one of the top franchises. We can't make the franchises contract a black head coach – that's not our job – but what we can do is give black coaches the skills needed to coach at that level and hope that the franchises and unions give them opportunities.

The SA Schools squad must be representative, so how do we achieve that? We start tracking players from under-15, and make sure there are talented black players in all the age-group squads. If you get it right with the Schools squad, the under-20 squad will become transformed. And eventually so will the Springbok squad.

When it came to schools rugby, we didn't have a say. That's run by the Department of Basic Education. We can't tell a school how to run their rugby programmes – the department must do that. But, with the EPD Pathway, an under-15 player would feel he was on our radar and that we're intervening to grow his talents. It's an entirely voluntary programme, however, and the youngsters don't have to be part of it if they don't want to be.

That's how we started to influence the development of players – both black and white – and educate them about the fundamentals of coaching and playing. All too often, rugby schools just say, 'Guys, play what you see,' and when those guys get to professional rugby they don't know what to do when faced with a wall of defenders. If you play what you see, then you must kick the ball every single time. But if we can get them to run against defensive lines at under-15 and under-17, they will know what to do in professional rugby. The EPD solved a lot of problems for us at an early stage.

I loved it, sitting with coaches and discussing tactics and strategy, going through coaching manuals, and watching the youngsters coming through the programme and achieving so much. These days, I'm not sitting with the managers as much because I've got to get women's rugby right and the Springboks must keep winning. SARU's top priority is always the Springboks – always. Let the Springboks do well, fix the Blitzboks, fix women's rugby. But at the end of the day, if the Springboks lose, transformation gets amplified.

We have to find that balance and that's when I blow my gasket … when we respond proactively to accusations that nothing is being done about transformation by putting plans and programmes in place to address it, and achieving great successes, yet we're sometimes accused of sitting around doing nothing.

The success rate was high for all the teams that reported to me as the high-performance manager: SA Schools, the Sevens, the under-20s … For all those teams, we had an 85% win record.

The only team that didn't report to the high-performance manager was the Springboks. I understood what we needed to do at the Springboks based on my track record with the team: as a player from 1997 to 2001, as a player at the 1999 World Cup, as technical adviser before the 2007 World Cup and for the duration of the 2011 World Cup. I could see obvious mistakes being made by Heyneke Meyer as he prepared for the 2015 World Cup, but he didn't have to act on what I told him. He reported to SARU CEO Jurie Roux, and not to me. All I wanted was for him to at least listen to my ideas as high-performance manager and for me to make suggestions on where I thought he was making mistakes. My mother always said, 'I've already learnt from my mistakes, don't make me learn from your mistakes.'

As I had seen with so many coaches before him, Heyneke tried to run everything: the coaching, the politics and the media. That's why Springbok coaches ultimately fail – because they're no longer focused solely on coaching. They get too involved in all the other issues, the politics and the pressure of the media. That's why my job as SA Rugby Director of Rugby now is to take the shit off Jacques Nienaber and let him concentrate on doing his job: coaching the Springboks. I'll shield him from all the noise that goes on around him.

I had learnt at the Stormers not to make decisions to please people making the noise, or to please the media and the fans. I thought Heyneke was doing exactly that. There's a fine balance between saying, 'Fuck everybody, I'm going to do it my way,' and choosing to listen to those you trust. That's why Jacques has been fairly successful, because he's got someone who can warn him not to please outside forces, or remind him to listen to the people closest to him. As we were heading closer to the World Cup, I could see that Heyneke started making decisions totally on his own, or decisions that pleased the media.

I felt there should have been more consultation with people from the MOBI unit who understood what a World Cup was all about.

In the 2015 World Cup, the Springboks lost to New Zealand 18–20 in a tough semifinal at Twickenham and finished the tournament in third place. As usually happens to the Bok coach, Heyneke Meyer was now out of a job, and the search was on for someone to take over. I thought, 'Fuck, I can do this.' But that would conflict with my role as high-performance manager, so I decided to take my name out of the hat and assist Allister Coetzee in getting the job. I have since been accused of setting him up for failure, but that is ridiculous. I did Allister's presentation and helped him get the job. I thought he and I would work together as we did at the Stormers, with him as head coach, and me as General Manager of Rugby at SARU.

Unfortunately, within six months, Allister appeared to fall at the same hurdle – all the politics and the media – and very quickly he was no longer concentrating on coaching. He should have told me about that. He started appointing assistant coaches, bringing in Matt Proudfoot as the forwards coach when I thought former French prop Pieter de Villiers would have been better. Later, he claimed he didn't have the right to appoint his own management team, which contributed to his failure. That's nonsense. In the end, Allister got all the coaches he wanted; we never blocked any appointment. And then I took that very same management team, and we won the World Cup.

When I saw Allister making the same mistakes as I had made at the Stormers, I said to Jacques, 'I'm not going to sit around for another four years and watch another guy fail to understand that he must just concentrate on coaching.' At the national level, a coach can't report to a financial person or to a board. When has there ever been a situation where a person who has played and coached at the highest level for 11 years is willing to assist the national coach by taking away all the political shit and allowing him to focus on the day-to-day coaching? That's what I was offering. The national coach must concentrate on building a team that wins consistently. Somebody else needs to worry about the long-term strategy and the politics. I quit the Stormers when I realised I was needing to handle all the bullshit and wasn't coaching any more – and that's exactly what I believe Allister stepped into. He stopped coaching and started getting distracted by all the other nonsense. I wanted him to trust me on this and let me shield him, but it felt like he didn't and wouldn't. I didn't want his job, but I did want to be part of a successful Springbok team. It wasn't going to happen if the national coach didn't actually coach.

Allister and I didn't establish the relationship I was suggesting, and I didn't have any input when it came to the Springbok team at all. I thought,

'Okay, I've tried my best here,' and I got on a plane.

By then I knew that there were jobs going at Harlequins in England and Munster in Ireland and applied for both positions. I flew out for the interviews, which were three days apart. I liked the way Munster spoke to me about the job and knew in my heart this was the place for me. And so, before Harlequins could even come back with an answer, I accepted the position of Director of Rugby at Munster.

They had never had such a position before. They always had a head coach, but now they wanted someone who handled the recruitment of players, did succession planning and reported to the high-performance director, David Nucifora, who worked for the Irish Rugby Football Union (IRFU). I didn't sign a contract with Munster; I signed with the IRFU and was seconded to Munster. That's how it works in Ireland. All players and coaches sign IRFU contracts and are seconded to the various teams. It's a very good system because there's proper succession planning in place. David ensured there was a supply of quality local and foreign players to the professional ranks. If a player wasn't good enough to be a professional rugby player, he didn't become one.

I reported to the Munster CEO, Garrett Fitzgerald, and a board, but I wanted to be involved on the field with the players as well and was given the responsibility of coaching the breakdown, working with the head coach Anthony Foley.

My family and I fell in love with Ireland immediately. Nikki and my three girls made our home in the beautiful little village of Castleconnell on the banks of the River Shannon, 11 kilometres from Limerick, where Munster are based. Limerick is a lot like Bloemfontein, with hard-working people. Comparing Dublin to Limerick is like comparing Cape Town to Bloem. Irish people are unbelievable, and we took to them immediately. As an Afrikaner, my English accent is terrible, but they don't care how you talk. They just want to see you working hard and loving Munster, and that was enough for them.

Everyone knew us at our local pub, The Black Swan, just outside Castleconnell, and they looked after us. We embraced the Irish pub culture and quickly learnt what a good pint of Guinness tastes like. We started understanding the Irish slang – knowing that a good time was *the craic* and 'grand' was what you said when you were enjoying something. The locals would attempt to mimic our South African accents, but simply couldn't pronounce my name correctly. It came out as 'Razzie' because they couldn't say 'Rrrr' and insisted on a hard sound for the 's'.

We planned to stay for the long haul as we wanted to qualify for Irish passports after three years. My twin daughters, Nikki and Carli, started high school in Limerick, while my youngest, Jani, started Grade 1 at a little school in the village. She developed an Irish lilt as she mainly spoke English, and even now she doesn't roll her Rs in the South African way.

Nikki stopped working as a professional senior nurse in June 2016, just two weeks before we left for Ireland. My mother had lived with us for about 14 years, and she moved into an old-age home when we left for Munster. Nikki would have needed a permit to work in Ireland, but she had her hands full running the home in Castleconnell anyway.

Things happened very quickly after I got the Munster job. I told Nikki that I had gone out looking for a house while I was over in Ireland for the interviews, but I actually found it on the internet, fully furnished, and paid a deposit then and there without physically seeing it. Munster thought we were arriving on a Monday. I didn't tell them, but I bought our plane tickets myself, and we flew over the Friday before. The five of us arrived at Shannon Airport where I hired a car and trailer to take us and our 14 suitcases to Castleconnell. I didn't tell Nikki I hadn't seen the house and pretended to know which one it was. I couldn't find the house and first went to the wrong place before someone on the street corrected me. The cat was out the bag.

There were a few things that we had to adapt to, like the weather and the fact that it gets dark early in winter and light early in summer. And, because of the rain, we couldn't braai as often as we did in South Africa. Everyone in our street was unbelievably good to us, though, and it wasn't just because we were involved with their beloved Munster – they were simply friendly people.

Having arrived three days early, I had time to settle in. I don't like it when people feel sorry for me and want to help. I prefer to organise things myself. On the Sunday before I was due to arrive at Munster's offices, I went shopping, bought myself a Munster top and walked into their offices at the High Performance Centre at the University of Limerick on the Monday, appropriately dressed and ready for work. No one was expecting me and the first person who walked past me without recognising me was Simon Zebo, who at that stage was probably Ireland's number-one winger and a Munster regular. I knew who he was, though, because I had studied every single player and learnt all their names.

Garrett Fitzgerald was at Munster's head office in Cork at the time, so I went looking for Foley's office. I had met him once before during the job interview and had had supper with him. When I walked into his office, he immediately jumped up, hugged me and slapped me on the back – maybe a little too hard because he was a big, strong man. He showed me around, introduced me to the rest of the management team, and then I went to my new office, closed the door, and for the first hour or two I thought, 'Okay, where do I start and how am I going to handle this?'

I persuaded Jacques Nienaber and his family to join us in Ireland. Says Jacques:

The decision to move to Ireland was easy for me because I was keen to work in a foreign country. I had been ready to go in 2014. I'm not sure Rassie was initially eager to go, but when he realised nothing would change and his vision for South African rugby wouldn't become a reality, he knew he had to leave. Rassie had discussions with Harlequins and he phoned me from London to tell me Munster were interested and that he

142

would fly to Ireland to meet them. When he walked out of that meeting, he phoned again to say, 'This is the place, this is like Free State.' I was working as defence coach for the Springboks and was preparing for the three-Test series against Ireland. I had built up profiles on the Irish players and shared my information on the Munster-based players with Rassie, so he was well prepared for that interview. We took a vote as a family on staying or going. I was keen, Elmarie supported me, my son — who was in Grade 8 at the time — was neutral, but it took some time to convince my daughter, who was in Grade 3, that this was a good idea.

12

I ARRIVED IN MUNSTER at the end of June 2016 as Director of Rugby, a three-year deal that saw me working with the head coach Anthony Foley, affectionately nicknamed Axel after Eddie Murphy's character in *Beverly Hills Cop*. Axel was a Munster legend, as was his father Brendan before him. He played for them 201 times and was captain when Munster famously beat Biarritz Olympique to win the Heineken Cup for the first (and only) time in the club's history, in 2006. He won 62 caps for Ireland as a loose forward, mainly at eighthman. He retired in 2008, and became Munster's forwards coach in 2011, a position he held for three years. By the time I joined the club in 2016, he had been the head coach for two years.

Four months after I started at Munster, we flew to Paris to play Racing 92 in our opening match of the European Rugby Champions Cup (previously known as the Heineken Cup). We checked into our hotel in the suburb of Suresnes, and Axel sent me a WhatsApp message recommending a podcast entitled *You Create Your Own Reality*, which I still use a lot these days.

The next day, Sunday, 16 October, the team met to go through the lineout strategy for the afternoon game at Yves-du-Manoir Stadium. This was part of the match day routine where the forwards and the backs had separate meetings. It was coming up for 12:30pm and Axel was late. I went to our technical analyst George Murray and told him I was worried. I hadn't gone to breakfast so I didn't know that Axel hadn't come down from his room that morning. I don't know why I said this, but my words to George were 'Please go to his room … I think he's passed away.' I had no reason to say this; it just came out like that.

George was gone for a few minutes, and when he came back down and stepped out of the lift, I could see he was pale and upset. He said he had found Axel lying next to his bed. I said, 'He's dead, isn't he?' and he nodded, 'Yes, I think he's passed away.' I was shocked and didn't know what to do. We alerted the hotel staff who called the police, and they went up to Axel's room.

The players didn't know what was going on, and I, very stupidly, suggested we keep the news from them, otherwise how would they be able to concentrate on the match? Team manager Niall O'Donovan just looked at me and said, 'Are you fuckin' crazy? You must tell these players, man. The guy is dead.'

I will never forget his words, and it shocked me that I had to break the terrible news. I hadn't experienced a death so close to me since my friend Murto had died, followed by my father when I was 18. I was unsure how to handle it. The players were eating lunch when I went into the team room. I looked at these players, whom I hadn't known for very long, prominent players like the captain Peter O'Mahony, Keith Earls, Simon Zebo and Conor Murray. I was trembling as I said, 'I don't know how to tell you this …' and then I just started crying. I had to ask Niall to help me as he knew the team better than me, so he broke the news as gently as he could. The players were completely blindsided. Their grief was immediate. We then had to make sure the news didn't get to the media before the family was notified.

The match against Racing 92 was called off, and we waited at the hotel while plans were made for us to fly home. We sat outside the hotel and Axel's father, who was staying in a nearby hotel, joined us. The authorities tried to zip Axel's body up in a bag, but he was such a big man that he didn't fit as they carried him out of the hotel.

Two days later, a French coroner ruled that Axel had died as a result of acute pulmonary oedema, a heart condition that had caused fluid to build up in his lungs. He was only 42 years old. The next day his body was flown on a specially chartered plane to Shannon Airport, just outside Limerick. Thousands of people lined the road as a hearse took Axel from the airport. A large emotional crowd gathered outside Munster's home ground Thomond Park and applauded as the hearse, accompanied by a police escort, stopped briefly. The crowd sang 'There Is an Isle', the anthem of his former club, Shannon.

As we prepared for Axel's funeral, our next rugby match was also postponed. I had never been to an Irish funeral before and was quite unprepared for what took place. I had been thrown into a situation I had never encountered before – I didn't even know how to carry a coffin or how the mourning process worked – but the Limerick people and the Munster players and staff guided me through it. Axel lay in an open casket in his house and mourners walked through to pay their last respects. It felt to me like the whole town of Limerick went to Axel's house to say goodbye. Later, we had a service, and never in my life have I seen so many people at a funeral. It was incredibly sad, but the days before and after were full of memories and stories of the legendary things Axel did, and then we took turns to carry his heavy coffin (he weighed over 100 kilograms) to the cemetery.

The experience brought home to me the reality of what death is, not having dealt with it since I was 18. In Ireland, the attitude is: 'We're going to celebrate this, and we're going to cry about this, and we're going to go to the pub.' But it's not over once the burial takes place. The Irish have something they call the 'month's mind', so after a month you mind him again, go to church and then back to the pub.

Our first game after Axel's death was at a sold-out Thomond Park against Glasgow Warriors in a European Rugby Champions Cup match. It was a deeply emotional experience, starting with us retiring his No. 8 jersey for the game. Our eighthman CJ Stander wore 24 on his back and each player had the name 'Axel' embroidered under the Munster crest on his jersey. The crowd of 26 000 fans observed a minute's silence before kick-off. In one of the big stands, the spectators sat in such a way as to form the name 'Axel' in white, against a red backdrop.

Emotions were high after renditions of 'The Fields of Athenry' and 'There Is an Isle'. In the 20th minute, Keith Earls was sent off for a dangerous tackle, but nothing was going to stop us winning for Axel, and we beat Glasgow 38–17, scoring five tries. After the final whistle, we all stood at the centre of the pitch, joined by Axel's two sons, and sang the club's anthem 'Stand Up and Fight'.

In Ireland I learnt so much about how to treasure a life. The Irish understand how to appreciate life and how to mourn a death. If a swan is killed in Limerick, it's on the front page of the newspaper. There's hardly any crime. In 2016, the first year we lived in Ireland, there were 37 murders in the whole country. In South Africa, there were 19 000 from 1 April 2016 to 31 March 2017. When someone dies in Ireland, you can expect a minute's silence. It made me appreciate life more.

We had to fill the void left by Axel, and again the players helped me. I called six or seven of the senior players in, people like Peter O'Mahony and Conor Murray, and asked them, 'What do you say, boys, what do we do, how will we handle this, what are we going to do in the next match?' We decided not to bring in someone new for the head coach position but rather divide up the work. We call it the coaching matrix, sharing the different responsibilities between us. I took on the position of head coach and handled the breakdown. Jacques was the defence coach. Jerry Flannery – a former Munster, Ireland, and British and Irish Lions hooker – who was the scrum coach, became the forwards coach. I had already signed Munster's fullback Felix Jones as the technical coach after he was forced to quit the game at the age of 28 after breaking his neck, and he handled attack. Felix is now the Springboks' assistant coach and will join England's coaching team after the 2023 World Cup.

I combined the head coach role with that of Director of Rugby. I was still the guy who was analysing the opposition, doing long-term planning, and signing players, but I was hands-on as well.

It wasn't difficult to motivate the team. We just played for Axel. When we spoke about the big thing that would win the game, it was called the axis of the game. We renamed it the Axel of the game. I talked to the players about creating their own reality from the podcast that Axel recommended to me hours before he died. We would ask ourselves, 'Where is our reality, and what would Axel want us to do?' There wasn't a single game, even in the following year, where we weren't playing for him.

From coming sixth in the Pro12 (the precursor to the United Rugby Championship before South African teams joined the competition) in 2015/16, Munster made it to the top of the log to earn a home semifinal the following season. We won 19 out of our 22 games, with a great one-point victory over Ulster in Belfast, where they are notoriously difficult to beat, and a memorable 29–17 Boxing Day victory over our arch rivals Leinster at Thomond Park. In the Pro12 semifinal, we scored three tries to beat Ospreys 23–3 in front of our home crowd.

Irish rugby fans are something else. They don't start booing or leaving the stadium if their team is losing. They'll take you out in the newspapers and they will be direct and to the point, but they will always keep the criticism fair and honest. It was just lekker to breathe again and get back to coaching without being pulled in different directions. It was just the team on the field and no other shit.

The Pro12 final against Scarlets at the Aviva Stadium in Dublin in front of 44 000 spectators was a bitter disappointment. Never in my life as a coach did the opposition team score 50 points against me and, in the final, I was really worried that this would happen. It was probably one of the few games where I thought, 'I hope this game ends soon.' We ended up losing 22–46. I was really surprised because we had been so competitive all season and were actually the favourites going into that game. To this day, I can't tell you what went wrong. In the change room after the match, we were all shocked. I remember my words to the players. I told them I couldn't work out what I had done wrong, but I knew it was me. I didn't see it coming at all.

In the European Rugby Champions Cup, we won five of our six games in Pool 1, including an incredible win over Leicester at Thomond Park when they were unable to score a single point. They got their revenge the following week, though, beating us by two points at Welford Road, for our only defeat in the group stage of the competition. We then thrashed Toulouse 41–16 in the quarterfinal, but came unstuck in the semis, losing to Saracens 10–26 at the Aviva Stadium. My run in both competitions ended at the same stadium.

I fitted in with Munster and Limerick so well. I got along with the players, the fans, and the local residents. I loved the lyrics of the Munster song 'Stand Up And Fight':

Stan' up an' fight until you hear de bell,
Stan' toe to toe, trade blow fer blow,
Keep punchin' till you make yer punches tell,
Show dat crowd watcher know!
Until you hear dat bell, dat final bell,
Stan' up an' fight like hell!

I'm a Despatch boykie. That's where I learnt to stand up and fight.

On 5 November 2016, my mom, sister Gerda and brother-in-law Willie, and Frikkie Erasmus came over from South Africa, and my sister Martlie and her husband Bert came up from London to celebrate my 44th birthday. We braaied outside and Frikkie made plankiesteaks for us, the typical South African way. They even came to watch Munster beat Ospreys 33–0 at Musgrave Park in Cork. My mother and sisters fell in love with Munster, the village, and the people.

Frikkie and I started talking about Springbok rugby and he asked if I would ever go back to South Africa and coach the Springboks again. I said I might, but only when I was 50 years old. I told him I didn't want to coach to keep people happy and deal with the politics around rugby. I wasn't talking about racial issues – I knew how to handle transformation. That was a challenge I enjoyed, and I could see that my work at the EPD Pathway was working well. I just didn't want to deal with the agendas of people who weren't part of SARU structures.

Frikkie said Allister Coetzee, the Springbok coach, was struggling. At that stage, he had lost five out of nine Tests, including the first-ever home defeat against Ireland in Cape Town against a 14-man Irish team, and a 15–57 thrashing by New Zealand in Durban. Things got worse the following year, including a humiliating 0–57 defeat to the All Blacks in Albany.

Frikkie suggested I apply for the position of Director of Rugby at SARU. I was against the idea, saying SARU never wanted that. I clearly remember being told that they didn't want a director, but they didn't understand what the job entailed. They thought a Director of Rugby was a director on the board, someone who sits in an office and does budgets. The Director of Rugby is actually a person who still coaches, but also handles the non-rugby issues so that the head coach can just get on with the job.

Frikkie asked if I wanted to go back. I was completely honest with him. I said, 'I love South Africa, Frikkie, but I'm really in a good place here. The job is going well, the people are fantastic, I've got a good salary, my wife is loving it, the kids are settled and have made friends, and it's such a safe place.' Why would I want to go back?

I had to admit, though, that I had this itch to scratch. I knew it would work if I was Director of Rugby and could work with Allister in the same way we did at the Stormers. I had been exposed to the professional way

Ireland ran their rugby and I liked it. They had 160 rugby players and were number one in the world. In South Africa, we had over 1 000 professional rugby players and were fourth in the world. I learnt a lot of things we could do better from Munster and their set-up. Frikkie said, 'Okay, you carry on here. I'll go and speak to the people.' I agreed, but with only 10% conviction. I thought SARU would just say, 'Fuck him.'

Frikkie and I had been through a lot together, so I totally trusted that he had my back. He went to speak to the president of SARU, Mark Alexander, and the CEO at the time, Jurie Roux. The first thing I heard back from Frikkie was, 'Can you get out of your contract?' I told him I wasn't prepared to have that conversation with Garrett Fitzgerald if the SARU position wasn't a real possibility. If nothing was going to happen, I didn't want Munster to think I was looking for a job somewhere else.

But Frikkie had everything under control. He knew my demands and he had them included in a contract between me and SARU, guaranteeing me the set-up I thought would work. I made sure that Jacques was also offered a job with SARU. After all, I had persuaded him and his family to come to Ireland in the first place. I needed to make sure he was part of the deal if I went home again.

I then faced the difficult task of telling my family and Jacques and his family that maybe, just maybe, we would be going back to South Africa. First Nikki and I sat down, and she said she didn't want to leave Castleconnell. The kids were more adamant – they simply did not want to go back.

I took Jacques and Elmarie to our local pub and warned them that Frikkie was talking to SARU and that we could find ourselves working with the Springboks again. I wanted to know if they would be in if we went back to South Africa. I remember Elmarie saying no, and Jacques saying, shit, he wasn't sure, and that they would have to think about it.

Then Frikkie phoned and said he had everything in writing. When I heard that, I called everyone together and told them what was on the table. I know it was a tough decision, but they all agreed that we probably wouldn't get this opportunity again.

It was also a tough decision for Jacques:

Rassie suggested we all meet at our local pub, The Black Swan, where he told me of the opportunity at SARU. Nikki and Elmarie were immediately against the idea of returning home because the children were settled at school and had made friends. About four weeks later, Rassie had more details and we met again at the pub. Initially, I wanted to stay in Ireland, because I had my eye on getting an Irish passport after five years, which opened up job opportunities in the European Union. I was also enjoying Munster and the successes we were achieving. Rassie was building a winning squad, which excited me. The club was struggling when we arrived and there was pressure on Rassie to get new players. He wanted to work with the existing squad and only brought in three players from South Africa. In the end, he convinced me to return to South Africa, and we had to have a few more tough conversations with our families to persuade them. It wasn't easy to move back.

There were a lot of tears when I told Munster. I felt super shit about leaving because they had been so wonderful to me, and we had achieved such wonderful success in such a short space of time. There was an escape clause in my contract where either I or Munster could end the agreement after 18 months for one of a variety of reasons: unhappiness, budget constraints, that type of thing. But I didn't use that clause. I was open with Garrett Fitzgerald (who sadly passed away in February 2020) about Frikkie's discussions with SARU. He reminded me that I had signed with the IRFU, not with him, so that was another conversation I had to have, with David Nucifora. Of all people, I think Nucifora understood my situation most personally, as he had once been in the running to coach Australia only to have his hopes dashed at the last minute when the Australian Rugby

Union gave the job to Robbie Deans. He told me not to worry about the legal issues and released me.

To make matters worse for me, I had signed new players, including Jean Kleyn from the Stormers. I had persuaded them to leave South Africa, and now I was on my way out. Jean has since gone on to qualify for Ireland and has played five Tests.

Munster were typically kind and understanding. It was so incredibly hard after 18 months to ask, 'Can I please go back?' And you know why they said yes? Because they're fucking good people.

In June 2017 Munster announced that Jacques and I would be leaving at the end of the year. We had agreed to stay on for six months so that we could give them a decent handover time and weren't leaving them in tatters. Before we left, we won five out of the eight matches in the Pro14, and had a win and a draw in the Champions Cup. Then we handed over to Johann van Graan, the former Bulls and Springbok assistant coach, who took over as head coach, and JP Ferreira, the Lions defence coach, who replaced Jacques. Felix Jones and Jerry Flannery stayed on as assistant coaches. They continued the good work at Munster, guiding the team to a successive Pro14 semifinal, but losing in a very tense match to Leinster 15–16.

I knew it was a good deal, but it was heart-breaking to leave Munster. Even now, I get so hartseer when I see pictures of Castleconnell and our beautiful home next to the River Shannon. I started to doubt myself. I was putting my balls out there because now my vision for the Springboks was going to be tested. I had been talking the big game for so long and the plan I was so sure about was soon to become a reality and be tested.

Even now, I still don't know if it was the best decision for my family to leave Ireland.

13

WE ARRIVED BACK IN SOUTH AFRICA in November 2017 with contracts that stipulated I was the Director of Rugby at SA Rugby, with Allister Coetzee as Springbok coach, and Neil Powell as Sevens coach, reporting in to me. Jacques's contract said he was the Assistant National Coach.

There wasn't a discussion with Allister at that stage if he was keen to work with me as Director of Rugby. When I left in 2016, I had my difference of opinion with Allister about his coaching team. He got the people he wanted, with Matt Proudfoot as his forwards coach, when I thought Pieter de Villiers – who had worked with me on the MOBI unit – was the better option. I had suggested he make Mzwandile Stick the off-the-ball coach because of his Sevens rugby background, but Allister made him the backline coach. I disagreed because I felt Allister had to do some coaching, and his job was taking charge of the backline. It seemed Allister wanted to manage like a football manager, overseeing the coaching set-up, but I feel that a coach must coach.

When I got back, I didn't phone Allister and ask him if he was okay with me coming back into this position. It wasn't my place to do so. I expected SARU to have had that discussion with him. It felt very uncomfortable. Once or twice I got the feeling that he wasn't happy, but we never had a frank discussion about it.

When we returned, the Springboks were on the end-of-year tour, which we weren't involved in. They came back having lost to Ireland and Wales, but had a narrow win over France and a solid victory over Italy. After the Wales game, Allister was adamant he wouldn't resign, despite his poor track record of a 44% win record: 11 wins, 12 losses and two draws from his 25 games in charge. He told journalists he would take the Springboks to the 2019 World Cup.

As always, there was a review of the tour and Allister's performance as coach, and I sat in on the part of that process dealing specifically with rugby. After that, he made the decision to resign. There was never a time when the two of us could start planning for the future.

I don't know the ins and outs of what Allister said to Jurie or to Mark, but he did claim in a letter to Jurie that I had been employed to replace him and that he would become a 'ceremonial coach', and described reporting to me as 'an indignity'. He further claimed that he was being 'set up to fail', and that unnamed officials had 'embarked on a deliberate attempt to undermine [him] from the word go'. I was totally blindsided and horrified.

That's what hurt most when I came back, when I was criticised for taking up the position as Springbok coach and accused of setting Allister Coetzee up to fail so that I could swoop in and take his job. When I saw people writing that, I just wanted to get on a plane and go straight back to Ireland.

After I had uprooted my whole family, persuaded my wife to leave her family and friends, asked my children to give up their schools and their buddies just so I could coach again; after I had asked Jacques and his family to make the same sacrifices, to say Allister's going to fuck it up and I'm going to come back? Really? *That* was my plan?

On 2 February 2018, SARU issued a statement stating that the two parties had reached an agreement and that Allister would leave with immediate effect. It was so sudden. We have probably WhatsApped each other twice since.

My plan was to put systems in place and have the best leaders in the

155

different departments as I started working as Director of Rugby, with Chean Roux at the Junior Springboks and Neil Powell at the Blitzboks. I also had to work at growing women's rugby.

The Springboks were always the priority and we needed someone to replace Allister. The common view was that it would be career suicide for any coach to take the job a year out from the World Cup. We really thought Allister would stay on and that we would help him prepare the Boks without any external interference, so I was taken by surprise with his decision to quit. In 2016, I had recommended that Allister be given the job. How would I know that he would quit two years later? He had the same job, same salary, same players, and same support staff. The only difference was that he was reporting to a rugby person and not a financial person.

I told SARU if they wanted to interview people for the job and find someone who would be willing to take a one-year chance on being the Bok coach at the World Cup, I would sit in on those interviews. But if they didn't find anyone, I offered to take over as coach and they could change my job description. I said, 'If we don't win, I know I will be fired.' The length of the contract period doesn't determine how long you are a Springbok coach – the administrators, players, media and fans determine that.

The High Performance Committee, which included Jurie Roux, Mark Alexander and James Stoffberg (who was chairman of the committee), made the decision to make me the head coach. I was incredibly proud to be given the honour, but I wasn't happy with the circumstances in which it happened. I didn't want a job where I was accused of moving Allister out. That wasn't the fucking plan. All the other structures kept going, and all the other coaches kept their jobs. Only the Springbok coach felt he couldn't report to me.

I had a six-year contract as Director of Rugby, but I made it clear that I would step down as head coach after the 2019 World Cup. Because I was being accused of planning this all along, since 2016, I gave my word that I would do the job for two years and then resign and step aside for someone else.

I took over Allister's coaching staff – the people he claimed were forced on him, which wasn't the case. Matt Proudfoot, who was appointed by Allister, was contracted. He wasn't my choice, but I liked Matt. He had been my assistant coach at the Stormers, so I knew him very well. His technical analysis is superb. But I also brought in Pieter de Villiers, the former prop, because I wanted someone who would add a bit of grunt to the forwards. I was looking for someone who would bring out the dog in the player, someone to say, 'You must stop this maul. I don't know where you're going to put your head, but stop this maul.'

Mzwandile Stick was retained, but moved to the position I felt was his strength as the off-the-ball coach, capitalising on his Sevens experience. Jacques Nienaber, who had been Allister's defence coach before joining me in Munster, went back into that role.

But I needed a backline coach because that had been Allister's job, so I decided to look at the franchises to see who was coaching the best. I certainly couldn't coach attack on my own, because I don't have those skills. I went for Swys de Bruin, who was doing wonderful things as backline coach with the Lions and had helped head coach Johan Ackermann take the Lions to successive Super Rugby finals in 2016 and 2017, which they unfortunately lost. So Swys became my attack coach.

I was confident I could be both head coach and Director of Rugby because I had the experience to handle both jobs. I knew how to tackle the issues of transformation and development of players and coaches. I had put systems in place to identify promising youngsters at under-15 level and monitor them as they progressed, as well as the systems to fast-track black coaches. I understood how it all worked. I was prepared to do it for two years, and I was determined to do it my way. I knew I would get fired if we lost (I even said so in public), but I knew where the obstacles were and how to avoid them. I knew what a Director of Rugby should be doing for their head coach. I told SARU and the players that I wasn't prepared to make any political decisions, and that I was going to be bold, and if my plans didn't work and I got fired, I'd go. This was the job I wanted when I was 50. Now it had been given to me at the age of 45.

We started the 2018 international season with a money-maker Test match against Wales in Washington, USA, but that wasn't our focus. England were coming out for a three-Test series, and that's where we needed to prove ourselves and get people to believe in the Springboks again. The Wales Test was intrusive but important because of the revenue it generated.

Every year you have 12 or 13 Test matches scheduled, and then you can organise an extra match outside the Test window. As it's an unscheduled match, you don't have all your top players available because their clubs aren't obliged to release them. The Wales Test was a commercial deal, but obviously it was still a Test match. I wasn't part of the decision to schedule it, but I wasn't going to moan about it. It came with the job.

When I became Bok coach, I knew what chances I had to take and that I had to put my balls on the line. I told my team we wouldn't complain about flying to Washington to play Wales and then flying back to Johannesburg to play England at Ellis Park seven days later. I don't think we even had five days of training with the players. I divided them into two squads; one flew to Washington for the Wales game, while the other stayed in Johannesburg to prepare for England. Eight players were involved in both games, starting the Wales game and sitting on the bench for the England one.

The coaches flew with the team to Washington, while I stayed in Johannesburg until the day before the Wales Test and then hopped on the plane, arrived on Saturday morning, and was with the team for kick-off. We lost the match 20–22 when Wales scored a try with six minutes to go. Then we were back on the plane on Sunday, arriving in Johannesburg on

Monday, and went straight into training for the England match, which was five days away.

It's an old cliché but it's true – every Test match is important, and it was disappointing to lose what I thought was a 50/50 game. I knew what the media would say about me if we lost to Wales, and I wasn't wrong. They said I'd had a terrible start, a disastrous start. You always think: if we had brought our strongest team we would have won. We would have had a week of satisfaction, arrived home with a tired and jet-lagged team and would probably have lost to England, and then the pressure would have been on again. I knew I couldn't just live from week to week, but had to do some forward planning. We wanted to beat England in the three-Test series, and that was more important than winning the Wales Test.

Not to say I disregarded the Wales game. It gave me an opportunity to try out some of the new players on the fringes of the Test team, and I gave 11 players their first Test caps.

Getting back, I now had at least four or five training sessions with my fresh starting XV for the England Test. It would have made no sense to have flown them to Washington. What was also important was that I saw how motivated the coaches were. They had to look fresh on Monday, forget the jet lag and get down to business. I knew then that I had a tight management team. The players didn't even know that we had all gone to the USA. I can't say, though, that the trip didn't stress me. I couldn't sleep properly because of the six-hour change in time zone. It was unbelievably hectic, and for the first time I felt the pressure of being head coach.

14

FROM THE MOMENT I WAS APPOINTED Director of Rugby, I started looking at the Springboks' schedule for 2018 in order to plan for the team's turnaround, with the goal of going from a world ranking of sixth at the start of 2018, back to number one. I had to get the belief back, both from the players and the public, and to do that we had to beat the All Blacks in New Zealand. We were due to face them in September in Wellington in the Rugby Championship. I had to believe that victory was possible, and I had to get the coaches and players believing that as well. Beating England was extremely important, but beating New Zealand in their own backyard – that was the big thing. Even if we finished 2018 with a 70% win record, but lost to New Zealand twice, I knew people would just dismiss us saying, 'Ag, you always lose to New Zealand.' I needed to fix that, and that was uppermost in my mind in 2018.

The first thing I did was speak to the players. We started with alignment camps rather than training camps. Instead of the players getting together for two or three days of training and then going back to their franchises, they came in for two days of talking about various issues, with them listening to us and us listening to them. We didn't even go onto the field; we were aligning.

That was so important because if you don't talk with the players regularly, there's a lack of communication and they don't have a chance to discuss issues that are bothering them. They start imagining things, and soon the devil is in their head. People outside of rugby talk nonsense to them, and they start reading misinformation in the newspapers and on social media. It's important to deal with those issues before they spiral out of control. Alignment means getting everyone on the same page. Do you believe what I believe? Do you see what I see? Do you see where we're going? Do you know what we're trying to do? Do you want to be part of this? Do you have another opinion? In the alignment camp, everyone has the chance to voice their opinion. From there we establish our plan, and then we ask, 'Do we all still agree?'

Being aligned means being dedicated to your team and its goals. You don't have to speak out if that's not the kind of person you are, but your eyes will tell us and your actions will tell us if you agree and if you are aligned.

Transformation was an important issue in the alignment process. I had to explain to the squad what transformation meant for me. If it was seen as white player out, black player in, it would always be controversial. Transformation starts with winning; transformation means being representative; transformation means the way we do things must change. I took on this issue in my very first presentation to the players and coaches. It wasn't this ninja presentation with flames coming out. It was a white sheet with black letters that stated the facts, with one or two video clips that meant something to me. In the middle was 'Winning', written in a big circle. Winning was our main priority. From that circle, there were three legs – 'change', 'squad depth' and 'experience'. When you get to a World Cup you don't want seven players with four or five caps. Experience means the bulk of the squad must have 20 Test caps.

We are lucky, with the World Cup in 2023 the average age of our players is 29 with 40-plus Test caps. Depth means that in each position we have two senior players, and a junior who's pushing really hard. So transformation, squad depth and experience can override team selection, and everybody had to understand that. That's how we started from the first match.

I had experienced quotas being a sham, where black players were on for seven minutes in the beginning of a match or came on for the last three minutes just to show they had played. It seemed to me that Laurie Mains pulled that stunt with Conrad Jantjes at the Cats. That was 2001, and we were now in 2018. I thought, 'Fuck it, are we really going to keep on bullshitting in the same way?' We couldn't be doing the same nonsense.

I explained to the squad how I saw things and I gave them a chance to talk back. Everything was done in front of everybody. I've never had a one-on-one with a player, except when he came to me with a deeply personal issue. I told them not to come to me individually with questions about why they were not in the team, or why they thought they deserved an opportunity. I know that in the past when a white player walked into a room with a coach for a one-on-one, or a black player walked in for a one-on-one, what that player and the coach came out with in their heads were two different things. And while those one-on-ones were going on, the rest of the players would start speculating about what was being said behind closed doors, and the rumour mill would start grinding.

Those are the issues we discussed as a team. I didn't want to know too much about their personal lives because I wanted to focus specifically on how they played, and I wanted to look at their roadmap. In a roadmap we gather information relevant to a player's rugby abilities both on and off the field. We look at his technical skills (tackling and passing, for example) and his understanding of the fundamentals of the game. We also look at his character: Is he a team player? Is he ego-driven?

We score each of the players on their abilities and update those scores as they progress through the age groups to see if they're advancing or going backwards. They might be a team player one year, but the following year they get a big head and are now a prima donna. That goes on the roadmap. They might lack the ability to pass both left and right one year, but perfect the skill the following year. That goes on the roadmap. We set them targets so they have something to shoot for as they get older, stronger and more experienced.

The roadmaps are an important guide to team selection. The moment I start feeling sorry for a player, I'm no longer picking him for rugby reasons. If I took everyone's emotional state into consideration, then everyone would have reasons to be selected and players would be favoured for all the wrong reasons.

They could go and suck up to the assistant coaches if they liked, but it wouldn't work with me. I told them I would be non-emotional and make sure we picked the best players. Whenever we had team announcements, the squad was up there on the screen for all to see.

For example, the discussion went something like this: 'Kwagga, you're starting against Wales for your first cap. Thomas, you're going to go to Wales, but you've got the kind of engine that means you can fly to the US, play the match and then play against England off the bench. Pieter-Steph du Toit, you will be our captain against Wales. Never mind the jet lag, you're like a dog chasing a piece of paper – you never get tired.' That's how I would talk. Obviously, I would never say sensitive things that would belittle a player. My big thing is I never want to be embarrassed or cause someone else any embarrassment.

I told them that if it didn't go well in the Wales Test match, we just needed to be sure that we were all aligned. Because I had been open and honest with the players, nobody believed they had been selected or not selected because I was trying to fix transformation. I had sound rugby reasons why each player was in the side.

It wasn't a case of this player is black or white, but rather if he's good enough under the high ball, or if he tackles effectively enough when he's the second-last defender, or if he cleans up well enough at the breakdown. When I had my doubts, they were never about race – they were always about ability on the field. Yes, in the beginning, of course we wanted to fix transformation, but I also had to fix people's mindsets about how I selected a team.

When I picked youngsters like Sbu Nkosi and Aphiwe Dyantyi, I knew I was being accused of taking chances on them in order to push transformation. But that wasn't the case. I might have been taking a rugby chance because they were young and making their debuts, but I wasn't taking a political chance. I was confident that both Sbu and Aphiwe were good enough.

When I selected the 23 players for the England Test at Ellis Park, I strongly considered Duane Vermeulen as the captain. Pieter-Steph had been captain in the previous Test, against Wales, but we had made it clear to him that it was a one-off. The captain the previous year was Eben Etzebeth, but he was injured, as was Warren Whiteley, who had captained the Boks in two Tests against France the previous year. My concern about Duane being captain was that he was based in France, playing for Toulon, and we weren't sure when he would be able to join the squad.

I needed someone who was immediately available. I also needed someone who played close to the action and could talk to the referee, so it couldn't be a flyhalf, fullback or winger. I felt that the captain needed to be a loose forward or scrumhalf. I preferred loose forward because that's a player who is usually on his feet and can see the game and is not stuck in a maul or doesn't have his head buried in a scrum. I needed someone who had the players' respect for the way he played. Siya Kolisi was the Stormers' captain, playing some of the best rugby of his career, and he was a loose forward. He ticked all the boxes. So I chose him to be captain. Those were my reasons.

I didn't tell him until we were all sitting in the team meeting. I put the names of the squad up on the big screen, went through it, and said, 'Siya, you're captain.' There wasn't a single moment where I felt, this is a historic moment – the first black captain of the national rugby team. Not one fucking bit. I really did not see this being such a big issue. I didn't have a discussion about it with the assistant coaches beforehand and I didn't pick up any emotion in the team meeting when I announced that Siya was the captain. Nobody – and I know a lot of people won't believe this – nobody came to me and said, 'Fuck it, hey, we have a black captain.' Not a single person said that to me.

I had known Siya since he was 18 years old, when he came to Western Province. As Director of Rugby, I was working with the under-19s, the under-21s, and at the academy when I encountered Siya for the first time. I saw immediately that he could carry the ball, hand off tacklers, and run over opponents. I was very impressed with his strength.

I wanted to sign him for Western Province, but his agent told me we had lost out because Siya had signed for the Cheetahs. I then got Frikkie to check the contract. He found a glaring problem that invalidated the contract, and we were able to sign Siya.

I got to know Siya very well as a player. One of the things that always impressed me about him was that he never let his head drop. I knew he could go off the rails, but I understood that, having been through the same thing myself as a young player when I was at the Cats and going out partying. Most players are in and out of trouble, so he wasn't unusual in that regard. I can't say I was a father figure for him – other people played that role – but I was there for him through good times and bad times, ready to give him advice based on my own past experience. He was always frank and open with me and told me straight up about things that irritated him. We established such a bond that I knew I could put my trust in him.

I sent the team through to SARU president Mark Alexander and CEO Jurie Roux on the Sunday before the Wales Test. I didn't speak to them beforehand and ask them if it was okay to appoint Siya because I didn't have to. We told the squad the same day, so they knew who was flying to the USA, who was staying behind to prepare for England, and who was going to be involved in both games. To avoid the story being leaked and creating unnecessary media hype and speculation, we released the squad announcement to the media the next day, Monday, 28 May.

When I read the team out at a news conference, there was no fanfare or heightened emotion as I made the appointment public. I simply read out the team, and then looked up for questions from the journalists.

That first news conference was just crazy. Our media manager Rayaan Adriaanse had drafted questions we could expect, and I wrapped my head around the way I wanted to answer them. I was honest with my answers and told the media that I knew Siya was a good leader and I was excited about what he offered the team. I dealt with the issue of transformation, saying that while we were trying to fix the wrongs of the past, Siya's appointment as captain had no bearing on transformation. I made it clear that all the players in the squad deserved to be there and I was not trying to fabricate things.

This is where I realised the captaincy is massive for so many rugby supporters. I don't expect the 12 million-odd people who follow rugby in South Africa to understand rugby teamwork 100%. I want them to support the game and give their opinions. But I don't expect them to analyse tackle counts or know how lineouts work or understand how much a captain does. They're supporters and fans; it's not their job to analyse the finer details. But I didn't properly understand what a black captain meant for the guy living in a shack in KwaNobuhle, or the oom on the farm in Grabouw. For me it was a case of figuring out how this team operated on the field.

I am often asked why a boykie from Despatch, coming from this racially conservative background, appointed a black captain, when two black coaches before me – Peter de Villiers and Allister Coetzee – didn't. I don't have an answer to that.

What I can tell you is that I know what embarrassment is, and I don't ever want to see a player embarrassed, humiliated or angered by discrimination based on his race, or social standing, or on what school he went to, or what language he speaks. I couldn't coach a team where people are made to feel that way. Embarrassment is something I feel very strongly about. I can tell just by the way he looks at me if someone has been humiliated. Our eyes tell so much about what's going on in our hearts. You can see in my eyes when I'm embarrassed and when I'm hartseer and when I'm happy. Even though I put on a show and smile, you can see in my eyes how I'm actually feeling. I learnt to look in my dad's eyes and could tell even before he spoke how drunk he was or if he was still capable of reasoning. I could see in my sister's eyes if she was panicking. I can see in players' eyes if they are under pressure or in control. Their eyes tell me who's there and who's not there, who's weak and who's in control.

Because of Siya's appointment I got accused of being a political person. It made me fucking angry. I had been biting my tongue for seven years, not saying anything while people made the same mistakes over and over again. Then I got accused of pandering to my paymaster, whatever that was supposed to mean. The only way I could confront that ignorant slur was to win and keep winning. It was so much easier to put those accusers in their place by simply telling them to look at the scoreboard.

Going into that game against England at Ellis Park faced with that kind of criticism, I felt the stakes had never been higher. I had to win to prove my detractors wrong, and I was confident we would win because of the team I had picked. We also had the advantage of playing England at altitude, where the bulk of the Springbok team had been preparing for over a week.

Apart from Siya, there was also media attention on the three debutantes: Sbu Nkosi, Aphiwe Dyantyi and RG Snyman. I wasn't going to allow any suggestion that Sbu and Aphiwe had been selected because they were black. While I was in Ireland, I had been keeping an eye on Sbu and knew he was close to making Allister Coetzee's Bok team. He was one of the stand-out wingers who was very physical on both attack and defence. Aphiwe had been a consistent performer at centre and wing for the Lions the previous season, while RG Snyman had proved himself to be one of the best locks in the country. It wasn't difficult to select them based on form.

When I woke up on that Saturday morning, 9 June 2018, I felt for the first time that I was in charge of a rugby Test. The Wales Test didn't feel like the first one. That morning I felt, 'Okay, Rassie, you always thought you had a plan, now your balls are well and truly out there.'

I don't know if you can ever be 100% happy with your team. We only had four training sessions, with a lot of alignment, and I wished we could have had another two or three weeks of preparation. We had done about as much as we could in the amount of time we had, getting my new assistant coaches Swys de Bruin and Mzwandile Stick on board with my systems, and getting the players to understand that it's all about owner-ship, not leadership. I was confident the leadership would come, but for now I just wanted the players to take ownership. On that morning, I felt confident this was the best I could have done, but, fuck, I was nervous.

The atmosphere at Ellis Park was the most intense I had ever experienced. There was no time to appreciate or enjoy what was going on. I was a bit hartseer inside, I don't know why, and felt a bit overwhelmed when Siya led his team slowly down the huge tunnel at Ellis Park and onto the field with fireworks going off. I stood in the coaches' box and tried to enjoy the moment when the anthems were sung. As the players got into position for kick-off, things slowed down. Everything seemed to be in slow motion. I had to focus on the start, and what I needed to tell Jacques, who was next to the field, over the walkie-talkie. While all of that was going on in my head, I looked at the people in the stand in front of the coaches' box, some of whom had turned around to look up at me with big, expectant smiles on their faces. I thought, 'Okay, fuck, now we've got to win!'

In that coaches' box, there is a TV camera permanently on you, record-ing your every emotion, and there's nowhere to hide. In the intensity of the game, I sometimes forget it's there. There've been a few times when I've been caught in a moment of high emotion yelling, 'P%#s, p%#s, p%#s,' for my mother to see. And the young fans.

Within 17 minutes, England had raced into a 24–3 lead. After just four minutes, Mike Brown shrugged off a tackle from Handré Pollard, fended off Damian de Allende and scored in the corner. Nine minutes later Elliot Daly had an easy run to the line, and four minutes after that, Owen Farrell scored another easy try when four Springboks were beaten by one pass, as commentator Joel Stransky put it. We just couldn't get into the game. Apart from the travelling England fans, the 55 000 fans who had sold out Ellis Park were silent.

Our defence was nowhere because the players were still getting used to our new system where the two wingers had to make big calls and trust themselves. If the wingers didn't make the important decisions, we looked like the most average defensive side in the world. Jacques came on the radio, saying, 'Ras, we can try to change this defence system.'

My reply was, 'We can't now – we're going with this!' I instructed him to tell the players to go harder and to make bigger decisions. That's what I was saying on the outside, but on the inside I was thinking, 'This can't be! How can I get it so wrong?' I thought to myself, 'Am I really making the same mistakes?' Was it because I didn't rate that specific England team that highly?

I didn't panic because those were the tactics I had believed in for so long. I had sold those plans to the players, and they were executing them on that field, and while the plans hadn't worked for the first 15 minutes, I knew the quickest way to lose the trust of the team was to abandon what I had spent so long convincing them about and getting their buy-in for. I had to give them confidence in the game plan by encouraging them to go harder.

I could have given up and said, 'Go back to what you've been doing your whole rugby life – use the touchline as the last defender.' But how would the players trust me after that? So the call was 'Go harder!' and that's exactly what Sbu Nkosi did in the 20th minute when his power and strength required three England players to block and stop him just short of the line. Faf de Klerk grabbed the recycled ball, and as England's lock Maro Itoje completely botched his tackle, Faf spotted a big hole in the defence to dash through and score despite Ben Youngs's desperate attempt to stop him.

I was nervous that England had gained too much confidence out of that early surge, and our players were in a state of disbelief. The message from Jacques to Siya and the players continued to be: 'Go harder – you'll get your opportunities.'

Once the first opportunity came, we started playing with confidence. As the half-hour mark approached, Sbu chipped ahead and when Daly failed to gather the ball in the in-goal area, Sbu kept his head and got a hand to it to score our second try. Go harder!

Four minutes later, Willie le Roux made a superb, angled run, drew the England defence, and flipped the ball to Aphiwe Dyantyi, who was speeding on his outside right next to the touchline. Aphiwe instinctively knew he would be tackled into touch, so he quickly flipped the ball back on his inside to Sbu and we had try number three. Go harder!

Five minutes later, Willie had a dazzling run and dived through two defenders for our fourth try. From 3–24 down, we were ahead 29–27 at halftime. It had been a dramatic turnaround.

By halftime I knew we would only get better, but I was still worried that England had 15 minutes in which to work out how they had got their first three tries and how to score them again. It bothered me that they would get their confidence back before we got better. We spent the time talking tactics, with the forwards coach, the backline coach, and attack and defence coach each getting three minutes to talk to the team. It wasn't about psyching them up – it was more about making sure they knew what to do next.

In motivating my team, I tend to make it personal. Personal emotions last longer. If your child is standing behind you and a vicious dog is coming at you, even though you're shit scared of that dog, you will stand there. But if a stranger is standing behind you, it's unlikely you will stand there. I tell the players they're playing for something important to them personally. If they understand that it's not about their egos, but about making their families proud, about playing for the people in their home towns or villages, for their fans, for their country, then you can hype them up. They have to understand that it's personal.

A coach who thumps his chest and shouts, 'Come on, guys! Let's go, go, go!' means nothing to me. A team talk must either be tactical or personal, but not emotional. You've got a team of players with their own goals and aspirations who want to play international rugby and make their families proud, and the moment they buy into that, you can psyche them up.

I told my players, 'Guys, you know what, there are people saying this team is only window-dressing. Fuck them, let's show them.'

In the second half, we stretched the lead to 42–32, courtesy of a try from Aphiwe, and Handré Pollard's boot, before England scored a late consolation try. Victory by 42 points to 39, and in the change room afterwards I could say with satisfaction, 'Guys, you've bought yourselves three more Test matches.'

I could now afford to be consistent with my team selection. The mood wasn't so much one of relief but rather of realising that the game plan was going to work. The players were so gatvol of being ranked sixth in the world, and hearing of how people were burning Bok jerseys in protest. We were over it and just wanted to get a solid rugby plan in place, play for each other and fill the stadiums again. I told the media afterwards that while I was worried when we fell so far behind, I was proud of the character the players had displayed, which we could work on for the next Test. Confidence was back and everybody was feeling, 'Fuck, this is going to work.'

I was particularly proud of Sbu and Aphiwe, our two inexperienced wingers on debut making big calls and going hard as we asked them to do. Sure, they made a few defensive errors, but that's understandable in that pressured situation. I know some of the so-called experts were saying they should have used the touchline as the last defender. But we were trying a new system and I needed them to understand that we had time to fix any problems.

In the build-up to the second Test, I worried that people would make a political issue out of their inexperience and turn it into a whole new drama. I just wanted that following Saturday to come so that we could get onto the field and do it all again. Among the coaches and players the vibe was: 'This is working, this is working.'

We went to Bloemfontein for the second Test where a familiar pattern unfolded as we fell behind in the ninth minute when Mike Brown scored for England, and even further behind three minutes later when Jonny May cut through our defence to score. As had happened at Ellis Park, our defensive systems were being exposed out wide. But the players refused to drop their heads and England never scored again.

Tendai 'Beast' Mtawarira, in his 100th Test match, made a storming break down the middle, RG Snyman showed his innovative ball skills by getting the ball back from the ruck, and then Duane Vermeulen used his brute strength to barge 22 metres past four defenders and score our first try. Handré's reliability with the boot was strangely missing until Siya opted for a kick at poles as halftime drew near, and Handré restored his confidence with a massive 60-metre effort to give us a 13–12 lead at the break. Our pack was incredible and referee Romain Poite awarded us a penalty try after we mauled them on their own line, which was followed by another Pollard penalty. Victory by 23 points to 12, and we had won the series.

Squad depth and experience were important aspects of my overall plan, so I made changes to the team for the third Test to give other players in the squad some game time. I brought in Schalk Brits, a player of many talents who had enjoyed a massive career at Saracens but had only played 10 Test matches up until then. He had retired from rugby and was sitting in the stands watching the first Test as a fan with a tour group before I called him up. I phoned and asked him to play for another two years until the end of the World Cup. I couldn't guarantee that he would go to the World Cup, but I wanted him to focus on hooker, his preferred position, and on loose forward. He was 37 years old, but he was the right player for that time. *Hire for aptitude + attitude.*

My philosophy has always been that the right player is not always the best player. Schalk was right for the time. I knew him inside out. At the Stormers, I played him at eighthman even though he was the hooker, and he excelled. He was one of the fittest, strongest players I had ever worked with. He is also a special person with a great sense of humour and is a fabulous team man. He was exactly what I needed to build the team culture I wanted. Schalk knew that if he played well and did what I wanted him to do, he would probably go to the World Cup, which he did, and he even captained one of the group games.

We lost the dead-rubber third Test in the rain and mud of Newlands in Cape Town 10–25, but I wasn't too concerned. Our kicking game was superior to that of England in the first half, but our finishing and discipline were poor. In the second half, England dominated and we battled to get out of our half. There were issues to work on, such as the lack of domination by the pack, which resulted in a lot of pressure on flyhalf Elton Jantjies. I had given seven more players game time and I was happy that the game plan was progressing. I took the blame for the defeat and conceded that we had to make some brave calls on team selection. The conditions gave me a chance to see who could perform in the wet, but our discipline let us down as we conceded too many penalties, which ultimately cost us the match.

My focus now shifted to the Rugby Championship and beating New Zealand away from home. But first we had to get past Argentina in Durban and in Mendoza. We scored six tries to beat them 34–21 at Kings Park, after trailing 10–14 at halftime. I gave Makazole Mapimpi a start for the first time since the Wales Test in Washington and he didn't let me down, scoring twice. We came unstuck in the return match in Mendoza, with Argentina building up a 20-point lead by halftime and eventually winning 32–19. I really felt that one, and I was a bit shaken because we had given them a good hiding in Durban. I couldn't even claim that we were jet lagged after the flight to Argentina because the Pumas were on the same flight as us.

Once again, I had used the matches as an opportunity to give other players a chance. I was measuring the improvement of our game plan not by using the scoreboard, which would have sidetracked me. It was too easy to look at the scoreboard and be disappointed, but I could see the growth in decision-making, in taking ownership, and in the way we were mauling and contesting the breakdowns and sticking to our guns tactically. Everything was getting better. I was also looking at the improvement of individual players, all the time preparing for the showdown against New Zealand.

We lost to Australia in Brisbane 18–23, failing to score a single point in the second half. I don't, however, want to create the impression that I didn't care about the match, with my focus being on the All Blacks. I was extremely disappointed with the defeat. Winning was the big thing. I never wanted to lose.

If those matches had been in South Africa, where you're subjected to a lot of noise and criticism, it would have been more difficult to stick to the game plan. We almost got sidetracked by outside influences after the two defeats, because the criticism gets to the players and they were feeling the pressure of the possibility of three defeats in a row. But, despite the losses, the team still had belief and were ready for New Zealand.

We went to the Westpac Stadium in Wellington under huge pressure. At the pre-match news conference, I said they could fire me if we lost that Test match. I wanted to take the pressure off the players and give them a clear signal that we were sticking with our plan.

In the Rugby Championship the previous year, the All Blacks had beaten us 57–0 in Albany and then 25–24 in Cape Town. Tactically, they would have been preparing to run us to pieces in the last 20 minutes because they were used to the Springbok game plan. We wanted to give them something they had never experienced before, a game plan they couldn't get used to. If we gave them the same tactics, they would just adapt to it and beat us in the final 20 minutes. As we did with England, we would be coming at them hard, not giving them time on the ball, not giving them time to work us out.

I reminded the team that we had beaten England with a radical system, the same system that most of the teams are using today. I had to get the players to believe it was working. We had come from behind twice to beat England, and we had beaten Argentina. But now we had lost to both Argentina and Australia away.

It might sound strange, but I thought that was a perfect set-up for the Wellington Test because New Zealand would have thought it was going to be the same thing again. I told the players not to measure our progress from the scoreboard and instead look at how close we were in those two defeats.

At that stage I had a 43% win record: three wins from seven Tests. I personally thought that even if the win record was 70% or 80%, and we were beating less-fancied teams, people would still say, 'Ja, but you're playing New Zealand in the first pool match at the World Cup, and you can't beat them.'

It was a juggling act dealing with the perception of win percentages. We could have gone balls to the wall against Argentina and Australia and won those matches, then lost to New Zealand, and we would be straight

175

back to where we were when it came to public perception when they put 57 points past us in Albany a year earlier. We had to get the belief back for the fans, and that's why we focused so much on New Zealand. I could see the improvement. I realised we were taking a chance, but it was a chance that needed to be taken.

After 17 minutes, the All Blacks had already scored two tries and we were down 0–12. Once again, we didn't let our heads drop and we came storming back with three tries in 12 minutes from Aphiwe Dyantyi, Willie le Roux and Malcolm Marx, all converted by Handré Pollard. Our defence had been solid and we had been powerful on attack. The players' confidence was high, and the New Zealand commentator described the team's performance as 'brutal'. We never lost the lead, although the All Blacks kept coming back at us, reducing the lead at halftime to 24–17.

Cheslin Kolbe came on after halftime, earlier than expected because Lukhanyo Am had sustained a serious shoulder injury. Cheslin was playing in only his second Test match and within a minute he showed the rugby world his incredible anticipation and acceleration. He stretched the lead with an intercept on the halfway line, showing his pace as he outstripped Ben Smith and Beauden Barrett to score our fourth try.

We led 31–17 going into the final quarter of the match and traded tries as Rieko Ioane scored, before Aphiwe got his second. Then the All Blacks came right back into the game with a try by Codie Taylor. Adding to the pressure was that we went down to 14 men after referee Nigel Owens gave Willie a yellow card for going off his feet in the 67th minute. We spent the rest of the game soaking up an incredible, prolonged onslaught by the New Zealanders, ending with Ardie Savea twisting powerfully over from a maul. The pendulum swung our way when Beauden Barrett hit the posts with his last two conversion attempts.

In those dying seconds, the tension was unbearable, with the All Blacks mounting wave after wave of attack and us clinging to a 36–34 lead. The hooter sounded, and we were desperately defending yet another attack when Aphiwe Dyantyi rushed up on Damian McKenzie, causing him to knock on. Franco Mostert dived on the ball and secured it. Willie le Roux retrieved it and kicked it high into the stands for a famous victory. We had secured that all-important win against New Zealand in Wellington.

In the post-match news conference, I admitted that the victory had given me the best day of my coaching career thus far, but conceded that we had been fortunate in a match where we had enjoyed very little possession. But that's international rugby for you. Against Argentina in Mendoza we had substantial possession, yet lost 19–32.

I was proud of the way the players had learnt to make the big calls, particularly Aphiwe, whose tackle on McKenzie was so vital. He was playing in only his seventh Test match and, due to inexperience, had made some wrong calls against England and Argentina. But he was learning fast and was able to rise to the occasion when it counted in those final seconds.

As I reflected on that Rugby Championship victory over the All Blacks in Wellington, I was already thinking forward to our opening game of the 2019 World Cup against New Zealand at Yokohama Stadium, which was in exactly a year's time. We had chopped and changed players to try out different combinations and see who could perform away from home. Our performance so far in 2018 had given me hope that we would be able to adapt and turn things around when times were tough. I knew, after the defeats to Argentina and Australia, that the critics were writing us off for the World Cup, but this victory had given us hope that we would be contenders.

We beat Australia 23–12 in Port Elizabeth but lost to New Zealand 30–32 at Loftus. I was helluva disappointed with that All Black defeat and had to take it on the chin. We had dominated them and built a healthy 30–13 lead with 20 minutes to play. But you can never write off the All Blacks. Within 17 minutes, Rieko Ioane, Scott Barrett and Ardie Savea had scored tries, two of them converted by Richie Mo'unga, and they held on to win the match. All I could do was console myself with the knowledge that we knew we could beat New Zealand, having won that critical game in Wellington. The next time we faced them would be in Wellington once again, in the Rugby Championship in nine and a half months' time, and then in Yokohama for our opening game of the World Cup two months after that. At least we wouldn't be written off before the game even kicked off.

15

IT WAS WHILE WE WERE IN NEW ZEALAND for the Rugby Championship in September 2018 that I started getting a dry cough and shivers, as if I had a bad cold. I felt feverish and had a tingling feeling on my skin like gooseflesh. I wasn't worried, though, because it didn't last long. The team doctor, Dr Konrad von Hagen, took my temperature, which was around 38 degrees. I don't like to moan about illness, but I told him I felt I had something in my throat that was causing me to cough. He wasn't sure what it was and put me on a course of antibiotics. The sensation would come and go. I treated it by having a bath, and my wife gave me injections of Voltaren. It was never so bad that I felt I couldn't get up in the morning.

I came home from the Rugby Championship feeling no better, and then one day we trained at Belhar Rugby Club in the rain. When I got home to Durbanville I told Nikki I was feeling very cold, so I had a hot bath to warm up. But when I got out of the bath I was shivering badly. I was really cold and climbed into bed, under warm blankets. After 10 minutes, I was sweating and had to get up. I still had the dry cough and the sensation of having swallowed something that wouldn't go down. Apart from Doc von Hagen checking on me, I didn't go and see my family doctor or a specialist. It didn't seem that big a deal.

We went on the end-of-year tour in November and still I had the symptoms, not every day, but I kept getting the shivers. I called it kouekoors – when you're not really ill, but you're feeling pap. I put it all down to stress of the job as Springbok head coach. I was used to stress, and I understood your body sometimes stresses more than your mind.

Normally I could train full-on with the players and do the drills with them. Sometimes, if they were short of numbers, I would pack down in the scrum or stick my head in a maul. But now I started to struggle to keep up.

We came back from the end-of-year tour and I took my family to Mauritius with Frikkie and his family. I was playing volleyball in the pool with the children when I started wheezing and feeling out of breath. The sensation of having something stuck in my throat was worse, and so was the reflex cough.

I thought that by relaxing in Mauritius and switching off from the stress of the job, my symptoms would disappear. But when I lay down on the bed, or even on a deck chair next to the pool or at the beach, I was breathing deeply like I was gasping for air. The fevers and the raised temperature were becoming more frequent. I had to admit to Nikki that I was struggling. She took a video of me sleeping at night, propped up with pillows and gasping and wheezing badly. I got a hell of a fright when she showed me the video.

We got back from Mauritius on Christmas Eve, and the next day we were supposed to visit my sister and her family in Baviaanskloof. But I had such a fever that I couldn't go. Instead, I went to our family doctor on Boxing Day. He did some tests and listened to my lungs, which were okay. He couldn't work out what was wrong, so he sent me to the emergency room at the Durbanville Mediclinic where I was examined by a specialist. He confirmed I had an infection but didn't know where it was coming from. I asked for some antibiotics so I could go home, but he insisted on admitting me. He wasn't going to let me go until he found that infection.

I needed this problem sorted out as quickly as possible, so that we could go to Baviaanskloof over New Year's. I was due back at work on

11 January and wanted to be back at full pace with the team by then. The doctor did blood tests, but he couldn't find anything that would be causing the infection markers in my blood to be so high and couldn't work out why I had the feeling that there was something stuck in my throat. I begged him to just treat the fever, but he was determined to figure out the problem and refused to discharge me.

I was in hospital for four days, but I wasn't particularly worried. I had been in hospital so many times that I was used to it. I just hoped I didn't need an operation. Then the doctor said he had found something in one of my blood tests. I had to see a pulmonologist who did a biopsy on my lung. We had to cancel the Baviaanskloof trip while we waited for the results. Finally, the doctor phoned and said, 'You'll have to come in.' You know it's serious when they ask you to come in.

He told me I had granulomatosis with polyangiitis, a very uncommon disorder that causes inflammation of the blood vessels in your nose, sinuses, throat, lungs and kidneys. In my case, it was in my throat. It was previously known as Wegener's disease, named after the German doctor who first identified it. Before medical science discovered an effective way of treating it in the 1970s, half of all patients who contracted the disorder died within five months. Today, with proper treatment, it is no longer life-threatening, but it was still extremely serious and required heavy treatment with drugs for the next nine months, which meant that I needed to be treated right up to the World Cup.

Wegener's disease is an autoimmune disease that attacks the immune system. The blockage I felt in my throat was actually in my windpipe. When the doctor did a scan of my oesophagus, its diameter was that of a nine-year-old boy's. It was that small. My body thought there was an infection and was sending cells down to fight it, causing my windpipe to close.

The way to treat it was to break down my immune system with a lot of cortisone until the disease went into remission. I also had to take medication to kill the cells, rather like cancer treatment. My hair didn't fall out, but it went from brown to amber, almost orange, and it thinned out a lot. I didn't go bald, but when I washed my hair in the shower, I could see that it was falling out.

The doctor said I could train as long as I felt up to it. He obviously knew I wouldn't feel much like physical exertion on those high doses of medication. I told him the World Cup was coming up, but his answer put paid to any argument about rugby. He said, 'I'm treating Wegener's disease, not the World Cup.'

I started swelling up from water retention caused by the cortisone and couldn't sit for more than an hour without having to go pee. I knew this would be a problem at the World Cup, during bus rides to and from the stadium, or when I was up in the coaches' box, but my bigger concern was with the disease getting into my lungs or kidneys, where the chances of survival are much less. I had to get the treatment immediately to ensure the disease didn't spread. The lung biopsy showed that my lungs were clear and only my throat was affected.

When I arrived at the first team meeting of the year showing the side effects of the cortisone, everyone could tell – it looked like I had picked up 10 to 15 kilograms – but they knew I was a guy who enjoys a kuier and braaivleis, so they drew their own conclusions about my appearance. I tried to stay active, but I couldn't train with the players. My skin became irritated and my face went red from hot flushes. I got hot when it was cold outside and I had to put the air conditioning on. My armpits sweat when I get excited or nervous – it happened to me a lot when I was young. It could be in the middle of winter, but under my jersey it was wet. When I was an adult and could afford it, I had Botox injections in my underarms to control the problem. Now the sweating was getting worse.

I was very self-conscious about it. I couldn't run with the guys, I was swelling up, I was breathless, and when I was doing presentations, I would start sweating like a pig in front of them. I thought, 'Fuck this, I'll have to tell the players.' I played it down and told them, 'I'm a little bit ill.'

I didn't want them distracted so I assured them it was nothing serious and that I was being treated, which explained the side effects. In terms of our policy of openness and honesty, I wanted them to be fully aware of the problem but also relaxed about it. I didn't want them sitting there asking themselves, why's Rassie sweating so much, why's Rassie so fat, why's he swelling up, and why isn't he so active on the training field?

That wasn't the end of my problems. I got fever blisters on the inside of my mouth and allergic reactions that I normally wouldn't get, like a skin rash out of nowhere. If anybody got a stomach bug, I was the first one to pick it up. Whatever was going around the team, I knew I would get it. But I never got to the stage where I felt like giving up on it.

In April, I asked my doctor if we could manage the treatment to make things a little easier when I got to Japan for the World Cup. What was getting to me was that when people saw me in public, they made assumptions that I was living the good life now that I was the Springbok head coach, eating and drinking and having so much fun. I didn't want to explain to everyone, 'I'm actually fucking sick, man.'

I became a bit withdrawn, not from the team but from the public. I also didn't want my children to know how ill I was – not that I was seriously ill. I was confident the doctor had it under control and went for check-ups every few months, including during the World Cup. He was prepared to compromise a little on the treatment, but refused to jeopardise anything by stopping the medication entirely during the tournament. I'm happy to say the disease did go into remission in 2022, but it's something I have to check all the time now because you never know what's going to happen next.

In 2018 I was about to leave for Japan with our operations manager Charles Wessels to do a recce on the hotels and training grounds for the World Cup. I was still getting the fevers and then suddenly I got an abscess in my jaw, right at the place where, 25 years earlier, I had a metal brace and plate inserted to repair my broken jaw after I collided in a club game with Dennis van Zyl, my first Cheetahs roommate. Now all of a sudden, my body was rejecting it. The doctors suspected it was because of the breakdown of my immune system caused by the medication. I had surgery to remove the metal, which was slightly problematic because, after so long in my jaw, bone had grown over it. The maxillofacial surgeon earned his money that day. The metal is now on display in my bar.

The day after the surgery, I flew to London to watch a Six Nations match between England and Scotland and then on to Tokyo to join Charles on the recce. On the flight, my jaw was really hurting, and I was desperate for pain medication. When I arrived at Tokyo International Airport, they told me my luggage had been lost. The first thing I did when I got to the city was buy pain meds and underpants.

Another suspected complication from the treatment for Wegener's disease was when, bizarrely, I contracted TB in my elbow and had to have surgery on the joint. I thought TB was a lung disease. I never expected it to strike in my elbow.

There was never a chance that Wegener's would stop me going to the World Cup, however. The doctor knew it was a big year for me. As long as the treatment was working and I was being tested regularly, he foresaw no problems. I didn't worry about battling to breathe, but it wasn't lekker not being able to train with the players, and sweating so badly when I was doing presentations. My ego was taking a dent. I hated being swollen up from the water retention. But the doctor brought me down to earth when he put my treatment into perspective for me. Wegener's disease is serious, and if it's not treated properly it has a high mortality rate. Yet I was only receiving something like an eighth of what a patient with a serious cancer receives. I couldn't moan.

16

IN NOVEMBER 2018 THE SPRINGBOKS went on the end-of-year tour to play England, France, Scotland and Wales. All our remaining international matches before the World Cup were used to test our game plan and combinations, and confirm that we had the right players in all positions.

Our first game was against England at Twickenham, one that ended in controversy. Predictably, it was billed as a 'revenge' game by the media after we had beaten England in the home series in June. Sbu Nkosi scored a try that gave us a halftime lead of 8–6. With four minutes left, however, we trailed 11–12 and Handré Pollard had a chance to put us into the lead, but his 48-metre penalty attempt glanced off the right upright. But we kept up the pressure and, with the hooter having sounded, launched another attack on the England line.

André Esterhuizen gathered a loose ball about 45 metres out and made a powerful, angled run across the field. Owen Farrell launched himself at him, and both men crashed to the ground. England got possession and their prop Harry Williams kicked the ball into touch to end the game. The ref, Angus Gardner, consulted with the TMO to see if there was foul play. If there was, we would have had another penalty attempt to win the game. They decided Farrell had enough of a wrap on Esterhuizen for the tackle to be legitimate and blew the final whistle. Even the English commentators were perplexed, with Stuart Barnes saying, 'Sorry, it doesn't matter what you are [*sic*], but that is not an attempted tackle.'

I was deadpan as Siya and I sat down at the post-match news conference. When the inevitable question came, I was asked what I thought about 'the shoulder charge on André Esterhuizen', as the journalist phrased it. I made light of the question and replied, 'Shoulder charge or tackle?' I laughed to indicate I was joking and added, 'If it was a shoulder charge, the referee would have penalised him and we had a chance to win the game. It was a good tackle and well done because I haven't seen André Esterhuizen being tackled back like that in a while. If it was all legal, which I didn't have a good look at on the replay, then we should start tackling like that. It's obviously something that's really effective.'

A few minutes later, the subject came up again and I was asked what worried me about the tackle. I said nothing worried or irritated me, and repeated my comment that if it was legal, we must tackle the same way because stopping André in his tracks like that is unbelievable. I said we should just practise that. The journalist challenged me about being sarcastic, but I denied it.

We might have lost the Test match, which has always annoyed me, but we knew we would face England at some stage of the World Cup the following year, and knew too that we would be able to beat them based on that performance at Twickenham. We didn't have a full-strength side, while they did. We were without a number of key players who hadn't been released from their clubs because the game fell outside the Test window. But we couldn't blame the Owen Farrell tackle for our loss because, as I said in the post-match news conference, we hadn't taken our chances and our discipline had let us down, leading to too many penalties.

Since we were without our scrumhalf Faf de Klerk, who was playing in the English Premiership for Sale Sharks that weekend, we had a chance to see how Ivan van Zyl and Embrose Papier played in front of 80 000 people at Twickenham.

As we prepared for our next match, against France at Stade de France,

I made good on my word about practising those tackles. We heard that Farrell wasn't going to be cited, which meant even the citing commissioner felt that the tackle was fine, so we decided to make a quick video of how we were practising it. For a laugh, we filmed Jacques Nienaber, our defence coach, and I taking André through some Farrell-style tackles on a tackle bag and telling him to tackle higher.

It really was meant as a joke, but it ended up on social media and caused a small uproar. I was interested to see the mixed reaction, with some former players accusing us of being unable to cope with calls that go against us, while others, like former England and British and Irish Lions centre (and now TV celebrity) Ugo Monye, understood exactly what we were doing. Monye commented that it was funny and clever because it highlighted the inconsistencies over what was acceptable and what wasn't.

We didn't moan about it or make a scene, but decided to have a laugh and move on. I might not have been sarcastic in the news conference, but I was certainly sarcastic when we made the video. I knew it would leak on social media, but I didn't care. It kept the debate going around the legality of such tackles. Six months later, World Rugby issued guidelines to clarify the issue of high tackles and shoulder charges, showing just how badly Angus and the TMO had got it wrong. To his credit, Angus publicly admitted his mistake, which I respect him for.

The referee for the next game was Nigel Owens and he showed just how observant he is. I noticed that the stadium clock wasn't stopping every time there was a time-out. France was leading 26–22 when they won a scrum five metres from our line in the 81st minute according to the stadium clock. There should have been much more time to play had the time-outs not been included in the playing time. Thankfully, Nigel had also picked up the problem and made sure that more time was added. That meant that France couldn't just win the ball from the scrum, kick it out and win the match. They had to play on. We managed to force a penalty when

Nigel blew them up for holding onto the ball. From our own tryline, Elton Jantjies booted the ball downfield but didn't find touch. Luckily for us, a French player touched the ball before it went out, so we had the lineout. Again Nigel checked the time because now 82 minutes had elapsed on the stadium clock, but he let play continue. From the lineout we won another penalty, which Elton kicked into the corner. We drove from that lineout and Bongi Mbonambi scored, Handré converted and we won 29–26.

It was an important victory because otherwise we would have been off to Murrayfield in Edinburgh having lost two in a row. Once again, the close margins of international rugby were clear. If Nigel Owens hadn't been aware that the stadium clock in France sometimes doesn't stop, he wouldn't have ensured more time was added and France would have won the game from the earlier scrum.

Scotland gave us a close contest but our power up front was enough to subdue them. Handré was excellent, scoring a try and kicking 13 points for a 26–20 victory. But we came back down to earth when Wales beat us for the second time that year, a 20–11 victory at Cardiff Arms Park. That defeat gave me a 50% win record in my first year as Springbok coach. Not great when compared with other Bok coaches before me, but we had won the games I had specifically targeted at the beginning of the year – the series win against England and the Wellington game against the All Blacks.

The World Cup year started with my first recce of the hotels and training facilities in Japan. I met up with SARU operations manager Charles Wessels, logistics manager JJ Fredericks, and S&C coach Aled Walters for a seven-day trip. With my luggage having gone missing after the flight, I had to buy some shirts and underpants and I was feeling a bit self-conscious because of the effects of the medication I was on. But our Japanese hosts were incredibly friendly and always well meaning, even if – when they helped me with the shopping – they gave me underpants that were too small and shirts that were too bright.

The trip was very interesting as we went to a variety of hotels, including old Japanese ones, where we were taught the ancient traditions and customs of the Japanese people. After the third day I knew which place ticked all our boxes. But Charles was adamant that we needed to go to every single hotel. He was determined to check every bed in every room, Aled wanted to check every gym and speak to all the chefs to check menus and report back to our dietician, and JJ wanted to check travel times on the bus to training grounds and stadiums. By the end of the tournament, we never flew once as our locations changed. We always travelled by train, usually the impressive bullet train that reached speeds of 300 kilometres per hour, which allowed us to use the train's Wi-Fi and work on our laptops. We got to know our liaison officers, Gents (as we called him) and Sajuri. Gents and I still WhatsApp each other.

As much as Japan is a beautiful country, rich in culture and a great place for a tourist, I have never been one for sightseeing. I seldom remember a hotel's name, or the name of a stadium where we played. I don't get impressed by such things. I've never gone to Paris and insisted on seeing the Eiffel Tower. I'm always focused on the upcoming game, how training sessions are going, and the team performance on match day. I don't remember much about Japan outside of our rugby activities. I'm a poor tourist in that respect.

I've still got the Despatch and Bloemfontein streak in me, so I'm not very sophisticated. I enjoy certain sushi, but in Japan we were taken to a special restaurant where they served high-class sushi. Charles, Aled and JJ were laughing so much because they insisted I use chopsticks, which I cannot figure out. I wanted a fork, but it's a bit of a cheek to ask for utensils like that there. They then closed a curtain around our table, which was tucked away in a corner of the restaurant. I knew I had embarrassed our hosts and I thought it was better to eat the food with my hands. It was the rawest sushi, some of which looked like it was still alive. My revulsion for fruit also applies to raw food. I battled to eat that sushi.

It reminded me of an experience I had with André Venter and Tokkie Kasselman when we were playing for Free State. We were in Cape Town to play Western Province and staying at the posh Ambassador Hotel in Bantry Bay. At the buffet table was a large silver bowl with huge prawns covered in ice. I had never been exposed to prawns before and had no idea how to eat them – and neither did Tokkie, who is from Wesselsbron in the Free State. The two of us watched André confidently put four big prawns on his plate. They were still in their shells, with head and legs attached. We copied him and sat down to eat. I watched André shove a whole prawn into his mouth. He bit down on it, with legs and feelers falling onto the table. He chewed and chewed until he could swallow it. Tokkie and I looked at each other, realising that we had to do the same. Copying André, Tokkie ate four prawns and then it was my turn. Nobody was looking strangely at the other. I managed to choke down two but gave up on the third. We left the dining room and André asked, 'So, how d'you like the prawns?' We lied and said, 'Okay. What were they like for you?' He replied, 'No, first time I've eaten prawns.'

Our World Cup was due to begin on 21 September against New Zealand in Yokohama, but before that we had three Test matches in a shortened Rugby Championship and one-off friendlies against Argentina in Pretoria, and Japan in Kumagaya in which to fine-tune our World Cup preparations.

My approach to the Rugby Championship was to win it. We believed we could beat Australia at Ellis Park and Argentina in Salta and in Pretoria. We also had New Zealand in Wellington for the second year in a row. I wondered why they chose to have back-to-back Tests there. I reckon it was to put the monkey off their back after the defeat the previous year.

I felt we were 80% to 90% on track with our team selection for the World Cup, but we didn't have all the answers, particularly when it came to scrumhalf, but I knew we would go into 2019 still experimenting here and there to make sure we had the right players. Of the World Cup squad of 31, I had already picked 24 or 25 players.

I spoke regularly to the South Africa under-20 coach Chean Roux, checking on who was coming through. We had roadmaps on so many young players, detailing age, height, weight and race, but also passing ability, tackle completion, kicking accuracy and ability to beat defenders. Some players were doing really well at their franchises but faded at an international level.

Chean alerted me to a youngster by the name of Herschel Jantjies from the University of the Western Cape. He had been part of the EPD Pathway, so we had been tracking him from an early age and he was now doing very well in the Varsity Shield and had started playing for the Stormers.

We sent a 14-man squad over to New Zealand early so that they would be acclimatised and rested for the Test match. We kept another squad in South Africa to prepare for the match against Australia. It was the perfect opportunity to give Herschel his international debut, where he performed like a player with many years' experience. In the 11th minute, Sbu Nkosi broke down the right wing, with Herschel keeping pace to take an inside pass and score under the posts. He showed vision and maturity beyond his years, chasing down a chip kick from Pieter-Steph du Toit (showing us Pieter-Steph's amazing versatility) and almost scoring his second try. In the second half, he scored a superb try, darting on the short side from a ruck and going over unopposed. Herschel showed us he had the temperament for the big occasion.

We won the game 35–17 but, not having played together as Springboks for close on eight months, the players were a little rusty. I was a bit frustrated with the stop-start nature of the game and knew that if we played like that at the World Cup, we wouldn't get through the playoffs. But I was delighted with Herschel's performance because we still had question marks about the scrumhalf position. Cobus Reinach also showed his value coming off the bench and scoring a try.

The coaches and 10 of the players from the Australia Test flew over to join the squad preparing in Wellington. It was another close-fought battle, and New Zealand were leading 16–9 with just over a minute to play when Cheslin broke down the right and put in a chip kick. Herschel was following up and, under pressure from Aaron Smith, went up for the ball, which bounced off his arm and then his chest. He grabbed it a second time and scored. I was elated, TV cameras capturing me with a look of almost disbelief on my face. First we had the agonising wait from the TMO, who quickly ruled that there was no knock-on, and then we held our breath as Handré lined up for a conversion to tie the game with the hooter having sounded. He has always been the man for the big moments and didn't let us down.

What impressed me about Herschel was not so much his tries, but the spark he brought to the game. He was the ideal person to back up Faf de Klerk. We hadn't seen as much as we would have liked from Cobus Reinach, who played for Northampton in England, but knew he had the X factor that we needed at the World Cup. His father Jaco was a Free State and Springbok winger who once held the South African record for the 400 metres. He was one of the stalwarts in the pub at Old Greys, where I got to know him. Tragically, he was killed in a car accident when Cobus was six years old.

I knew Cobus from his Sharks days, very stocky and with a great ability to steal balls. But Herschel was this unknown guy the opposition hadn't yet had time to analyse, and who popped up everywhere. He would dart around the blindside and could break the mould out of what was happening on the field. That solved our scrumhalf issue – Cobus and Herschel would both go to the World Cup.

We, however, suffered a setback when our attack coach Swys de Bruin announced he wanted to leave the Springbok squad. We weren't expecting the decision, but we knew that Swys had taken a break from the Lions because of stress earlier in the year. I respected his honesty and could never judge him for his decision. If you haven't worn somebody else's shoes, you can't say what he's going through and the personal battles he's having to fight. Swys left us after the New Zealand game and resigned as assistant coach a few weeks later for personal and medical reasons. He later said another reason for leaving the Boks was that he had a different game philosophy, so it was the right decision to make.

We had six weeks to go until our opening game of the World Cup, so I made a quick decision to bring in Felix Jones from Munster to replace Swys. Felix and I were good friends and I knew that his work ethic and rugby knowledge were exceptional. We were also expecting to play Ireland in the playoffs, so Felix's knowledge of the Irish set-up would be invaluable. When I phoned him, he didn't think twice and jumped on a plane to join us in Japan. That's how sudden it all was. There was no time for him to meet the players or get used to our systems in South Africa.

Just before the game against Argentina in Salta, we heard that Australia had beaten New Zealand 47–26 in Perth, which meant a draw would have been good enough for us to win the Rugby Championship title for the first time in 10 years. Handré had a fantastic game, scoring 31 points to set a record by a single player at the tournament. We won 46–13 and lifted the trophy.

It was a great feeling and we celebrated the victory knowing no country had won the title (or its precursor the Tri Nations) as well as the World Cup in the same year. But that wasn't an issue for us; we would just break that pattern. I knew that all these earlier results meant nothing unless we won the World Cup. We wouldn't be judged on winning the Rugby Championship; we would be judged on our performance at the World Cup. It was a case of being back to square one, and building on what we'd achieved.

By now I was close to picking my final World Cup squad. Every Wednesday before a Rugby Championship Test match we selected our 31 players, plus seven on standby. I wanted to see, week by week, whether we would make any significant changes. Did any player who was on standby one week make it into the squad the following week? If so, what changed? I wanted to be in a position where we were satisfied with the 31 names that we announced, so we tested our choices over and over again.

We had a very important camp for three days in Bloemfontein before the squad announcement. I wanted to be sure that everyone was 100% aligned. It was more about getting all the players to understand what we were doing and why we were doing it, and giving them the chance to raise their opinions on things that were bugging them.

I chose to do the camp in Bloem because that was the right environment. I was about to tell players who had worked so hard if they were going to the World Cup or staying at home on standby, and I wanted to do that without any distractions. We had one training session at Shimla Park, which was a closed session so we didn't have people watching, and nobody could speculate on social media who would be in the squad and disrupt the players' concentration and confidence. Only one journalist reported on the camp.

We drove to Shimla Park without traffic police escorting us, and stayed at a lodge just outside the city where I got the players together and told them I wanted one last meeting with them before I announced the squad to them. I had the whiteboard ready and I explained to them that they had to tell me if there was anything that they wanted to get off their chests. I went around the room. We got about four items on the board and the room went quiet, so I got a case of beer in for the guys who drank alcohol, cooldrinks for the non-drinkers, and we continued. Eventually we had about nine or ten items on the board.

One player said he wanted to raise the issue of why I don't have one-on-one meetings, another wanted to discuss the songs we play on the team bus, another player wanted to talk about the songs the guys sing in the change room. A lot of personal issues were listed on the whiteboard.

Some of the newer players weren't used to me not having one-on-one discussions. I told them I preferred to talk to everyone together so everyone understood what was going on, and no rumours started about what might have happened between me and a player behind closed doors.

I also made a distinction between habit and tradition. If we did something because it had become a habit and it wasn't universally liked, then we could scrap it. It was harder to get rid of something that was a long-established tradition. For example, there were objections to a certain song that hadn't even been written when I was a player, which meant that it wasn't a tradition. The song was played in the last few minutes of the bus ride to the stadium and was timed to end as we drove through the gate. That meant someone had to push 'Play' two and a half minutes from the stadium so that the song ended at the right time. The song had the line 'Ons vir jou, Suid-Afrika' (We are for you, South Africa). It gave me goosebumps, but it was Afrikaans and part of it sounded like the old volkslied. For a Xhosa guy, it obviously wasn't relevant, so we discussed what to do about it.

The music on the bus was a big thing. I suggested that the solution was easy: we make Franco Mostert the DJ and he would play CDs of their favourite songs. The guys all laughed at me: 'What the fuck's a CD?' I told them I got irritated and had to bite my lip when they never played a song past the second verse and flicked to the next song. I could also under-stand an Afrikaans song irritates a Xhosa guy, or a Xhosa song irritates an Afrikaans boy because they don't understand the words.

We spoke about families and agreed that wives and children could come along and stay in the same hotel as the players, but that they would have to pay for it. Why would we take adult men and trust them to make the right decision in front of 80 000 people, but not trust them when it came to being with their families?

We spoke about alcohol and came up with a system of three stages of drinking that the players had to buy into. Stage one meant no alcohol at all. Stage two was when you wanted a couple of beers together, or a glass of wine with your wife after the team dinner. We expected them to avoid drinking alcohol on a Thursday night before captain's practice and on a Friday night before a game, but we were happy if they wanted a couple of beers on a Monday or Tuesday evening. Stage three was when we had an eight-day turnaround and the guys could have a lekker kuier if they wanted to.

We also scrapped the system of fining players for indiscretions such as arriving late for the bus. I told them they all earned a lot of money, so fining a player R5 000 for being late didn't mean anything. Instead, we used common sense. If a player was late, common sense told him he was late and he had to explain why in front of the whole team. Let everyone hear his excuse. Why would you be late if everyone else is on time? If the answer was that he had overslept, the reply was don't oversleep again. But if we saw that a player didn't care about oversleeping, then the option was to go home. We still had our kontikis, or fines meetings, where punishment in the form of downing a beer was handed out, but those were joke fines and not aimed at embarrassing a player. Disrespecting the team was a totally different thing.

We discussed dancing in the bus when Siya and some of the other players would get going. We got him to explain the dance and how it worked. For some players, it was something new that they wanted to understand and get used to. No one was compelled to dance, and no one was compelled to listen to an Afrikaans song. And don't judge the guy who puts on his headphones, because he's not trying to ignore you – it's just not his thing.

I was about to announce the World Cup squad, but of course I also had to tell the seven standby players that they hadn't made the cut, so I broke my own rules and did it one-on-one. Those were the toughest discussions I have ever had. The players were so tense and there were plenty of tears from both sides. For some, it was touch-and-go whether they would make the cut or not. I couldn't give them specific rugby reasons why they weren't going because it was so close between them and the guys who made it.

Sometimes I wasn't even 100% sure we had made the right call, and I'd be honest with the player and tell him that.

They were all extremely hartseer. None of them was angry, and nobody, as far as I know, talked about me behind my back, because that gets back to you. A lot of them are still with us for the next World Cup. I know that some people, who believe I play politics with my selections to meet racial quotas, will claim I cut players because of race. That never happened and, in any case, I simply would not do it. I had done the hard work the previous year to ensure the team that went to the World Cup represented South Africa and all selections were made on purely rugby grounds. There were both black and white players among the seven who were cut.

Despite being open and honest in all my dealings with the media and the public, there would always be accusations of me having political agendas or obeying higher political authorities. I tried to let people know what I was thinking and feeling by simply being honest. All I could do was give the fans the correct information and they were free to make their own decisions and treat me the way they felt.

Eventually, two standby players were called up after the tournament started. Thomas du Toit replaced Trevor Nyakane, who tore a calf muscle, and Damian Willemse replaced Jesse Kriel, who injured his hamstring, both players being injured in the opening game against New Zealand.

17

BEFORE I EVEN LEFT FOR THE WORLD CUP, I had to make
sure I was healthy enough for the tournament. My doctor tested me
and was satisfied that the medication was having the desired effect. The
disease wasn't in full remission, but he was prepared to lower the dosage
so that the side effects wouldn't be as severe. I still had to pee a lot and
was swollen from the water retention, but my main concern was ensur-
ing that the players weren't affected by my illness. I didn't want them to
think I was panicking because I was sweating so much. I made sure they
understood I was sweating because of the fucking pills. I struggled to sleep
and had to take a sleeping tablet every now and then, which made me
groggy in the morning. I was aware that, when you consider what some
people go through with illness, I really had very little to complain about.
I could manage the symptoms of the disease and deal with the effects of
the medication.

It would have been nice to explain my situation to every person who
walked past and chirped me, accusing me of partying too hard or telling
me I had become fat. But, I thought, 'How would they know?' They had
seen me running with the players or sitting in news conferences the
previous year, and now I looked different. The abuse came mainly after
the Springboks lost and the fans were emotional and angry.

But, on the flip side, there were many other people who were just the
opposite, like the ou tannie who came over to say, 'My kind, is jy okay?'

(My child, are you okay?), or those who just wanted to shake my hand or give me a hug. I can't complain about negativity when there were so many positive reactions.

The constant peeing was an issue, though, and sometimes I had to get the bus to stop quickly for me to dash off and relieve myself. I had to plan the trip carefully and never give up the chance to have a pee because we couldn't just stop at the side of the road. It wouldn't project the right image if passers-by saw a busload of Springboks and the coach peeing at the side of the road. Sometimes we stopped at a petrol station and I jumped off, but because everybody was impatiently waiting for me and I was under pressure to get the job done, I'd get stage fright and we'd carry on without me having peed.

During matches, when the situation was tense and I needed to concentrate, I couldn't just run off to the toilet. During the World Cup in Japan I had a chaperone everywhere I went in the stadium, so I'd run off with my chaperone chasing after me, be unable to pee because I couldn't pee under pressure, and run back to the coaches' box, only to rush back a short while later to try again.

Thankfully, I never missed a critical passage of play on any of those mad dashes, and there were quite a lot of them. Sometimes I kept in touch with the action by watching on my phone while I ran, which wasn't ideal because there could be a 30-second delay. In the end, the dashes to the toilet didn't have a big impact on my ability to do the job.

The scenario reminds me of an absolutely legendary coach, Oom Tat Botha, who coached me at Free State under-21 level and at Shimlas. He got so nervous during a game that he couldn't watch it live. As we ran out, he went off to sit in the toilet. When he heard the home crowd cheering, he'd listen at the toilet window to appreciate the volume of the roar. But if it was an away game, he would flush the toilet to drown out the noise of the opposition supporters. On one occasion we were at Newlands playing Western Province under-21. They scored in the dying minutes to take the lead, and Oom Tat, having heard the cheers from the Province fans, flushed the toilet a few times and then made his way from the toilet to the field. He didn't realise that we had scored straight away from the kick-off and won the match. As we walked back to the change room after the final whistle, Oom Tat was waiting for us, shaking our hands and commiserating, 'Bad luck, boys … Sorry, boys,' and getting confused handshakes in return.

I didn't get into the players' personal lives in an effort to understand them better. I think a lot of people would want to paint me like that. Some players would say I was a father figure for them but, in my mind, I never was. I made sure I understood where each player was coming from, but I didn't ask them to go through their background story for me. I liked to know which school he came from and which clubs he played for. It might be wrong for me to admit this, but I love working with players who haven't had it easy. I know this can seem unfair, because it comes across as not giving a proper chance to someone who had it easy growing up but is a brilliant player. That's not the case. I pick the guy based on his rugby talent. But (and this might be a personal flaw) if you give me two players and I see one has travelled a gravel road and the other has travelled a tar road, I'll take the one from the gravel road.

My own road was tarred in places, but there was also quite a lot of gravel. Maybe I enjoy working more with players where I can see something of myself. I can make the desire to win more personal for such a player. I've had teammates who had good pedigree, but when things were tough and dark out there, the pedigree disappeared. I want players who never back out of trying really hard for their team and offer no excuses for poor performances.

Take Franco Mostert, for example. I used to coach his brother, JP, who was also a brilliant No. 4 lock, and could play flank and eighthman. Then he had a terrible car accident, breaking his neck, which left him in a wheelchair, paralysed from the waist down. Franco – or Sous, as we call him – tried taking up golf professionally but didn't make it, so he threw himself into becoming a world-class rugby player. I know that every time he plays for South Africa, he's playing for his brother as well as his country.

I remind the players about this constantly. They're playing for the people from their hometown or village, for their family, for the people they care about. We used photographs of their families to make up the number on the back of their jerseys. It wasn't my idea, but what we were trying to say was that you, as players, are identified by your Springbok position and its number, and you are playing for the people on that number. It turned into a nightmare logistically because it takes a bit of time to get the jerseys made up, and if we changed our selection at the last minute, we had to get the jerseys changed. Our operations manager Charles Wessels nearly went over the edge with some of the late changes.

Makazole Mapimpi gave us photographs of himself, not of his family. I didn't know his background story outside of rugby, so I asked him what was going on. He told me he didn't have anyone else in his family. He didn't know his father, his mother had passed away and his brother had died after being electrocuted. Makazole grew up in a life of violence, as did Siya, which is what makes them both so passionate about creating awareness around domestic violence. It was very emotional for me to learn this story, and when I compared it to what I was experiencing in Japan with my wife and children with me, and he had no one, it was such a strong reality check.

Less than two weeks before announcing the Springbok squad, we played Argentina in a friendly at Loftus. This was Siya's first game back, having missed the entire Rugby Championship through injury. I gave the captaincy to Schalk Brits to prepare him for the job in one of the World Cup pool matches. It was a good chance to experiment a little with the side and confirm that we had the right players for the World Cup. Sbu Nkosi scored twice, and we won 24–18.

There was no big fanfare when I let the other players know they had made it into the World Cup squad. They worked it out themselves because they hadn't been called in to say they were on standby. I didn't make an announcement followed by jubilation in the room. It just didn't work out like that. But that night we did have a proper kuier – stage-three drinking. The players who had been cut from the team partied with us and only left the following day. I have a memory of scrumming with RG Snyman at some stage that evening. The next day I spoke to the 31 squad members and told them they could now go and phone their families with the news, but warned them they couldn't call too many people because we had to do an official squad announcement live on SuperSport later that week.

We were the first World Cup team to arrive in Japan, landing in Tokyo on Sunday, 1 September and travelling by bus for over four hours to the city of Seki to prepare for our friendly against the host country. We had set up the match for two reasons. The first is that I expected Japan to qualify for the playoffs. I worked out a scenario where we would top our group, Japan would come second to Ireland in their group, and we would play them in the quarterfinals. I wanted to have a good look at them and there was no better way than playing them in Japan. The second reason was that it was a good money-spinner for us, as Charles Wessels warned me that we didn't have the budget to do all the things I wanted to do.

England's World Cup budget was probably more than our entire rugby budget for all our teams. We simply didn't have the money; we were sixth in the world. It made sense to get to Japan early, become accustomed to the conditions, get to know the people, understand their culture, play the hosts, and earn some money.

After a 25-hour flight, we arrived at our first base in Seki, a city of about 90 000 people, where it was hot and humid, with temperatures reaching 29 degrees Celsius. We got straight down to work because we had the warm-up match against Japan in Kumagaya five days later. I had a lot of respect for the Japanese team and was reminded by local journalists more than a few times about Japan's famous 34–32 victory over the Springboks at the 2015 World Cup. Japan had reached their highest world ranking of ninth place, and had recorded victories over the USA, Tonga and Fiji, and won the Pacific Nations Cup. They were both well coached and well conditioned. I told the media that I knew a movie had been made about their World Cup victory – our job was to make sure there wasn't a sequel.

We scored six tries in the 41–7 victory over Japan in the warm-up friendly in front of 22 000 fans, but the win did nothing to dampen the locals' enthusiasm for the Springboks. In the cities where we were based, residents wore Springbok jerseys. I don't think they expected their own country to progress that far in the tournament and so adopted a second team to keep their interest going. Or perhaps it was because we arrived so early, and so got the publicity first. What I do know is that the Japanese are unbelievably good people and when you open up to them, they give the support right back. It wasn't a show they were putting on; their support and love for the Springboks were real. They even learnt our national anthem.

We had an official welcoming ceremony, which, because of our early arrival, didn't interfere with our preparations for our hugely anticipated opening match against New Zealand. This was the game I had been preparing for when I was winding down my job at Munster less than two years earlier. The win and draw in Wellington had given us a healthy dose of hope, even though they beat us at Loftus by running over us in the last 20 minutes.

The match against the All Blacks was as big as we expected. It was billed as the game of the group stage and the hype around it was massive. For the first 15 minutes we pinned them back in their own half, but the All Blacks did what they are so good at doing, and they came back at us, scoring 17 points in five minutes, including two tries by George Bridge and Scott Barrett, and suddenly we were chasing our tails. They led 17–3 at halftime, but we stuck to our guns and kept up the pressure. That paid off as Pieter-Steph scored under the posts, with Handré kicking the conversion and adding a drop goal, and we were back in the game, trailing by just four points. They conceded just two penalties while we gave away 11, and we lost 13–23.

I had expected it to be a 50/50 match. We knew exactly what we had done wrong, and we knew how to fix the problems. There were no surprises about the way in which they scored their tries, winning turnover ball from bad kicks, spotting a hole in our defence and capitalising on a missed tackle. I always felt we were in the game and expected us to spark at any minute. We had our chances, and only a great tackle by Richie Mo'unga stopped Cheslin Kolbe from scoring. Even though we were trailing, we knew we had come back against them before and I felt we would still be able to do it. But when the final whistle went, we were well beaten.

We were disappointed but never dejected. We definitely didn't feel all was lost. There were suggestions that this was the dress rehearsal for the final because both teams were expected to remain undefeated right up until then, in which case we would meet again. Much was said in the media about the fact that no team had lost a pool match and then gone on to win the trophy. But that meant very little to us.

The defeat did mean, though, that we were under huge pressure to win our group game against Italy. We knew we would beat Namibia and Canada, the other teams in Pool B. But if we lost to Italy, who had beaten the Springboks three years ago, when the Boks were under Allister Coetzee, we would be eliminated from the tournament. Our third match just became a monster of a game.

I already had my plans in place in case we lost to the All Blacks. When we did our recce of locations at the beginning of the year, I asked Charles Wessels to make sure we were in a remote place, far from distractions ahead of the game against Italy, so that our preparations would be solid. I didn't even tell the other coaches about my concerns. I told Charles and Aled that we needed to be in a remote venue where we could focus on ourselves. We then found a hotel with a golf course that was perfect, the nearest shop a 15-minute drive away.

First, we had to contend with Namibia in Aichi, an hour's drive from our base in Nagoya. For that match we held back on fielding our best team and gave some of the other squad members a game. Our plan was to play a full-strength team against New Zealand and Italy, and a fringe selection against Namibia and Canada. Schalk Brits captained for the second time while Siya got more valuable game time off the bench. Schalk was delighted to captain the Boks at a World Cup, giving me a hug and a thank you. Then it was back to business for him. That's how he is: happy for himself, but then it's the team first again.

We beat Namibia 57–3, scoring nine tries and restricting Namibia to just one penalty. Our performance was not as clinical as it could have been, but it gave us a good springboard for the next game, against Italy in Shizuoka.

We then moved to our remote base, and apart from one open media day, shut ourselves away. If we had beaten New Zealand, the players would probably have been pissed off that we were so far away, but now we effectively had a playoff match against Italy and they knew we had to prepare properly.

In that match at Shizuoka Stadium, we played one of the most brutal games I've ever seen from a South African team in tackling, at the breakdown, and at scrums. I was a bit nervous at the beginning and was concerned that the scoreboard didn't tick over as quickly as I would have liked. But then we got a couple of first half tries from Cheslin and Bongi, and we started getting stronger and stronger. With every big hit, Italy were getting papper and papper. Two of their props went off with injuries, which meant we played uncontested scrums after half an hour.

We led 17–3 at halftime and never allowed them to score another point while we added five more tries, three in the final 13 minutes. Italy got a red card in the 43rd minute for the most blatant foul, and Duane Vermeulen was penalised at a ruck, but after referee Wayne Barnes blew his whistle, Italy's two props Andrea Lovotti and Nicola Quaglio picked Duane up and dropped him on his head. Barnes, with the TMO's assistance, sent Lovotti off. It wasn't clear why Quaglio didn't join him because both had committed the exact same foul.

By this stage, we were so dominant in all areas of the game that even if they didn't get the red, it was just a matter of time before we would overpower them. The final score was 49–3, and the bonus-point win all but confirmed we were through to the quarterfinals. Our pack had been incredible, playing with such ferocity. The only problem came right at the end when Cheslin Kolbe, who had scored two tries, hobbled off with an ankle injury.

We had managed to get through two games of the World Cup without any controversies, and then one erupted that I did not see coming. It happened at the end of the Italy game while the players were still on the field. A video clip captured the moment when Makazole Mapimpi walked towards a group of six white players in a huddle celebrating the victory. He approached the group but then turned away, giving a dismissive wave. This was seized on back in South Africa as a racist incident where white players were perceived as excluding a black player from their celebrations and telling him to get lost.

The truth was a lot simpler. The six players were all members of the Bomb Squad, the group of reserves who came on as impact players. They formed their own camaraderie in a match, and celebrated their achievements together. There was nothing racial about it. It just happened that six of the eight Bomb Squad members in the huddle at that moment were white. Frans Steyn, who was in the huddle, had already told Lood de Jager, a white player, to get lost, which the camera didn't capture. It had become their joke that since Lood had been promoted to the starting team, he was no longer a Bomb Squad member and no longer welcome in the group.

When I heard that a racial shit storm had broken back in South Africa, I asked Siya to come to my room. Schalk Brits, who was captain of the fringe team, joined us. I felt so helpless and said to them I didn't know what the fuck to do. When I looked at the video in isolation, I saw all the reasons why people would say it was racial. But I knew exactly what had taken place. If it had happened to any other team, made up of only black players or only white players, it would have looked like some petty bullying. But because it was South Africa, it came out differently, and I realised how far we still had to go, and how far we were from people understanding the team. It should have been so easy to explain, but at that moment it was so difficult.

Schalk asked if we even needed to explain it when no one had done anything wrong. I said we had to, because if I used only my common sense and looked at this incident as a South African, and knowing our history, I understood why this would be misinterpreted by people who had never been in a team environment and who didn't know what the Bomb Squad was all about.

Makazole came to my room because he was getting messages from back home. He said he would put out a message explaining what was going on. I said to him, 'I don't care what you're going to say and how you're going to say it, but just say the truth.' Siya went with him and together they made a video, which went out on social media. I know many people who wanted to believe we were a racially divided team rejected Mapimps's explanation and claimed he only said it to protect his position in the team. That is utter rubbish. But sometimes, when people make up their minds, they don't like the facts to get in the way. I let Mapimps do his own thing because the moment I told him what to say or how to explain it, then it wasn't his version of the truth. I didn't want to get involved unless they asked me.

Mapimps posted a video on Instagram in which he explained what the Bomb Squad was and that they had their own team spirit and their own calls. He said in the video that the Bomb Squad had come together after handshakes with the opposition: 'As I walked towards them I realised they were about to do their call. I wasn't part of it, so I decided to move away. There was nothing wrong there with what they were doing – we are united as a team.'

I felt so dejected. I thought, 'Ag no, fuck man, this can't be.' I knew there was nothing in this, but I fully understood why people could see everything in it, and that was making me feel a bit broken at that stage.

I addressed the issue the next day when I named the team to play Canada in our final Pool B match. I explained what the Bomb Squad was all about and how it was sad the video clip had been misinterpreted.

I said, 'It's so sad that somebody could see something negative in that because I can give you my word that as a head coach I would not allow anything like that in the team. There is nothing like that in the team. For those who want to see something negative in the team, I guess they will find something. But I can guarantee to the other 95% of the people in South Africa who want to know the truth that that is the truth. This team is such a closely knit team. We are representing a country that has a lot of problems, but I think this team is representing this country with a lot of pride.'

The controversy may have blown up in South Africa, but it didn't affect preparations for our next match, against Canada. We were now seeing the benefits of having arrived early in Japan, which gave us time to settle down, and the system of alternating our teams from game to game. The players were in a rhythm, the humid conditions didn't worry us and, apart from Trevor and Jesse in the first game and now Cheslin, we didn't have too many injuries.

We made 13 changes to the team for the final group match, against Canada in Kobe, and blew them away in the first half. Cobus Reinach got a hat-trick within 20 minutes and we led 47–0 at the break. Canada were simply not in our league and their problems worsened when one of their players got a red card just before halftime. The final score was 66–7, and we finished second in Pool B behind New Zealand. We had to wait until Sunday to find out if we'd play Ireland or Japan in the quarterfinal, and that depended on the result of the final game of the group stage, between Japan and Scotland.

We weren't even sure the game would go ahead after Typhoon Hagibis hit Japan, with terrible consequences, the day before the match. According to Japan's Fire and Disaster Management Agency, at least 98 people died and almost 350 were injured in the storm. The insurer Munich Re estimated the losses at US$17 billion. Three games were cancelled, but the tournament organisers delayed an announcement over the fate of the Japan–Scotland game for several hours before deciding to go ahead. Japan continued their incredible journey after beating Ireland in their second pool match and topped their group with a 28–21 win over Scotland. Ireland finished second and played New Zealand in the quarterfinal. We played Japan.

I had been 90% sure we would face Japan and had been analysing them in depth. The warm-up game before the tournament started was useful when it came to looking at the speed with which they played the game, but I knew what we had to do to beat them. I had done all my homework on Japan, and also worked out a strategy to get the players up for the game. I knew what it felt like to lose in a quarterfinal as we had done in 2011, when everything comes to a sudden stop and you just fly home.

I told the players how brutal it was. In the back of everybody's mind was the fact that Japan had beaten the Springboks at a World Cup before, in 2015, and they had beaten Ireland, ranked number one in the world, as well as Scotland, who were ranked seventh. We had improved our position since 2017 and were now ranked fourth, while Japan were 10th.

Japan had these very quick players and it's difficult to get into a battle with them because they're all over the field. If that was how the game panned out, we would be in trouble. I felt our maul would be a key weapon.

We had 12 days between our last group game and the quarterfinal, so there was time to spend on specific aspects of our game. I took out my 2005 manual on mauling, which I used with Free State when we beat the Bulls in the Currie Cup final. The technique is based on the V-formation of birds in flight. I enjoy learning lessons from animals because there's no ego or politics involved. When birds fly in a V-formation, the bird that leads rotates to the back because it takes the most drag or headwind. The birds at the back are protected in the slipstream of those in front and they are able to regain their strength. When birds fly in a V-formation, they are all aligned and can achieve 60% more range. They honk to encourage each other. With geese, if one of them is forced to the ground for whatever reason, two geese go down with it and wait either until it is dead or ready to fly again so that they can form another V-formation again.

Together with our forwards coach Matt Proudfoot, we showed the players how to rotate positions in a maul so that the guy in front fell to the back. It was pouring with rain, so we found a room big enough to accommodate us as the forwards walked through the moves. I asked Charles Wessels to get us two cases of beer and told the players no one was leaving until we were all aligned on the mauls. I asked Matt if I could take charge of the session and took them through the manual and tactics that beat the Bulls.

We went through each player's role, from the jumper taking the ball to the way each person packed down. Everybody was involved in analysing the tactics, drinking their beers, giving their ideas, pointing out things that didn't work, perfecting things that did work and writing ideas on the whiteboard. We walked through the maul over and over again for two to three hours. By the time we walked out of that room, we knew we would score a vital try against Japan using the techniques we had perfected.

During the session, I desperately needed to pee because of the medication I was taking and the toilet was about 10 minutes away. In Japan, you can't just sneak off and pee behind a bush, but I was bursting so I ducked between some trees and relieved myself. A short while later, our liaison officer Gents approached me with a very serious face and said, 'Mr Hassie [he couldn't say his Rs], I have something important to report. You were urinating next to the trees.'

He looked at me without a hint of a smile. I stammered out an apology, making all sorts of excuses. Then his whole face broke out into a broad smile, and he said he was only joking. What made it so much more amusing is that Gents never made jokes. This was the first. He was also surprised that we wanted beers for the training session, so I told him it was quite normal. Because of the long turnaround between the matches, the guys wouldn't have trained that day anyway, so having a dop was okay.

Japan had achieved beyond most people's expectations, and their style of play had attracted a huge support base. I felt it was us against the world. Very few rugby fans, apart from the South Africans, were rooting for us. We had to make the game personal to motivate our players. The problem was that the Japanese people were so incredibly nice to us: they had learnt our anthem, they had worn Springbok jerseys and they had been the most wonderful hosts.

In the final team talk, I told the players to be physical against Japan, to bully them. I pointed out the differences between us and them. Japan had mental toughness and worked with coaches who focused specifically on their mental state. But we played for different things. I was quite blunt when I said, 'These guys do it because they want to grow the game of rugby. We want to do it because we want to save our fucking country. We've got fucking 58 murders a day. Women get raped every day. These guys are playing rugby to get it on the map. That's their motivation. They've got 120 million people and they're one of the richest countries in the world

– that's their motivation. It's pissing me off that they think that gives them the right.'

Just for this game, I wanted our players to stop appreciating the Japanese people and everything they had done for us. Japan's motivation was to establish rugby in their country. We were playing to bring a country together.

I wanted our players to intimidate the opposition right from the start. 'Don't smile at them. Please don't smile at them. Siya, when you get the toss, let them get the idea, "I'm here to fuck you up." If you guys walk out of here and think that this is a joke, then you're joking with the country and you're joking with South Africa. I want you to take this seriously and I want you to fuck them up physically for 15 to 20 minutes.'

Within four minutes at Tokyo Stadium, we did just that and pushed Japan back at a scrum. Faf fed Mapimpi on the blind side and he brushed off two defenders to open the scoring. A few minutes later we were in trouble as Beast tip-tackled Keita Inagaki, and referee Wayne Barnes, without consulting the TMO, gave him a yellow card. How different it would have been had he given Beast a red card – Tendai was an important person in our maul. In a pre-match TV interview, I said the game would be a battle of the different tactics, and that's what happened as we dominated them up front and their speedy backs ran at us. Time was up for the first half when we mauled them once again, allowing Damian de Allende a dash for the line. He was brought down by three defenders, but got to his feet, continued his run and dived over the line. Barnes disallowed the try, ruling that Damian hadn't released the ball in the tackle, and so we went into the break with a slender 5–3 lead, having missed some chances to take the game away from them.

We turned the screws in the second half. Handré banged over three penalties to give us some breathing space, and then came the moment we had rehearsed on that day off in training. In the 65th minute, Lood de Jager won the ball in a lineout five metres inside our half. Malcolm Marx came round to the back of the maul and the drive was on. I had a sense of déjà vu as it happened. It was like the 2005 Currie Cup final all over again. I could see how Japan's forwards kept falling away as the maul kept moving. The drive was unrelenting and we got to their 22-metre area. The defence fell apart and Pieter-Steph, Siya and Malcolm had no one in front of them. Malcolm broke away, gained some ground and flicked the ball inside to Faf, who handed off a desperate defender and dived over near the upright. It was clinical and precise, and exactly what we had planned. I had predicted we would score a vital try from that move and that's what happened. Our hard work in that classroom won us the match, without a doubt.

In the 70th minute Siya and Francois 'Flo' Louw secured a turnover, and Handré and Willie le Roux had great runs down the middle before Mapimps ran 30 metres, shrugging off a defender to score his second try. We high-fived each other in the coaches' box, knowing that that was the game. Victory by 26 points to 3 and into the semifinal to face Wales at Yokohama Stadium.

Willie le Roux took a bad knock on his shoulder during the game, which affected his play. He dropped a number of up-and-unders, and received a lot of unpleasant criticism from the fans, who didn't realise he was injured. They also didn't appreciate the incredible role Willie played in the team, organising the defence and providing support for the younger players with his vast experience. He was suffering tremendous discomfort but refused to give up and trained through the pain in preparation for the Wales semifinal. We managed to secure specialist treatment in Japan to get him right.

As we were leaving for the semifinal, Willie came up to me and said if I was having to cover up too much for him because of the negativity back home, then I should drop him from the team. I wasn't prepared to do that. I had organised a highlights package of Willie's best moments in the previous four games and showed the video to the team. None of the players was in any doubt that Willie's contribution to the team was immense. That gave him the confidence to carry on, and he was one of the outstanding players in those final two matches.

What people don't know about Willie is that he is a perfectionist and very competitive. He cares a lot, which is why you see him so animated on the field, waving his hands and directing the players. His communication with his teammates on the field is on another level. He creates the tries; he often makes the second-last pass before the try is scored. That's what he brings to a team.

I wanted to pick Cheslin for the Wales game, but he was still recovering from an ankle injury he had picked up in the Italy Test. He missed the Canada game but was cleared for the quarterfinal against Japan, where he strained the ankle once more. Our team-selection protocols were that if a player was unable to train on a Monday, he couldn't be selected for the game later that week.

Cheslin wasn't available for training on the Monday and so I announced the team for the semifinal with Sbu Nkosi in his place. But by Thursday, Cheslin was back to full fitness, stepping us all over the place. I asked him if he was ready for Wales. He looked at me in surprise, almost angry. He didn't say anything, but I could tell by his expression that he was challenging me for even thinking of breaking my own team-selection protocols.

I went to Stokke (our nickname for assistant coach Mzwandile Stick) and Jacques to get their views. They confirmed that Cheslin looked in great form, but pointed out he had been ruled out on Monday. I argued that he was ready, but Stokke was adamant: 'No, Rassie, you can't pick him now.'

This is why you must have people around you who believe in your methods, so when you break your own rules, they will correct you. Stokke said to me, 'Is jy mal?' (Are you mad?) You're going to lose the whole team if you pick Cheslin now and we get into the final. What are you going to tell the team on Monday when you select them for that game?'

Stokke was right. I had to be honest with the players. I couldn't mess with their minds and change things because I wanted to. I went to Cheslin one more time and asked how he was feeling. He just said, '*Ja-nee, ek's reg, maar Sbu is gekies*' (Well, I'm all right, but Sbu has been selected). It showed great character.

I expected Wales to beat France in their quarterfinal. We had played them twice the previous year and lost both games. They were the team that played the most like us, and we knew how tough they were. They can play beautiful rugby but they can also grind you. They had won the Six Nations by strangling the life out of the opposition, and we expected them to try to do exactly the same to us.

I can only describe the first half of that Wales game as a war of attrition. We led 9–6 at halftime from three penalties by Handré. In the 56th minute, Damian used his power and strength to break through three defenders and score a vital try, but then Wales hit back late with a try by Josh Adams. We were level at 16–all, with Wales on the attack, when Flo Louw – who had just come on – won a crucial turnover ball from a ruck, which allowed us to clear our lines. It was a massive moment in the game. We were under a lot of pressure before Flo was able to steal that ball and win us a penalty.

We gained territory, controlled the ball from a lineout and then won a penalty from a driving maul when a Welsh player came in from the wrong side. Referee Jérôme Garcès played advantage and Handré tried a drop goal that was just out of his range, knowing he'd be called back if he missed – which is what happened. The penalty was about 30 metres out and Handré put it straight down the middle: 19–16. At that stage I was feeling a bit numb, almost going through a loss of reality for a few minutes. All I could do was thump the table in the coaches' box before high-fiving my colleagues.

We were in the final, and I was now in unchartered waters as a coach.

18

I WAS A PLAYER AT THE 1999 WORLD CUP, losing in the semifinal to Australia. Then I was an assistant coach at the 2011 World Cup, losing in the quarterfinal to Australia.

But reaching the final of the 2019 World Cup was something else completely.

We had watched England dominate New Zealand to win their semifinal the day before we beat Wales. But those games don't make a big impression on me. It's irrelevant what other teams do against each other because their strengths and weaknesses have nothing to do with our own strengths and weaknesses. England were very organised and played a well-structured game, but we were very different to New Zealand. I didn't think England was suddenly this great team, but I knew how good the All Blacks were, and for England to beat them was impressive. We knew England, having played them four times the previous year, winning twice.

We usually prepared for our opposition more than a week ahead of the game, but with knockout games you don't know who you'll be facing the next week. In preparing for the semifinal, we would face either France or Wales, so some coaches prepared for France, others prepared for Wales. For the final, we knew it was either England or New Zealand. Even before the semifinals were played, our coaches began preparations for England. We focused on them, not because we didn't rate New Zealand but because we already had plenty of analysis on the All Blacks from the pool match

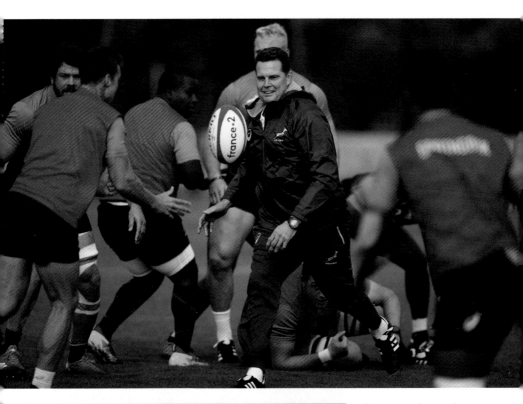

Getting stuck in with
the forwards during
training at the INSEP High
Performance Centre in
Paris before the Springboks'
victory over France on
10 November 2018.
STEVE HAAG SPORTS

A happier time with Wales
coach Warren Gatland
at Cardiff's Millennium
Stadium on 24 November
2018 before the Springboks'
final Test of their European
tour against Wales.
STEVE HAAG SPORTS

With three crucial members of my coaching team, off-the-ball coach Mzwandile Stick, defence coach Jacques Nienaber and attack coach Felix Jones in 2019.
RUSSELL BELTER

Celebrating our victory in the 2019 Rugby Championship after beating Argentina in Salta on 10 August 2019, with operations manager Charles Wessels, defence coach Jacques Nienaber and strength and conditioning coach Aled Walters.
RUSSELL BELTER

Arriving in Japan on 1 September 2019 for the World Cup and looking slightly puzzled at the amount of Springbok team luggage at Tokyo International Airport. ANNELEE MURRAY

The job I was never comfortable doing – facing the media on 18 September 2019 at the Tokyo Bay Hotel to announce the Springbok team for our opening World Cup match against New Zealand.
STEVE HAAG SPORTS

With captain Siya Kolisi at Fuchu Asahi Football Park in Tokyo during training in the week building up to our World Cup quarterfinal against Japan on 20 October 2019. STEVE HAAG SPORTS

Lost in my own thoughts before the World Cup semifinal against Wales on 27 October 2019 at the International Stadium in Yokohama. STEVE HAAG SPORTS

The Springboks pose for the traditional team photograph at the Hilton Hotel in Tokyo on 1 November 2019, the day before the World Cup final at the International Stadium in Yokohama. STEVE HAAG SPORTS

This is the moment when TMO Ben Skeen tells referee Jérôme Garcès to 'stay with your on-field decision' to confirm Makazole Mapimpi's try in the World Cup final and I breathe a sigh of relief. Technical analyst Lindsay Weyer on the left. RUSSELL BELTER

The moment we knew we had won the World Cup as Cheslin Kolbe scores his amazing try. Lindsay Weyer on the left, Matt Proudfoot and Felix Jones embrace behind me, Mzwandile Stick out of picture on the right. RUSSELL BELTER

Minutes after the World Cup final whistle I, overcome with emotion, walked out to join the players on the field, and was embraced by my good friend, operations manager Charles Wessels. RUSSELL BELTER

As the feeling of victory sank in after the final whistle at the World Cup, this seemed an appropriate way to acknowledge Jacques Nienaber's role. RUSSELL BELTER

Celebrating with the Webb Ellis Cup shortly after the trophy presentation. Lood de Jager, his arm in a sling after being injured in the match, shares a moment with RG Snyman. STEVE HAAG SPORTS

Acknowledging the crowds during the World Cup trophy parade on 7 November 2019 as we stopped off at our sponsors MTN for lunch. MTN

On the trophy parade through the streets of downtown Johannesburg. These scenes were replicated in every city we visited to celebrate the World Cup victory. ANNELEE MURRAY

My birthday cake made specially for my 47th birthday, which was two days before the trophy parade. ANNELEE MURRAY

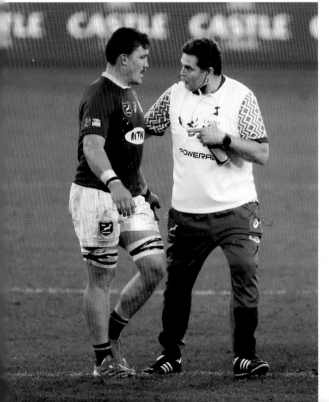

Doing my job as water boy (and more) with Willie le Roux, Faf de Klerk and Morné Steyn during the South Africa A match against the British and Irish Lions at Cape Town Stadium on 14 July 2021.
STEVE HAAG SPORTS

The job that caused so much controversy – carrying the water and passing on information to Jasper Wiese during the second Test against the British and Irish Lions at Cape Town Stadium on 31 July 2021. STEVE HAAG SPORTS

In Hartenbos with my sisters, Gerda (left) and Martlie (right), and our mother, Maria, in November 2022. PERSONAL COLLECTION

My rugby-loving mother, Maria Erasmus, watching the Stormers play Munster in a United Rugby Championship match at Cape Town Stadium on 15 April 2023, a match that Munster narrowly won. Her loyalties were divided on the day. PERSONAL COLLECTION and from the Rugby Championship in 2018 and earlier in 2019.

In our last training session, I told the players that our game plan wouldn't be perfect; we'd still have to grind it out. But I needed them to understand that they couldn't lose this just because they hadn't given it their best shot. We had worked so hard to get where we were; they couldn't give it up now because of nerves.

We had more than an hour's drive from our hotel in Tokyo to Yokohama for the final at the International Stadium, the same venue where we had lost to New Zealand and then beaten Wales. I didn't want to give the team talk at the hotel because by the time we arrived at the stadium the talk would already be an hour old. I wanted it to be fresh in their minds. I had to make it personal for each player. If you get him to understand why the match is so important for him as a person, something switches in his mind and motivates him.

I had never played in a World Cup final, but I knew the difference between a Currie Cup semifinal and final. In those finals, I felt some of my teammates gave up, their legs were heavy, their handling was terrible and they were almost too nervous to make a mistake. It felt like they were overwhelmed by how big the game was.

Some of my best games were the big moments, like the 1997 Currie Cup final when we lost to Western Province but I was Man of the Match. Or the 1999 World Cup semifinal when we lost to Australia. Or even when we were going for the record 18th Test victory in succession and I refused to give up. I am most proud of my performances in those games, even though we lost them. I had seen how the pressure of a big game could suck the confidence out of a player. They would allow themselves to be pressured by the media or by the coach, or even a teammate. I had to make sure my players didn't freeze because the game was too big for them; instead, they would be able to rise to the occasion.

So we didn't chat at the hotel. We drove to the stadium and had the team talk there. I didn't write anything down about what I wanted to say. I've never done that. What I feel at the hotel is different to what I feel at the stadium. Things change in my mind after I've seen the fans outside and picked up some of the atmosphere. For me, a specially prepared team talk makes the players go, 'Oh fuck, let me just switch off.'

I stood in front of the whiteboard in the change room with the warm-up timings written on it, and spoke to the players. I told them they didn't have the right to worry about their mistakes because that was windgat, an ego problem. They weren't representing themselves in the final – they were fighting for things that happen in South Africa, the hardships people face on a daily basis.

I told Siya he was fighting for the next youngster from his home township of Zwide so that kid doesn't have to suffer like Siya suffered. I told Lukhanyo and Mapimps they were playing for the kid who didn't get the opportunities that they eventually got. I could have gone through the whole team, picking up individual traits and issues that were personally important to each player, but time was against me.

I emphasised that no one had the right to drop their head if they were playing badly because it wasn't about them. If they lost a lineout, they had to jump up and make the next tackle. If they missed a tackle, they had to jump up and make the next cleanout. I wanted them to show me they understood by either saying yes or nodding their heads when I asked, 'Do you agree you are not representing individuals today and that no one has the right to worry about themselves?' I told them not to worry about their mistakes; that was my job.

With the talk over, I went out to watch the teams warming up. I wanted to see what England were doing because they might do something in the warm-up that they would use in the game. I didn't watch our team warming up and left that to our coaches. The referee, Jérôme Garcès, came to talk to us briefly. We were satisfied that he was in charge because we were used to him. He had refereed our opening match against New Zealand and

218

our semifinal against Wales. We knew the way he controlled the game, and he understood how we played. Where we had contentious issues from those two matches, we received clarity from the committee that handled refereeing queries, headed up by Alain Rolland, the former Ireland scrum-half and Test referee, which worked effectively and efficiently.

I sat down in the coaches' box, joining our technical analyst Lindsay Weyer, who had already set up his laptop. I felt quite calm and started making notes in my notebook. The assistant coaches, Stokke, Felix and Matt joined me. I felt the emotion of our national anthem, which Stokke sang loudly next to me. We all shook hands and then I put on my headphones, checked my communications to Jacques and Aled, both at the side of the field, and went into work mode.

In rugby, every single move is like a chess game. Some people think rugby is just 'play what you see'. It isn't. If you play what you see, you will always just kick the ball because you won't see the space. So it's always chess … If they're competing with four men, we bring in five men. If they're kicking off short, how do we react? When the game starts, everything you've planned and analysed goes into motion. Jacques looks at the defence, Stokke looks at the off-the-ball work, I look at the players' discipline. I'm constantly thinking, 'Are they still productive? When are we going to put the Bomb Squad on? Should we give a player another seven minutes to empty the tank before the next guy goes on?'

Within a minute we showed how hard we would play and won a penalty when Courtney Lawes didn't roll away at a breakdown. I saw how strictly Jérôme Garcès would police the breakdown and gave instructions for Siya to tell the players and to say it loudly in front of Jérôme so the ref knew that we understood. Handré's penalty attempt was slightly wide. Two minutes later, Mapimps took a high box-kick and went on a run, surging between England defenders Maro Itoje and Kyle Sinckler. In the tackle, Itoje's arm caught Sinckler on the jaw, knocking him out for a few seconds. Straight away I knew Sinckler was gone and told Stokke, 'No way will he pass the HIA [head-injury assessment].' It was a significant moment, because Dan Cole then came on as a replacement a lot sooner than England was expecting. I knew he didn't have the wheels to play against Beast, Steven Kitshoff, Frans Malherbe and Vincent Koch for 73 minutes in a World Cup final. I wanted the players to keep Cole moving all over the park.

I was delighted with our start. Mapimps had bullied England with that great carry. I told Jacques to tell the players I wanted 80 more minutes of that. England were already down a player, and we needed to keep bullying them. We were showing our dominance in the scrum, putting England under constant pressure. Within nine minutes, Handré slotted our first penalty from right in front of the posts. We were preventing England from settling down, and they were making simple mistakes with wayward passes.

Then Bongi Mbonambi got a knee to the head tackling Courtney Lawes, and I saw immediately that he was out. I called down to Jacques to get Malcolm Marx ready so Bongi could get checked for concussion. That disrupted our plan of using Bongi for the first half, and Malcolm for the second half, but it was vital that Bongi have the HIA. I was hoping he would pass the test and so rest for 10 or 15 minutes at the same time, but he failed the HIA and wasn't able to carry on. We needed to be prepared.

Malcolm's great strength is in contesting the ball on the ground, but that's also where he's vulnerable to getting a yellow or a red card if a referee misinterprets his actions. We told him to be careful not to be sent off because we didn't have another hooker and would be forced to go to uncontested scrums if he was carded. We'd also have to bring on a front-row forward and take off another player, which would have been hugely disruptive. So Malcolm went on with instructions to be reserved, which went against all his instincts. He's a great all-round player, he makes good decisions, and he loves to steal a ball. We didn't want a ref reading it wrong, so we told Malcolm, 'Don't bite too hard, because if you get a yellow card now, we are fucked!'

To add to our problems, Lood de Jager's World Cup came to an end at the same time as Bongi's when he suffered a bad shoulder injury and Franco Mostert replaced him. We now had two replacements in the pack and were only 20 minutes into the game.

After Cheslin played the ball on the ground, England won a penalty, which Owen Farrell converted to make the score 3–all after 22 minutes. But three minutes later, Handré kicked a second penalty to give us a 6–3 lead.

In the 30th minute there was a turning point in the game as England launched wave after wave of attack on our line. For four minutes, with Garcès playing a penalty advantage to England, their big forwards drove at the line. Every time, our big forwards pushed them back. It was unrelenting pressure, but our guys never wavered. They were doing exactly what I had asked them to do, jumping up after making a big tackle, ready to do it again. Eventually England gave up and opted for a kick at goal, which levelled the scores at 6–all. Their players had worked so hard for so long and their only reward was three points. Handré kicked another two penalties shortly before the break to give us a 12–6 lead at halftime.

England brought the heat and we handled it. We didn't even have to make dominant hits. They were close to our line, but not close to scoring because we were making positive tackles every single time. We hadn't fired any shots yet, but we'd taken plenty of bullets, and now England had emptied their supply. Come the second half, it was our turn to fire the shots and see if England could handle it. It was such a lekker feeling.

The psychological impact of withstanding that onslaught was huge. We looked at what England had achieved. Did they outsmart us with unexpected moves, in which case we would make a plan, or did they overpower us, in which case we would step up? But they had done neither. It was like a double blow to them. They had neither outsmarted nor overpowered us, despite their best efforts.

We were focused but relaxed in the change room at halftime. I went over to the forwards and told them, 'What you are doing is fucking unbelievable. Give us another 40 minutes of that and we'll win the World Cup.' Then I spoke to the whole team and was blunt about what they had to do. 'The next thing is to be fucking physical and mental. No technical shit from now on.'

The assistant coaches gave their input and then I spoke to the players one last time. I emphasised the importance of discipline and not turning the ref against us. So far, he had been very fair, and I didn't want that to change. I also stressed the players' body language. I didn't want to see players holding their hamstrings or nursing a sore knee. 'Get up and get in their faces. For 40 minutes, use your body language and then you're world champions!' There were shouts of agreement as the players clambered to their feet and started moving out.

As we came out for the second half, we had to make sure we fired decent shots when we got the opportunity. I was still nervous about the players freezing in the big moment. I wanted them to believe in themselves and never die wondering, 'What if I had gone harder, or faster, or stronger?'

Handré and Farrell kept the scoreboard moving with two penalties each. I was particularly pleased with the penalty we won in the 56th minute with a move we had never practised on the field, but only in a hotel room. We called it 'The Move'. We set up a maul in the middle of the field with seven players waiting to bind and drive. Faf de Klerk took the ball from a ruck and then passed to Duane Vermeulen, who was at the front of the V-formation, and the other forwards packed in behind him. We mauled the ball up to England's 22-metre line, forcing them to concede a penalty that Handré booted over. Once again, practising our mauls behind closed doors had paid off.

With us leading 18–12, there was a significant turning point in the match. In the 66th minute Willie le Roux took a high box-kick by England scrumhalf Ben Youngs under pressure and went to ground as the forwards piled in to support him. Faf recycled the ball on the short side to Lukhanyo on the halfway line. Lukhanyo found Malcolm on his shoulder. In the tackle, Malcolm then fed a quick pass to Mapimps who put in a superbly timed chip kick. As England turned to chase, Lukhanyo surged past Youngs, picked up a perfect bounce and, with England players floundering in his wake, was free to run in and score. Instead, he calmly flicked the ball to Mapimps sprinting up on his left. England's fullback Elliot Daly was in no position to counter the move, and Mapimps, as cool as you like, trotted in to score our first try, which Handré converted, 25–12 to South Africa.

The way Lukhanyo, Malcolm and Mapimps attacked on the blind side was so calm. Mapimps chipping ahead perfectly, Lukhanyo running on to the ball and giving it back to Mapimps to score – it was beautiful. In the heat of the moment, I didn't fully appreciate just how nonchalant Lukhanyo was, like he was at the practice ground. That's exactly how I wanted them to play in tough situations. They were so relaxed.

In the coaches' box, we were all up out of our seats shouting at the tops of our voices as Mapimps scored. But we nervously sat down to wait for the TMO, Ben Skeen of New Zealand, to rule if there had been any forward passes. I bit on my pen as Lindsay checked on his laptop and gave me the thumbs-up, but we needed the official version from Ben. As the agonising wait dragged on, I started planning ahead, calling for Frans Steyn to replace Willie le Roux. The chess game continued. Ben told Jérôme, 'Stay with your on-field decision,' and I gave a small fist-pump in celebration.

Eight minutes later, we scored again. England launched several attacks from inside their own half, spreading the ball left and right but each time encountering a Springbok brick wall. As the ball came down the line from a ruck for the fifth or sixth time, Malcolm put in a big hit on Henry Slade who spilled the ball forward. Lukhanyo dived on it and popped it up to Pieter-Steph, who passed to Cheslin on his outside. Cheslin, who was close to the touchline and still about 35 metres out, appeared to have nowhere to go, with five England players bearing down on him. He gave a little skip that flummoxed Joe Marler, spotted Farrell moving to his right to block him, and stepped inside him, leaving the England captain for dead. Suddenly the space opened up in front of him and he was free to sprint in for a glorious try.

This time our celebrations in the coaches' box were much more exuberant. We knew that that was the game. I hugged Stokke, almost grappling with him like a wrestler and shouting at the top of my voice. Felix and Matt slapped me on the back. As I sat back down, I grabbed my headphones and squeezed them tightly in sheer joy and relief.

Cheslin did everything we were used to seeing him do. I didn't fully appreciate how brilliantly he evaded Marler and stepped past Farrell because that's what Cheslin did so often. It was almost as calm as Lukhanyo's pass to set up Mapimps. That's what made that World Cup final so special for me, watching these guys under pressure playing with such assurance.

We were leading 32–12, but I couldn't relax. I'd experienced opposition teams bouncing back in the final quarter to win a match. I remembered the All Blacks at Loftus the previous year, scoring three tries in 17 minutes to beat us by two points.

I radioed down to Jacques to tell the players to keep composure. 'A lot of things can still happen; no stupid penalties,' I told him. Matt wanted to go down to the side of the field, but I wouldn't let him, saying, 'We're going to need advice at scrums and shit.'

I was worried that this could still be ripped away from us. I asked Stokke, 'Can we still lose this match?'

'Aikona, no ways!' he said. 'They can't score two tries.'

When he said that, I felt calm. I radioed down to Jacques to substitute Faf with Herschel. At the Springboks, we don't just change things to keep people happy, and Faf was in control and playing exceptionally well. There was no need to inject Herschel's brilliance into the game. But I thought,

'Hell, if you have the luxury of giving a guy a chance to experience the joy of winning a World Cup, let's do it.'

I could finally enjoy the last minutes of the game and gave Stokke a kiss on the cheek. Lindsay and Felix were packing up their equipment, but I was still staring at the field as play went on. As the dying seconds ticked away, I had one more moment of doubt and asked Stokke, 'They can't win it any more, can they?' He gave me a reassuring pat on the shoulder. Ben Skeen came over the comms to Jérôme Garcès, telling him there were two minutes left. I smacked the table in relief, packed away my radio and made my way down to the field.

As Handré booted the ball high into the stands to end the game, I joined the players for the celebrations. I walked out of the tunnel onto the field, to be met by the support staff who were hugging, cheering and crying. I gave Charles a big hug, but I was overcome with emotion and became tearful. I went back up the tunnel to compose myself. I was reluctant to join the players; it was their day and I wanted them to enjoy the moment. As we waited for the trophy presentation, I walked among them, hugging, laughing and joking with them. I gave Jacques a kiss on his bald head. We had come a long way together.

When we gathered on the podium and Siya raised the trophy high, with fireworks going off and confetti flying into the air, I stood at the back of the group, with everyone jumping up and down in front of me. I was jubilant, but I didn't want the limelight. I looked for Nikki standing at the side of the field, and watched the reactions of people in the crowd. We walked around the stadium, bowing in thanks to the Japanese people for being so unbelievable. I remembered how strange it felt the first time we had done it and how nice it felt the last time.

I look back at that victory with a mixture of emotions.

I remember the feeling I got when we played England in the first Test at Ellis Park, when Siya made his debut as captain and I faced a backlash from some quarters, when we were down 3–24 after just 20 minutes. Back then I was stunned, thinking, 'This can't be how life works, disrupting my family by going to Ireland and then coming home, working so hard to achieve transformation through the EPD Pathway, developing strategies and tactics, and believing how it was going to work, only to see it all unravelling in front of me.' I had told myself that I couldn't feel sorry for myself and couldn't have excuses. I remembered how we didn't give up; we went hard, and by halftime we were back in the game, and ultimately won the series.

And now, 16 months later, we'd just beaten England in a World Cup final, and I felt, 'Fuck, it was worth it!' All the fighting and disagreeing and convincing, disrupting the family and Jacques's family, getting programmes aligned, getting players and coaches through the systems I put in place, building a team that represented the whole country, playing a game that took us from number six to the top of the world, it was worth it.

I thought back to the moments when I doubted myself and thought I was arrogant because I presumed I knew better than other people, when the gun was against my head in that first Test against England, and when we almost lost three Tests in a row and I promised to resign if it happened, yet I kept going with my plans. Even if we had lost the final, I would have known I lost it the way I wanted it done. It was all worth it. *Uiteindelik!* (Eventually!)

My father once told me a story when I was leaving Despatch to go to Bloemfontein. He told me about a man who was at the beach, catching crabs. As he caught them, he chucked them in a bucket. His friend came past and warned him that his bucket was filling up and the crabs would crawl up the side of the bucket and escape. The guy said, 'Don't worry, they're South African crabs, they'll drag each other down.' I think that's what my dad experienced his whole life. The moment he was about to achieve something, someone came along to drag him down. I feel, in

South Africa, that there's a bit of an illness, that the moment somebody makes it, they get dragged down.

Now I felt almost vindicated. Maybe the correct word is 'relief'. I said to myself, 'Fuck, I told you!' I have made many mistakes in my career and have doubted myself and felt sorry for myself many times. I can now admit this to myself. I constantly thought, 'Is anybody going to get this, will it work out eventually?' And then it did. Thank God it worked out.

Winning the trophy was great, no question. It's wonderful when you win. But a photo of me holding up the Webb Ellis Cup wasn't the biggest thing personally. Rather, it was Lukhanyo making that pass almost in slow motion for Mapimps to score, Cheslin dancing past the England players, our forwards mauling the Japanese back, seeing the plans working. That was what was special.

Siya and I took the Webb Ellis Cup with us to meet the media at the post-match news conference, where the first question was what the moment meant to me. I felt proud as I sat there because we hadn't been given much of a chance to win the World Cup. I explained how, as a team, we had decided we would have to be together for 20 weeks if we wanted to win the trophy because we were so far behind the other teams in building a competitive squad. We didn't see that as a sacrifice but rather as an honour. I said we had just completed week 19 out of the 20. We still had the trophy tour around the country the following week. Charles came up with this great suggestion when we were making our plans at the beginning of the year. He insisted we factor in a victory parade around the country. That's how thoroughly we planned.

I spoke about dealing with pressure, which I had driven home in my team talks with the players. I explained what I understood pressure to mean. In South Africa, pressure was not having a job, or one of your close relatives being murdered. Rugby shouldn't be something that puts pressure on you; it should be something that creates hope. We had the privilege of giving people hope; it wasn't a burden. But giving hope wasn't just talking about it and posting a nice picture on social media. We gave hope by playing well and giving people the chance to put their differences aside so that, for 80 minutes, they could enjoy something special. It wasn't our responsibility to do this – it was our privilege.

I also had the opportunity to pay tribute to Siya sitting next to me. I told the journalists of his struggles, not only to get opportunities to play rugby, but also to get food, shoes to wear, and a way to get to school. I continued, 'And then you think, here he sits as a captain, and he led South Africa ...' – I paused to control my emotions as I nudged the Webb Ellis Cup towards him – '... to hold this cup. I think that should sum up what Siya is.'

It was taking a long time for the realisation to sink in that we had won the cup and were now the world champions. I was caught up with what the players had spoken about in the weeks before the final. Mapimps talked about the young woman Uyinene Mrwetyana, who was raped and bludgeoned to death at a post office in Claremont a week before we flew to Japan. We spoke about so many problems back home. But we had this thing where I said, 'Stop saying you want to give hope and inspire people if you're ranked number six in the world.' I said we must never use those phrases until we were actually in a position to do something meaning-ful. Now, as world champions, I felt we had a little more power to say, 'If we work together, we can be successful.' I was feeling somewhat over-whelmed that we had done it.

I missed the bulk of the celebrations in the change room when the players were drinking champagne out of the Webb Ellis Cup, Frans Steyn was challenging Prince Harry to a down-down, and Faf was walking around in his underpants in the colours of the South African flag.

The next night we attended the World Rugby Awards in Tokyo where the Springboks won Team of the Year, Pieter-Steph won Player of the Year, and I was named Coach of the Year. I received my award from the great All Black captain and fellow loose forward, Richie McCaw.

I then had a chance to pay tribute to the other coaches nominated in my category. I spoke about how the All Blacks had set the bar very high over the past 12 years and how we had to be like them. I said we had enjoyed the 24 hours since winning the World Cup and promised we would enjoy the next two weeks, but then we had to get back to work to try to emulate New Zealand.

While the relief and satisfaction of winning the World Cup was still sinking in, I was already planning for the next big challenge, which was winning the three-Test series against the British and Irish Lions in 2021. When I took over the Springbok job, I had 618 days to prepare for the World Cup. We now had 614 days to prepare for the Lions. We needed to be consistent. We had lost seven out of 14 Tests in 2018, but only one in 2019. There was precious little time to sit back and enjoy victory. We had work to do.

Little did I know that the Covid pandemic was just four months away, and how devastating its impact would be.

I had experienced a trophy tour once before when I was the coach of Free State and we brought the Currie Cup back to Bloemfontein. It was incredible to see the emotions of the Cheetahs fans who hadn't seen the Currie Cup in their home city for 29 years. Now, as the Springbok coach, I saw what winning the World Cup meant to South Africans from all walks of life. I remember a young girl running barefoot next to the bus for five or six kilometres, loving every moment because everyone around her was happy. I saw the young boy who wept when Siya signed his boots. I saw people who surely had no reason to be happy with their lives but were happy for those few seconds as we passed by. The trophy tour was important for ordinary South Africans to come together and celebrate.

There was so much happiness that week as we travelled around the country. But happiness doesn't change anything. Happiness doesn't take away your poverty.

Why am I hanging in here in 2023? It's not so I can say we've won another World Cup. After the victory in 2019, I thought somebody would drive this unity we were all feeling, but here we are in 2023 and we're still battling with a lot of things in South Africa.

I'm not sure I can appreciate my place in history. People don't talk about transformation in rugby as much these days. It's not such a big issue any more, and I'm very happy about the role I have played in that. I feel that was much bigger than lifting the World Cup trophy. I got transformation right, even when people said Siya shouldn't be the captain, when people criticised me for playing Sbu and Aphiwe, claiming they were inexperienced, when people told me my players were racists because they chased Mapimps away from their celebration.

For me, the massive achievement has been the EPD Pathway. I did it not because I thought one day I'm going to coach the Springboks. I did it because I could do something to give people an equal chance. Wouldn't South Africa be a better place if everyone were given an equal chance? And if they don't take their chance, they don't make the team.

I think we were lucky that we won the World Cup. The margins between winning and losing are so small, three points here and three points there. But I was trying to fix something much bigger than that. I want people to recognise that we succeeded because we had so many supporting the team, because we were not picking from just white players – we had black talent there as well. People can say, 'Had you not won that trophy, your efforts would have meant nothing.' Yes, we won it, it's symbolic, and the fans have something to hold onto. But it drains you when you think, 'Fuck, what if we hadn't?' Sometimes I feel so frustrated that we weren't able to capitalise on our success and appreciate just how much rugby had changed.

19

IN DECEMBER 2019, the first reports appeared of an outbreak of a coronavirus in Wuhan in China. It was the first time we had heard of Covid-19, but I paid no attention to it initially, and why would I? On 30 January, the World Health Organization (WHO) declared Covid-19 a global health emergency, which meant nothing to me as I was watching the South African franchises in Round 1 of Super Rugby, which kicked off the day after the WHO announcement.

We managed to get through seven rounds before the world shut down. All Super Rugby matches were cancelled as Covid started to spread around the world and South Africa joined other countries in going into lockdown, throwing rugby into a crisis. The South African Rugby Employers' Organisation, to which all the provinces belong, negotiated a salary cut with the players in an effort to keep professional rugby alive.

Tours to South Africa by Scotland and Georgia in July were cancelled, followed by the Rugby Championship and then the end-of-year tour when we would have played Italy, Ireland, France and Wales. Thirteen Tests in 2020 were wiped out and, along with them, a wonderful chance to show-case the Springboks as world champions.

The shutdown also disrupted our plans for the 2021 British and Irish Lions tour and affected our preparations for the 2023 World Cup. There were still a few positions that I wanted to review, and I felt we hadn't had enough time to sift through all the players and test them under extreme conditions. I had planned to use the incoming series against Scotland, and the Rugby Championship to see which players came out on top. Suddenly those games were gone, with a huge financial loss for SARU.

Personally, the Covid pandemic affected me tremendously. I was continuing my treatment for Wegener's disease and my comorbidities were a constant worry. I really had to hide from the virus. I decided not to take any chances and stayed at home. I think I left my house three times that year. When my children went back to school after lockdown, we wore masks inside the house.

By December 2020 I was feeling less apprehensive, and we visited Frikkie and his family at Pringle Bay. When we came home, I could feel my body was aching and I was exhausted. I just wanted to sleep. My twin daughters were also feeling terrible. I had a Covid test, which was negative, and so we went off on the traditional Erasmus family holiday to Baviaanskloof. Still I wasn't feeling great, so I phoned Frikkie to check on him. His whole family had tested positive.

We just knew we would be positive as well, so we packed up and drove straight back home. For six days we felt so pap. That was the main symptom – utter fatigue. I never developed a cough or a fever, though my blood-oxygen level was around 91, which was a bit worrying. The fifth day was the worst in terms of the fatigue, but then we all started improving.

Because of Wegener's, I was quite anxious about my health, and googling for information didn't make things easier. I was fortunate in that I had the disease in my throat and not my lungs. After six days I felt much better, and fortunately did not get Covid again.

We couldn't do much in terms of rugby. For most of 2020, we couldn't have training or alignment camps. A local version of Super Rugby, called Super Rugby Unlocked, was held in October, and the Currie Cup returned from November to January, all without spectators. At least our top local players were getting some game time. We had to be creative to keep playing games and changed a few laws to make the contests interesting.

There was also the off-again, on-again debate about the fate of the British and Irish Lions tour scheduled for the following year. Various options were discussed: holding the series in Dubai, then in London at Twickenham, then somewhere in Australia. I said we were willing to play anywhere. There was a big financial incentive for us, but more importantly, we didn't want to miss the opportunity of playing the Lions, which comes around once every 12 years in South Africa. After much discussion, a decision was reached in March 2021 for the three-Test tour to take place in South Africa in July, but in accordance with strict Covid protocols and at empty stadiums.

When the 2021 international season finally started for the Springboks on 2 July 2021, we hadn't played a single Test match since the World Cup final on 2 November 2019. We were the only Tier One nation not to play Test rugby in 2020. We were scheduled to play Georgia twice, while the players in the British and Irish Lions team had played the Six Nations in 2020 and 2021, and the Lions team itself played a warm-up Test match against Japan at Murrayfield before flying over.

When their squad was announced, I noticed they had only selected three hookers, but I felt they needed four. I had an online meeting with the Lions coach Warren Gatland, with whom I was very friendly, and suggested he select a fourth hooker. I gave him a scenario in which one hooker started a game, one was injured, and one had Covid. He would then have no back-up player in a key position. A game couldn't continue if they didn't have a full front row of specialist forwards. I didn't want a situation where we would have uncontested scrums. He understood the problem and so picked a fourth hooker.

We were totally naïve in the way we handled Covid protocols. Unlike the British and Irish international teams, who were used to travelling in Covid conditions playing in the Six Nations, we were pretty clueless on what to do and how to behave. By the time the Lions arrived in South Africa on 28 June, the players were already used to the pitfalls of Covid and their protocols for testing and preventing the disease from spreading. We were far behind them in understanding what it takes to get a team through Covid. The Lions arrived in a country where there were growing Covid numbers, a 9pm curfew, a ban on the sale of alcohol and cigarettes, and restaurants were only allowed to serve takeaways.

We had a camp in Bloemfontein before travelling up to Johannesburg to prepare for our first Test of the season against Georgia at Loftus Versfeld. In accordance with Covid protocols, we booked into our hotel in Rosebank five weeks before the match. It was very frustrating for us, with the constant testing and long hours hanging around in the foyer waiting for the test results.

Our preparations for the Georgia Test were disrupted when two players, Vincent Koch and Sbu Nkosi, tested positive, while Herschel Jantjies was cleared after initially returning a false positive. In the week leading up to the game we were cleared to return to training. At the same time, a Currie Cup match between the Cheetahs and the Bulls – the Lions' opponents in a few weeks' time – was cancelled because a Cheetahs player got Covid, causing even more consternation.

Three players made their debut in that Georgia Test – Aphelele Fassi, Rosko Specman and Jasper Wiese – as we used the match to work on our goal of squad depth. The players were a bit rusty after a 20-month layoff since the World Cup final, but after half an hour, they started to click and they put in a good performance to win 40–9, scoring six tries.

It was strange playing in an empty Loftus Versfeld, but most of the players had already experienced the lack of crowds playing for their overseas clubs, in Super Rugby Unlocked or in the Currie Cup. But we weren't going to allow the lack of crowds to demotivate us, so we adapted as we went. We tried to look for the positive, which was that we could communicate easily on the field. You couldn't do that when there were 85 000 cheering fans. You couldn't even hear the player next to you. But now, with quiet stadiums, you could shout to a player who was more than 30 metres away. It was like a schoolboy match where you could hear the noisy father on the other side of the field.

Then, just as we were starting to find our rhythm, we were hit by a devastating wave of Covid that swept through the squad after the match. Eleven people tested positive – five players, including Siya, and five members of the management team, including Jacques, as well as a masseuse. Four Georgian players tested positive, as did their coach, Levan Maisashvili, who ended up on a ventilator and in a serious condition in hospital. And so the Ministerial Advisory Committee (MAC) that controlled all Covid-related matters decided that the second Test against Georgia should be cancelled, which was a devastating blow to our preparation plans.

The MAC wanted us confined to our hotel. The only people there were us and the hotel staff, but we weren't able to maintain a secure bio-bubble effectively and all too often somebody in our group came into contact with another person who was positive or who had returned a false positive, which required them to go into quarantine. Our doctor, Jerome Mampane, was one of those who had a close contact, so he had to isolate, which meant we didn't have a team doctor. We then flew in Dr Konrad von Hagen, who was our team doctor at the World Cup, to help out. But then he contracted the virus and ended up seriously ill on a ventilator in hospital. Our dietician, Zeenat Simjee, also had to be admitted to hospital. We then called SARU's medical manager, Clint Readhead, for help, but soon after he started work he had a close contact and had to isolate, which meant that we were still without medical support. The Lions, by contrast, had included four doctors in their touring squad, so they were well looked after.

We became preoccupied with the time-consuming Covid protocols. When our doctor wasn't in isolation, he had his hands full treating players who had tested positive. Once a player tested positive, we had to check who had been in close contact with him. I spent hours at night with Lindsay Weyer, our technical analyst, searching through videos of training sessions, trying to identify anyone who had been in close contact with that player for more than five seconds. If they had gone through a whole training session, that applied to just about everybody. The thing that baffled me was what about the ball? Wouldn't an infected player pass on the virus through the rugby ball? Nobody could answer that one for me.

The players were so fit and in such good shape that many of them didn't know they had Covid until they were tested. It was so frustrating for them to sit alone in their hotel room, doing their exercises on their own, eating food delivered on a tray and left outside their door. They became bored and irritable.

We were all locked in our rooms, while the Lions, because of their experience with Covid protocols during the Six Nations, were moving around with a bit more freedom. We were playing the Lions in three weeks' time and I promised we would produce 23 players who were Covid-free to make up the Springbok team.

We were now at a disadvantage because we had lost that crucial second Test against Georgia as preparation, while the tourists were getting invaluable match practice against the local Lions team at Ellis Park, and against the Sharks at Ellis Park and again at Loftus. To add to my frustration and confusion about Covid protocols, one of their coaches, Gregor Townsend, got Covid but was back at work after just seven days. If any of the Boks got Covid, he had to be in isolation for 11 days.

Because we had 11 people with Covid, the MAC said we couldn't fly to Cape Town for the South Africa A game against the Lions because if somebody on the chartered plane had Covid, everybody would get it. I repeated my promise – even if we played against the Lions with a Western Province team, we would find 23 non-positive guys.

This is probably where the tour started turning sour. I called a group of players and the management to my room and asked them to trust me. I said we couldn't continue under the current situation where we were stuck in the hotel while the Lions were playing rugby. I said, 'How the fuck are we going to play against the Lions if we don't play this SA A game in Cape Town?' We were going to get a beating because we weren't match fit and needed that game before the Tests.

I then wrote a letter to Jurie Roux in which I told him that Jacques and I were resigning because we couldn't just throw away the Springboks' name like that. I said we were in an impossible situation, and while I knew that we were on life support financially and SA Rugby needed the series to go ahead, we couldn't carry on. We were saying that he could find new coaches, but we weren't the people who would be irresponsible and put the Springboks up against international opposition and get 50 points scored against us because we hadn't played enough rugby.

Jurie was very upset. I was fighting hard. I said, 'Let's get on a call with the Lions management and the MAC and let me hear all the rules and protocols and how they're supposed to work.' My issue was that when we got Covid cases, we were isolating for 11 days from when the person tested positive, while when the Lions got Covid cases, they were isolating from when they first got symptoms, which turned out to be a shorter quarantine period. Their experience of Covid protocols during the Six Nations stood them in good stead. All I wanted to do was fly 23 healthy players to Cape Town and play the game on the Wednesday. I asked why the Lions could fly to Cape Town and not us.

The players agreed with my approach. We got onto a Teams call on the Sunday morning, and I could see on Jurie's face that he was despondent. Everyone was keeping quiet. I spoke up. 'I have something to say – Covid won, and we give up. We just can't operate like this. My players are getting depressed, they can't socialise, or see their families, or have meetings together. They're training in their rooms, doing sit-ups and push-ups using hotel furniture. We're doing everything virtually, and now we want to just get onto a field and train. We can't do that, yet you guys are flying to Cape Town.'

The Lions raised the issue of our 11 positive cases. I said I'd fly the players who didn't have Covid to Cape Town, but they objected. We had to wait until Thursday, they said, but that would mean the South Africa A game would be cancelled. I asked how we could play them after just one Test match against Georgia while they'd had four warm-up games. Their response was for us to organise our own warm-up game against someone.

'Who?' I asked. Against Western Province or something like that, was the response. I must add that they weren't being arrogant; in fact, they were talking very nicely to me.

I said this didn't make any sense. If we didn't leave that Sunday night to Cape Town, the tour was off. And they said, 'Well, then the tour is off.' I said, 'Okay, thank you for everybody's input, thank you for listening, and thank you for trying.'

Then, as I was about to click on the red 'Leave' button, I heard a member of the Lions management team speak up: 'Whoa, whoa, whoa, we are here to find solutions.'

Finally, we agreed to have another round of Covid tests, and all the players who were negative would then fly to Cape Town, and those who were positive would stay behind. Most of the management team were positive, so Stokke and I coached the team.

The Lions were properly set up at the Arabella Hotel outside Hermanus, a 90-minute drive from Cape Town. They had the place to themselves and could play on the fabulous golf course. We, on the other hand, were in a Cape Town hotel, unable to afford the same luxuries as the Lions because SARU was cash-strapped as a result of Covid and no Test matches in 2020. The hotel had a high fence around it, stopping people from wandering in and out, and the players couldn't walk around in the streets outside. We improvised as much as we could, setting up gym facilities and training bikes in the hotel's basement parking.

In the end, we were able to field a near-Test-strength side that wasn't short of experience; 16 of the team had played at the 2019 World Cup and had 522 Test caps between them. Lukhanyo captained the side, which included Morné Steyn, the hero of the Springbok team 12 years earlier when he kicked a last-minute penalty to give the Springboks victory in the second Test match of the 2009 British and Irish Lions tour, which clinched the series.

I caused a controversy when I decided to become one of the three water carriers. We always had Jacques next to the field passing on instructions to the players because, as a qualified physio, he wasn't confined to the technical area. But now he was the head coach, confined to the coaches' box, so it made sense for me to take over Jacques's role. I could only go onto the field when the clock was paused, but without the noise of the crowds, I could easily shout instructions to the players. I didn't have to run onto the field or get into a huddle to be heard over 60 000 fans.

I was then accused of wanting to be seen on TV, which was a strange criticism because I don't enjoy the limelight. But what I did want to do was give the players accurate information from Jacques. I could easily shout his instructions in Afrikaans, and if the Lions winger Duhan van der Merwe, the boy from Outeniqua High in George, was nearby, I would say things in Afrikaans that I *wanted* him to hear.

Sbu and Lukhanyo scored first-half tries, and we led 17–3 at halftime. Despite the healthy lead, I was concerned the players weren't feeling the flow of the game because of a lack of match practice. We were winning, but they couldn't seem to see *how* they were winning. I warned the players at halftime: 'The Lions will get a spark somewhere, and they're going to fucking light up.' It was as if the players were plodding through the game, waiting for try-scoring moments that didn't come. The momentum soon shifted between the teams. We were up at the start and then started sliding slowly down as the Lions gained confidence and energy.

Faf de Klerk and Marco van Staden were sin-binned, and then the

Lions staged a second-half comeback. We didn't score in the second half, but managed to hold on for a 17–13 victory. It was a huge result for us after all the uncertainty over the fate of the game: being stuck in our hotel rooms in Joburg, flying down late on a chartered flight, having only one warm-up game. Yet we had beaten a team that was living at the Arabella and had played four warm-up games.

After the match, Warren Gatland had plenty to say. He told a post-match news conference that Faf's yellow card should have been a red. Faf had been penalised for a no-arms tackle on Josh Navidi, and the referee Jaco Peyper asked TMO Marius Jonker to check if there had been contact with the head, which would have meant an automatic red. They decided that Faf had made no contact with Navidi's head, but Gatland said someone was watching a different picture to him. He said he was having a meeting with the referees the next day to get some clarity. He also made a comment about me acting as a water carrier. There was nothing in the rules that said I couldn't do the job, but Gatland was clearly not happy. He said that if I was the water boy, I better make sure I was carrying water. The first shots had been fired.

This is where the whole refereeing debacle started. There wasn't a World Rugby referee manager in South Africa, nobody to give us guide-lines or protocols if refereeing problems arose. I asked for information regarding referee protocols – how and with whom do we raise any prob-lems we might have? I knew that Gatland could phone the match referee the morning after a game and they would give him feedback. So that's the way I thought I would be able to do it as well.

I was active on Twitter and made a comment about wanting clarity on an incident of foul play in the game so that we could get alignment with the ref, so I retweeted a video clip that had been posted by a person calling himself Jaco Johan. To my amazement, people started suggesting that I was Jaco Johan, simply because he posted similar videos and had similar views to me. I have never hid behind a pseudonym to make my views heard. I was pretty honest and direct in my own tweets without having to disguise myself. I don't know who Jaco Johan is – if that's even his real name!

We managed to play another game on the Saturday, this time against the Bulls at Cape Town Stadium, before the first Test. Jacques and the other players who had tested positive finally flew down to join us, and we made 12 changes to the side so everyone had a run before the first Test. Only three players who were involved in the Lions game the previous week were retained. The Bulls won 17–14.

On the Thursday before the first Test match, I asked for a conference call with World Rugby's referee manager Joël Jutge and Director of Rugby Joe Schmidt. Jacques and Siya were also on the call. We had three items on the agenda. The first was a request that both sides handle referee issues in a positive way, because I wasn't happy about the way Gatland was talking about Faf and red cards. I didn't want to cause fights, which is why I'd phoned Gatland prior to the series when I thought he didn't have enough hookers in his team. I had prevented it being a problem. I wanted Jutge and Schmidt to ask him to stop moaning in the media.

The second item on the agenda was to remind them that they hadn't seen us playing since the World Cup. They hadn't been exposed to Siya, Jacques, me or the players for over a year. I wanted them to treat us with respect. We had worked hard prior to the World Cup to show we weren't dumb, arrogant, in-your-face people, but intelligent, passionate players. I said, 'Siya would never approach the ref if there wasn't something really bothering him.'

The third item was an invitation for them to raise anything they needed us to know about interpretation of the laws. I wanted to know if they had seen anything in the South Africa A game that worried them.

I raised Gatland's comment about me being the water boy and asked if there was a law against it. I pointed out that the Lions kicking coach Neil Jenkins was carrying water for them. Jenkins was my age, had played against me, and was doing more coaching than me. Yet it wasn't a problem for him to carry water. I said I didn't understand why Gatland was moaning about these things. It was surely common sense when there were no crowds that I passed on information to Siya. Why wouldn't you use that advantage if it's not against any protocols? As far as I knew, only the head coach was not allowed onto the field during a game.

Schmidt said it was a bad look for the game, so I suggested they keep the cameras off me. The problem couldn't be that I was intimidating or influencing the referees because I didn't speak to the referee at all, only to the players. My role was practical, but it was also tactical, just like it was for any other team that had someone at the side of the field passing on instructions from the coach. I said I would stop being the water boy if it was fucking up the game. But until then, I would carry on. World Rugby subsequently changed the law in 2022 to exclude the Director of Rugby from being a water carrier.

Jutge and Schmidt promised me that they would talk to Gats, as they called him. Even in that meeting they couldn't give me a protocol on how to communicate with referees after a match. It struck me as incredible that Jutge wasn't even in South Africa. To my knowledge, it was the first time in history that a referee manager wasn't physically present at a British and Irish Lions series.

20

A FEW DAYS BEFORE THE FIRST TEST, the decision was taken to play all three Tests at Cape Town Stadium because both teams were in secure environments, and it was felt that travelling back to Joburg would increase the risk of positive cases. That decision took away our advantage of playing at altitude.

Things got heated when Marius Jonker was appointed as TMO for all three Tests. He was the guy who had said Faf's tackle on Navidi wasn't a red, which had upset Gatland. We knew Gatland was unhappy that neutral TMOs weren't available. The original TMO, Brendon Pickerill of New Zealand, couldn't come after New Zealand Rugby recommended that their match officials should not travel to South Africa because of the Covid situation. There was also a concern that Pickerill might not be able to return home due to New Zealand's strict Covid rules.

Gatland was careful not to say anything in public, but it was widely reported by different rugby journalists that he was unhappy. The Lions' assistant coach Robin McBryde took up the issue and complained at a media briefing that World Rugby had no plan B, and that there was a reason why the TMO should be a neutral appointment. It was blatant intimidation of Marius, though World Rugby would later say his comments – while unhelpful and against the spirit of the game – didn't meet the threshold for formal charges to be laid against him.

I took up the issue publicly and said it didn't sit well with me that

Marius's integrity was being questioned because he was a South African. He had a lot of experience, having refereed 25 Test matches and been the TMO in over 40 other Tests, including a World Cup semifinal. During the 2020 Rugby Championship, they had local TMOs and there was no problem. I told the media that if New Zealand referee Ben O'Keeffe made wrong decisions in the second Test, we wouldn't say it was because he was a New Zealander and so was Gatland.

Ahead of the first Test, we had a good 20-minute meeting with Nic Berry, the referee, getting clarity on his interpretation of some of the laws. We asked for the opportunity to give feedback after the game, so that we understood where we had gone wrong and could work on correcting those faults. We asked Berry to show us as much respect as he would the Lions. They had a lot of leaders on the field, including at least three national captains, so we suggested that only the captains and vice-captains on the day speak to him. From our side, they were Siya and Handré.

We played the Test at an empty Cape Town Stadium and the Springboks were ahead 12–3 at halftime, all through penalties. But we were lacking energy. Not just fitness, but mental energy. We couldn't see that we were giving the Lions a bit of a pounding. But with no crowds getting excited (apart from me shouting from the side of the field), the team seemed unresponsive. Nobody had a spark in their eyes.

Just after the break, the Lions mauled us from a lineout on the five-metre line and their hooker Luke Cowan-Dickie scored. Two minutes later, Willie went over after chasing down a grubber from Lukhanyo. Berry sent the decision upstairs to Marius, who looked at the various angles and, after a long deliberation, decided that while it was very tight, Willie was ahead of Lukhanyo when the ball was kicked forward. Offside – try disallowed.

Three minutes after that, Faf went over for a try. Once again Marius was called upon to make a ruling. There was a question over whether Pieter-Steph had knocked on the ball while trying to gather a grubber from

Mapimpi. Marius said there was no indication the ball had gone forward and Faf's try was given. We led 17–10. Dan Biggar then kicked three penalties in the next 11 minutes, and we were trailing by two points, 17–19.

Then, in the 71st minute, the Lions centre Robbie Henshaw fumbled a pass under pressure from Lukhanyo. The ball went loose and Mapimps kicked it on. Lukhanyo followed up at speed, gave the ball another kick forward, and Damian de Allende scooped it up and scored. It had been a bit of a scramble with a bouncing ball, so Berry once again sent it upstairs to Marius. Marius went all the way back to the start of the move where Cheslin had contested a high ball, and saw that he had knocked it on. Another try disallowed.

We tried to get back into the game, but silly errors gave Owen Farrell an easy penalty opportunity that he didn't miss, and we lost 17–22.

I saw in Siya's body language – in his eyes, in the way he spoke, and the way he stopped speaking to the referee – that something was seriously wrong. I knew Siya's face when he was unhappy, and I could see he was pissed off during the match. He would approach Berry to ask him something but never seemed able to get Berry's full attention. I got the impression that Berry wasn't doing the same thing to Alun Wyn Jones. I could see and hear what was going on from my position on the side of the field. I didn't discuss it with Siya at the time, but I was amazed the ref seemed to treat him like this when all he wanted was clarification on an issue. I knew Siya had been brought up to respect people in authority, which is exactly what he was doing. But it felt to me like Berry treated the two captains differently.

I don't think Nic Berry is a cheat – not at all – but I feel he didn't understand Siya and how he talks. I wasn't asking that he give South Africa an advantage, but I felt he had to be aware of our history. Here was our captain, who was black, whose first language was isiXhosa, talking to a white referee, with two white touch judges, a white TMO and a white captain of the Lions. I wanted the ref to be aware of how it looked if he wasn't giving Siya a chance. I want to be very clear – I am saying Berry appeared to me to be ignorant of the sensitive racial politics in South Africa and the perceptions he could create by dismissing Siya as easily as he did without a fair hearing. I have no doubt that his actions were not intentional, but I felt he should have been more aware.

South Africa was going through a particularly bad time. We were battling with increasing Covid numbers, the country had been in flames just a week earlier when violence and looting hit KwaZulu-Natal and parts of Gauteng, former President Jacob Zuma had been imprisoned for ignoring a subpoena, the media was filled with seemingly never-ending stories of massive corruption revealed by the Zondo Commission of Inquiry, and there was an electricity crisis. I sometimes wonder if there was a subconscious bias against this team from the Third World country that couldn't afford to stay at a fancy golf estate and battled to even have a team doctor available.

I thought Marius had made a terrible call regarding Willie's try and blamed the pressure Gatland had put him under. But I bit my tongue and said that's fine, some things go against you. I sent Marius a WhatsApp voice note in Afrikaans after the game in which I told him I understood his difficult position. I said Gatland had been quite clever (or 'sharp', as I put it) in putting pressure on him. I reminded him we were good friends and that I would always value our friendship. I told him I knew he always did his best and had made some really tough calls. He replied, *'Dankie, Rassie. Dit was tough, ons praat in die week. Waardeer'* (Thanks, Rassie. It was tough, we'll talk in the week. Appreciate it).

I wasn't angry or frustrated. I thought our performance was a culmi-nation of a lack of match practice, no in-person pre-match meeting with the referee, not knowing what the protocols were, and not getting Berry to understand what I was trying to say about Siya. Because my job was to make sure that everybody was in sync, I felt I had failed. I had let the team and the country down. I was thinking, 'Fuck it, there're a whole lot

246

of things we must fix before we see these players again on Monday.'

I wanted to keep a positive mood, so I tweeted my congratulations to the Lions and acknowledged that some calls go for you and some go against you. I felt we were set up nicely for the second and third Test matches. All good.

The next day, we did a full video analysis of the match, and that evening the coaching staff met to discuss issues we needed to work on and to select the team for the second Test. Before we gave feedback to the players and named the team, we needed clarity from Berry on specific things that had happened in the game.

The thing that still bothered me, and where I cracked a bit, was the way I believed Siya had been treated. I have fought so hard for people in South Africa, particularly some white people, to accept Siya as a captain who deserves the position. He had proved himself by winning the World Cup. This was an urgent matter that had to be sorted out quickly. I was concerned that Siya's own players would think the referee didn't respect him. I wanted to phone Berry and ask him if he had a problem with Siya. I asked Deon van Blommenstein, who was the referees' liaison officer, to send him a message.

Berry was in the bath when Deon messaged him, but he later contacted Deon and requested the video clips. Shortly after that he sent another message, saying he wouldn't have time to discuss them that evening but would do so after he had spoken to Joël Jutge. Berry then called me on AJ Jacobs's phone and asked me to send him the video clips before a proposed meeting between him, Jutge and my coaching team. We then transferred the files to him.

He came back to me half an hour later and said he couldn't have the meeting with me. He said he hadn't received the video clips yet. I told him they were still transferring. He then said he didn't have permission from Jutge to discuss the clips. I later learnt that Jutge had told him my request was 'highly unusual' and 'out of protocol'. My response was that I needed his feedback urgently to assist us with our team selection and give the players clarity, but he wasn't interested. I told him that I didn't want to go the Lions route and talk in the media about this, as they had done with Faf's yellow card and Marius's appointment. I told him we didn't want to fight in the media.

I found it all quite strange because Berry had always been happy to chat through things. He and I exchanged emails in which he confirmed he got the video clips and would complete the review the next day. He said he didn't feel the delay would influence our selection. But I wasn't happy and told him it didn't work for us in terms of our timelines. I wrote that we felt the pressure the Lions attempted to put on the match officials through the media actually worked well and that we would be doing the same that week. He replied that anything put in the media has no effect on the match officials, last week or this week. Of course, my comment about not wanting to fight this in the media would come back to bite me when World Rugby accused me of threatening Berry.

I tried phoning Jutge but got his answering machine, so we had to delay our team selection. He then got back to me and complained that I wasn't following protocol. Yet they hadn't told us what the protocol was, despite me asking. I told him I didn't know what the big deal was – I just wanted to talk to the referee. Gatland had been free to talk to the referees after the Lions' midweek games. Why was this any different?

I realised I was getting nowhere. We were gatvol, so I decided we should just forward some video clips, about 28 of them, to Jutge, showing where we had problems with Berry's refereeing. We sent the clips on the Sunday evening. There was no response on the Monday, which was frustrating because the players wanted feedback and we wanted to select our team. All we got was an email from Jutge giving us, at last, the guidelines for communicating with referees. That morning, we were told the protocol for engaging with referees would be the same one used for the Six Nations. This was now two days *after* the Test match. The protocol said referee feedback would be given on a Tuesday.

When Jutge finally replied on the Tuesday morning, he forwarded us the answers Berry had sent him. I wasn't satisfied that Berry had given us any clarity. It was as if he hadn't given his answers much thought. I knew the laws of rugby and I knew where he was simply wrong.

I sat with my assistant coaches and discussed what to do next. I said, 'Okay, there's only one way.' And so I made the fateful decision to make a video that explained our problems precisely. I asked our videographer, Russell Belter, a long-time colleague who had worked extensively for us at the 2019 World Cup creating videos and filming our training sessions and alignment camps, to help me.

Here's how he remembers what happened:

The Sunday after the first Test, all the coaches met to discuss the game as they usually did. Rassie was properly agitated. Felix Jones, the defence coach, is an incredible analyst and had already cut all the video clips from the game.

The coaches – Rassie, Jacques, Felix, Deon Davids [forwards coach], Daan Human [scrum coach] and Mzwandile Stick – all agreed the ref was shocking, and the way he treated Siya really upset Rassie. Rassie was trying to get hold of Jöel Jutge, but he had no luck.

What upset Rassie, and he kept coming back to it, was that they needed to select the team for the second Test. They always picked the team on the Sunday night and announced it to the players on the Monday morning. Rassie said: 'If I'm wrong about the way the referees are blowing the game, then I have to change my team selection. But if the referees have made a mistake, then I have to choose this team.'

Because he wasn't getting feedback quickly enough, he was getting more and more frustrated. The coaches spent much of the evening going through Felix's video clips and asking: 'Are we wrong or are the referees wrong?'

Rassie constantly played devil's advocate, saying, 'Let's look at this from a referee's point of view. Could the referee see the infringement from where he was standing?' Then they looked at the infringement from the TMO's perspective and finally analysed the decision according to the laws of the game. They went to bed that night frustrated that they weren't getting any answers from World Rugby.

At 7am the next morning, the coaches had their usual Monday meeting. I was in the room with them, filming it. They still hadn't received responses from any referees, so they checked on the injury list with team doctor Jerome Mampane and selected the team with all the assistant coaches having a say. Then they had another discussion about how to deal with the referee issue. Rassie said: 'If they're not going to answer my emails, I'm going to shoot a video and insert the clips of the incidents we're unhappy about.'

He asked me to produce [the video using the clips from the match] and to put in graphics like circles and arrows, slow the play down, and zoom in on certain things to highlight the point. The coaches went off to do the team announcement and the players left for training.

The next day, Tuesday, Rassie, Human Kriek [one of the video analysts], and I started work on the video.

I positioned Rassie in front of the camera with his laptop where he had a timeline of all the things he wanted to talk about. We filmed his talk and then started adding the graphics, which took about eight hours to complete.

The video had a 15-minute intro because I wanted to set out the background. Because of the restrictions caused by Covid, we were in an isolation bubble, and I felt I needed to provide context for our grievances to those people who weren't physically with us. I started off addressing the issue of me being the water carrier. I pointed out that World Rugby had increased the number of water carriers allowed on the field from two to three, and that the only restriction was that the head coach couldn't be one of the three, and that I wasn't the head coach – Jacques was. I also said I understood why Gatland would raise this issue because it was all part of the mind games, and that was okay – we took it in our stride.

I raised what I referred to as 'a little bit of a grey area' when Gatland spoke openly in the media about wanting to get clarity from World Rugby about dangerous tackles, referring particularly to the complaints about Faf's yellow card in the South Africa A game. If they could raise this issue in this way, surely we were allowed to show instances where we felt aggrieved by the ref's decision. I had posted a couple of clips on social media and regarded it as part of the banter.

I spoke about an issue that particularly concerned me, which I referred to as the narrative that the Springboks are a dirty team that always wants to be physical. I also referred to the complaints in the media from the Lions about Marius Jonker's appointment as TMO. I said that I wanted this Test series to be played in a positive environment and didn't want more ill feeling in a country where we already had so much negativity.

I listed the people who I wanted to see this video – Joël Jutge, Joe Schmidt, Nic Berry, the other two referees Ben O'Keeffe and Mathieu Raynal, Marius Jonker – and then I hesitated briefly and added, 'Uh … SuperSport, maybe if you guys get this eventually, I'm not sure who this is going to.'

I was later accused of threatening to leak the video when I said I didn't know where the video was going. What I meant with my comment was: 'Take me seriously, look at this video, give me genuine answers, don't brush us off like we're a Third World country.'

I understood there would be consequences to making the video and said that if it meant I couldn't be the water carrier, I would step away from the role. If it meant we got a fine, I would step away from the team management. If the Springboks were in trouble, I would take sole responsibility and say I was acting on my own.

I wasn't accusing Berry of being a cheat; I just wanted clarity on issues of concern, which I felt I hadn't received, and I wanted the Lions and the Springboks to get equal opportunities for a fair contest.

Then I went through 38 different refereeing incidents that raised concerns for us. The video contained the same clips I had sent Jutge before. I hoped that I was doing it in such a way that they understood our frustration that we weren't getting real answers, preventing us from coaching properly.

I showed Lions flanker Tom Curry's late hit on Faf, which was punished with a penalty, and asked if we shoulder-charged like that, would it always just get a penalty? I was inferring that it should have been a yellow card. I showed side entries and foul play by the Lions that weren't penalised, and inconsistencies in the way high tackles were policed. I analysed footage of a tip-tackle by flanker Hamish Watson on Willie le Roux where Watson didn't get a yellow card, and a similar incident involving winger Duhan van der Merwe, which also escaped attention.

I went through a series of ruck infringements and showed the inconsistencies between what Berry told us before the match and how he actually refereed the game. I took issue with the pressure applied to Marius Jonker, which I felt was the reason he disallowed Willie's try for offside.

The big thing for me was showing the instances where as I saw it the ref and his assistants blatantly ignored Siya and disrespected our players. I described the difference in the levels of respect shown by the assistant referees towards the Springboks compared with the Lions as 'comical'.

I dealt with a number of issues of player safety, which is a big concern for World Rugby. I showed an incident, right in front of Berry, where Curry, from the flank position, scrummed onto our loosehead prop Ox Nché, forcing him up and causing a neck injury that ruled Ox out for the next two Tests. Not only was Curry's action not penalised, but Berry awarded a penalty to the Lions.

At the end of the video, I repeated that I didn't know where the video was going or even where I would be after this because I was expecting a huge backlash. I said, 'If you think this is going over the top and it shouldn't go out to the media, then I did this in my own personal capacity, not as part of the Springboks, and I'll withdraw myself from the Springbok management team.' I offered to stand down if I was wrong.

For the rest of that Tuesday, Russell edited the video and later he sent me a link to the finished product. Russell recalls:

Rassie stayed in the room the whole time while I was editing, pacing up and down behind me. He never looked at what we were doing, but he listened. Every now and then he asked me: 'Hierdie video sal privaat wees, nè?' (This video will be private, won't it?) He was concerned about that.

We finished the video, and once Rassie and Felix had watched it from start to finish and approved it, I uploaded it to my Vimeo account. From 2019, I had been giving Rassie videos on Vimeo with a private link to distribute to the players. My private Vimeo account has never been hacked, and no unauthorised person has ever found a video on that account. The name I gave the video was a series of nine random numbers, so it would be anonymous. Only the people with the private link would be able to access the video. It was impossible for anyone to search for the video using a search engine unless the person was already in possession of the link.

I didn't think we needed password protection for the video. I know from experience that many people are technophobes or ignorant about technology. If you make it too difficult for them to watch a video, they simply won't watch it. If you add a password that contains a mixture of letters in upper- and lower-case and a variety of symbols, people invariably get it wrong. It was important that Jutge could simply click on a link and the video would play immediately. Rassie didn't want Jutge to have a reason to say he hadn't watched the video because he couldn't access it. If someone wanted to leak the video, they would simply leak the password as well.

We also wanted the video to play on any device no matter how bad the bandwidth. That's why I chose Vimeo, which detected a low bandwidth and delivered an appropriate quality video. YouTube was a dangerous platform because it was too accessible to the broader public.

I shared the link with Rassie shortly before 10pm on Tuesday night. He told me he would send the link to the people he wanted to view the video.

Just after 7am on Wednesday morning, I sent an email with the Vimeo link to Nic Berry, Joël Jutge, Joe Schmidt, Jacques Nienaber and Jurie Roux. I also sent the link to the Springbok players and coaches on our WhatsApp group.

Jutge emailed me shortly after 2pm that same day and complimented us, saying it was 'a big and good work [sic]. You have good competencies around you.' He said he agreed with most of the issues we had raised. He also took my point that the review had to happen earlier and said it would now take place on the Monday morning after a game, and the refs would be available by the afternoon.

I was satisfied and thought, 'Job done!' They now knew we were serious. They'd seen the video and they'd heard what I had to say.

On that Monday morning after the match, before we made the video or had any feedback from Jutge, I wondered if we should change the captain for the remaining two Test matches. It was, however, a very brief thought and we swiftly moved on with complete confidence in Siya as our captain.

While waiting for the feedback on our video clips we did our normal reviews, and on Tuesday morning we gave the players time off while we worked on the video. When they got back together again, we wanted to have answers for them. We couldn't coach the players if a referee penalised something we were training them to do. We needed to understand what the referee's interpretation of the law was and how strictly they would police certain aspects of the game, so we could train properly in the build-up to the next Test. We couldn't ask them to trust what we were showing them at practice when they were experiencing something totally the opposite from the ref on the field. We weren't dealing with children; we were dealing with 35 adults. We couldn't bullshit them.

Russell comments:

I kept an eye on the number of views to see where it was being viewed. On that Wednesday morning, two and a half hours after Rassie sent out the link, I saw it had been viewed 31 times in South Africa and alerted Rassie via WhatsApp. Seven hours later, at 1.48pm, I sent him another message to tell him the video had been viewed 54 times, twice in Cahors, France, where Jutge was, three times in the United Kingdom (Bristol, Reading and Palmers Green), and eight times in Brisbane, Australia, where Nic Berry was from. He replied: 'Hoe de fok in Australië en UK?' (How the fuck in Australia and the UK?) I replied, 'Geen idee, die refs deel miskien jou mail' (No idea, maybe the refs are sharing your mail).

Within 36 hours, the number of views shot up incredibly. People all over the world were watching it, downloading it and, I presume, copying it and sending it on again. It started appearing on social media and on YouTube. That's when we lost control of it. I started getting calls from international broadcasters for a broadcast-quality version. I ignored the calls and told Rassie I was now password-protecting the video. But it was too late – the video was already out there.

It is impossible, from a technical aspect, to determine who leaked the video. I could see in which town or city it was viewed, but it was impossible to know who shared the video. Password-protection was meaningless because the person sharing the private Vimeo link could also simply share the password.

From what I could see, the video was played in 65 countries around the world, including surprising places like Iraq, the Cayman Islands,

Vietnam and Malta. Most of the views were in South Africa, the UK, Ireland and Australia.

We have tried to find out where the video was first leaked, but no one can tell me. No one can tell me where or when it became public knowledge. I can tell you this: after that video, nobody spoke about how badly Berry had refereed that match.

I'm not accusing Berry of leaking the video. It could have been anyone. I just can't believe that people would think that, after I had got the result that I wanted from Jutge as the referee manager, I would now go and fuck it up by leaking the video. That would totally sway the referees against us.

I did not leak that video. I would never have leaked that video. I had nothing to gain from doing that and I knew it would cause big trouble for me if it was in the public domain. However, I had to get World Rugby's attention and the referees' attention. They needed to know that they couldn't just look at the clips and ignore me. They had to take their time and give me proper answers. I wanted Jutge to know that if he didn't respond properly, it could end up on SuperSport. I felt that if I said that, he would not brush us off.

This is how Frikkie saw the situation:

The general perception is that it was Rassie who leaked his video, even though he did not release it publicly. Rassie sent the video with its link to a restricted group, only comprising Joël Jutge and Joe Schmidt of World Rugby, Nic Berry, Jurie Roux, Jacques Nienaber and some 40 Springboks and coaching staff.

There is, however, email proof that within 33 minutes of Rassie sending the link, and even before Berry could have viewed the full 62-minute video, Berry forwarded the link to his personal referee coach in Australia, Mitchell Chapman, who in turn forwarded it to four other Rugby Australia officials.

*This is proof that the video was released by Berry to someone outside
of Rassie's restricted group. Analytics of the Vimeo platform showed
that, of the first views of the video, eight were in Australia. Berry is not
accused of any malice in providing Mitchell Chapman with the video. In
fact, his email to Chapman reads: 'Just so you're in the loop. I don't want
this to disrupt Ben's presentation so let's be smart how we handle it.'*

*The [World Rugby] Judicial Committee did not find that Rassie
leaked the video. The Committee found that Rassie's action in sending the
link to the restricted group, without password-protection and without a
privacy setting, amounted to publication and that he therefore published
or caused the video to be published.*

The reaction to the video was overwhelming. Some journalists described
it as 'a rant'. One writer said it was one of the most controversial moments
in recent rugby history. I was accused of turning the Lions series toxic.
Rugby Australia accused me of abusing Berry and said, 'The attack on
Nic's integrity, character and reputation is unacceptable.' The condemna-
tion was widespread and furious.

I found support from South African fans and some rugby writers, who
felt I was justified in standing up against bad refereeing, and from former
players like Bob Skinstad, who said the video was risky but I had a point.

The reaction to the video on the Wednesday morning was a massive
distraction. But I had to put it behind me because we had to prepare for
the second Test. All I can say is that I experienced so many different emotions in the build-up to the game. I had never, ever in my life been so
nervous as I was before that match. By the way they were looking at me, I
knew the players were concerned.

My philosophy of having the Director of Rugby act as a shield for the
head coach to protect him from all the noise was put firmly to the test and
it worked as I had expected. Jacques and I always worked well together.
I took all the shit away from him and the team, and he concentrated on

coaching and making sure the team was properly prepared. In the first news conference after the video appeared, I told Jacques I would go with him to field all the questions about the video, and then he could handle all the rugby issues.

The fallout from the video wasn't a factor for the players in their preparation. They knew they had played badly in the first Test and allowed the Lions back into the game in the second half. Our scrums and our ball-carries had to be better. We told the players we would clarify the refereeing decisions as the week went on. We told them there'd be no moaning about the ref during training. It was time to fix ourselves.

I knew, though, that the leak upset the players. I confronted them about it because they all received the link. I said, 'If some of you leaked the video, please come and tell me. Don't let me make my name asshole, don't let me lie to people. If one of you WhatsApped the link by accident, tell me.' I was satisfied the leak didn't come from a player. They wouldn't do that to me.

21

AFTER THE LONGEST WEEK, we finally played the second Test. Within two minutes, the tension that had been building all week bubbled over. Alun Wyn Jones objected to something Mapimps did in a ruck, and grabbed him by the jersey. Immediately, other players joined in the scuffle. It was nothing more serious than pushing and shoving, with Eben Etzebeth and Jones eyeballing each other from close range and grinning at each other.

Referee Ben O'Keeffe stamped his authority on the game immediately by calling Siya and Jones away from the other players to explain why he gave South Africa a penalty. He put his foot down and told the captains: 'I'm going to give you both a simple and clear message.' I was satisfied he was giving Siya as much respect as he was Jones.

Then came two yellow cards, one for each team. Duhan van der Merwe was sin-binned for kicking Cheslin, despite assertions from him and his captain that he was trying to kick the ball while being nowhere near it. A few minutes later, Cheslin was blatantly wrong in his clumsy attempt to field the ball and clattered into an airborne Conor Murray to earn a yellow card. The incident unleashed another wave of anger as players from both sides piled into each other. Again the situation didn't escalate and a confrontation between two of the biggest players, Eben and Maro Itoje, ended in nothing more serious than a smiling, staring contest.

Marius Jonker was called on to rule on a Lions try shortly before halftime. The replay showed Robbie Henshaw gathering a chip over the top by Murray and falling over the line with three Springbok players smothering him. He was confident he had scored, and the Lions ran back to the halfway line. Marius took his time and saw that Henshaw had knocked on.

With so much attention focused on the match officials, they were leaving nothing to chance. They took their time with all their decisions, and frequently went upstairs to Marius to review contentious moments. The result was that the first half, in real time, was 62 minutes long – longer than my video.

At halftime we were 6–9 down, with all the points coming from the boots of Pollard and Biggar. Even though we were trailing, I wasn't worried because the feeling among the players was different from the first Test when we had led at the break. In that game, I knew we would lose because the players didn't realise they had the upper hand and allowed the Lions to turn the game around.

But in this second Test, the feeling was the opposite. We were down by three points but we were dominating. The players could feel they had momentum. They were determining the pace of the game and going in harder. They were in total control of when they ran and when they kicked the ball.

Four minutes after the break, Handré put through a perfectly timed crosskick to Mapimps on the left wing, who cut back strongly, breaking fullback Stuart Hogg's tackle and scoring.

We led 11–9 in the 60th minute when the forwards set up a powerful driving maul to within five metres of the Lions' tryline. Faf collected the ball and put in a neat grubber for Lukhanyo to dive on and score just inside the dead-ball line. I felt the Lions couldn't come back after that. After all the problems we had faced to get this far, I finally felt we had a fair contest. Handré then kicked three more penalties, and we won 27–9.

While Jacques and the assistants in the coaches' box high-fived each other, I ran into the change room and hid behind the Jacuzzis. I had so much pent-up emotion that I lay down and cried with relief. We hadn't won the series yet, but I had stuck my neck out such a long way and was really feeling the intense scrutiny.

Someone had leaked the video and now I was being called a sore loser, unprofessional, pathetic, a terrible sportsman, every insult you could think of. I was being asked, 'Is that how you want your kids to look at you? Is that what you teach your players?' I guess the thing that hurt most was that people thought I could be so sharp in the way I played and coached rugby but so stupid in life, damaging my career and the Springbok name by leaking a video. It was so insulting. How stupid do you have to be to send a video to the referees, get the feedback you wanted, and then anger those same referees by leaking it anyway and making the world hate you?

The stress had been unbelievable and I had a lot of self-doubt. I wasn't sure if I had done the right thing in making the video in the first place, and initially I wasn't convinced my own players believed me when I said I didn't leak it. I knew many people around the world had already found me guilty, but that's how it works in the court of public opinion.

I received some encouragement from some of the Irish players I had worked with at Munster. They came up to me before the game and shared some light banter, a wink and a smile. I was feeling quite alone at the time, and those gestures made me realise that the hatred I was experiencing wasn't universal. I didn't feel completely isolated because I was getting a lot of support from South Africans from all walks of life.

Once again, I sent Marius a voice note, saying no matter which way the calls went, I would never point a finger at him. I told him that the way he handled the situation took balls, and he was a man with balls. He replied, 'Well done, Rassie. *Geniet die oomblik*' (Enjoy the moment).

For the first time in the series, we went for five forwards and three backs on the bench for the third and final Test, instead of the usual 6–2 split we had used for the first two Tests. We brought in Morné Steyn because I knew he would kick a last-minute penalty to win the match and the series. Lions series are always incredibly tight, and I was convinced we needed a goal-kicker who could slot the big one, which Morné had done many times before, most famously to win the Lions series in 2009.

We were mentally prepared for this match. Most of the Springbok players had been in the World Cup final, the semifinal and the second Test where, if they had lost, it was over, so they understood the pressure. The Lions were now in the same boat. They also had a gun to their head. The pressure and the tension were extreme for both teams going into that final week with only one match standing between the players and destiny.

The Lions made the first significant breakthrough when they overpowered us at our own mauling game and hooker Ken Owens forced his way over for a try. Handré kept us in the game with two penalties and we were behind 6–10 at halftime.

Sixteen minutes into the second half, Cheslin produced another moment of magic that we often take for granted. Willie made a break down the right-hand touchline and passed outside to Cheslin, who still had 30 metres to the tryline and fullback Liam Williams and Cowan-Dickie to beat. He stepped inside Williams, leaving him sprawled on the ground, and then backed out of Cowan-Dickie's attempted tackle before sprinting to the line to score. It was a magnificent try and gave us a 13–10 lead. In the TMO's box, Marius took a long look at the build-up to the move when Jasper Wiese failed to control a high ball that bounced off him. Marius ruled the ball went up and not forwards. The try stood.

Lions replacement flyhalf Finn Russell levelled the score when Jasper was penalised for a shoulder charge. Then Morné came on for his first Test in five years, and almost immediately kicked a tricky 35-metre penalty from the right-hand side of the field, before Russell brought the Lions level again: 16–all with six minutes to play. The game was now unbearably tense, and the fate of the match and the series depended on one mistake either way.

That mistake came from the Lions with only a minute left. Morné stepped up to take the crucial penalty to win the series as he had done 12 years earlier. As with the Loftus penalty, it was straight down the middle. He struck it perfectly and the Springboks led 19–16 with a minute left to wind down the clock. The hooter sounded when the Lions won a last-gasp scrum. The match was still in the balance. Our forwards, under intense pressure, were magnificent in winning a penalty and all Morné had to do was tap the ball and kick it high into the stands. The series was ours.

As the Springbok celebrations erupted on the field, I again ran into the change room and hid behind the Jacuzzis. Once again I was overwhelmed with relief. If we had lost, the backlash would have been extreme. None of the previous battles would have been worth it. But we had won, and I felt, 'Okay, shit, the Springbok name has been saved.'

I can't tell you why I had this hunch about Morné kicking the vital penalty. I can't explain why I can sometimes predict events happening on the field. No one believes me.

Jacques has experienced it many times:

Over the past 30 years of working with Rassie, I've become used to his hunches and how accurate they are. I'm a man of science, and this is something I can't explain. On the day we selected the team he said to me we must pick Morné. He said it wasn't a hunch; he could see it.

This had happened before when we coached Munster for the last time before returning to South Africa. We were playing Racing 92 at Thomond Park in terrible weather conditions. The halftime score was 3–all. In the change room Rassie said to our scrumhalf Conor Murray, 'Keep putting pressure on the kickers; I see a charge-down and a try being scored.' He didn't say, 'I think there will be …'; he said, 'I see …' Early in the second half, Conor charged down a clearance kick from Racing's flyhalf Dan Carter and scored a try. We ended up winning the game.

When we played the All Blacks in Wellington in 2019, just before halftime he instructed me to go onto the field and tell Duane Vermeulen that we shouldn't play between the two 10-metre lines. His words were: 'I see them turning the ball over, spreading it wide and scoring a try. Please tell them to kick the ball dead and keep the pressure on them.' But I couldn't get onto the field in time to pass on the message. Rassie was going ballistic, shouting on the radio, 'Jacques, I saw a turnover coming! You guys don't trust me, I'm seeing it!' The next thing, Duane was tackled, the ball spat out, the All Blacks gathered, threw two passes out wide, and scored. Just as Rassie had predicted.

Another time he could 'see' something happening was when we were watching the Barbarians playing New Zealand on TV and he 'saw' the final score. I took a video on my phone of what happened. The video starts with Rassie sitting on the couch saying the Barbarians have the upper hand, and he tells me to point the camera at the screen. The video shows the score is 17–5 to New Zealand in the 32nd minute. I then point the camera back at Rassie. He says, 'The final score will be 31–22 to New Zealand, and after this you can call me Nostradamus.'

We left it there and went outside to have a braai, forgetting about the game. Two hours later, the game had finished, and Rassie suddenly remembered his prediction. I looked it up. Same score.

So when Rassie said he could 'see' Morné kicking the final penalty, I knew what he meant and we brought him into the squad.

We had been against the ropes so many times in the past two years. Trailing England in successive Test matches in 2018, losing to New Zealand at the World Cup, down and out against the All Blacks in Wellington, but each time we emerged victorious. History remembers Willie John McBride in 1974. Now history would remember Siya Kolisi in 2021. After all the battles, the bitterness, the controversy and the insults, the feeling of victory was incredibly satisfying.

But I still had another battle to face.

22

FIVE DAYS BEFORE THE THIRD TEST, World Rugby informed me I would be facing a disciplinary inquiry and sent me a summary of the charges. The following week, when World Rugby sent me the charge document, I got the full details of what I was up against.

I faced six charges of contravening World Rugby's Code of Conduct and Regulation 18 relating to misconduct (in essence, making statements that are insulting and that bring match officials and/or the game of rugby into disrepute). All the charges related to what was now being called the 'Erasmus Video', and the accusation that I had threatened Nic Berry that unless a meeting took place, I would publish video clips of his performance. I was charged with 'making good on that threat' by publishing the Erasmus Video or permitting it to be published. On top of that, I was also charged with denigrating the game, impairing public confidence in the integrity of the match officials, and bringing the game into disrepute by releasing the video.

While I prepared for the disciplinary hearing, the Springboks were involved in the Rugby Championship, winning both matches against Argentina in Port Elizabeth and then flying to Australia's Gold Coast to play Australia and New Zealand. My presence with the team would have been a major distraction, so I decided not to go and watched from home as we lost three games in a row, twice to Australia and once to New Zealand, before winning our final match against the All Blacks. Three of the games were decided by a last-minute penalty, including the win against New Zealand. We ended up coming third in the Rugby Championship, winning just three of our six matches.

I was in France, looking at venues for the Springboks at the 2023 World Cup, when the disciplinary hearing took place on 27 October and on 30 and 31 October. A couple of weeks earlier, given the huge publicity around the issue, I applied for the hearing to be held in public. I wanted the opportunity to present my version of events to World Rugby and the public at the same time, and for Berry to have the same opportunity.

Too many people told me that there was no way I would be found not guilty, and I felt a public hearing would provide transparency and openness. In my application, I said a hearing behind closed doors would impair public confidence in the integrity of World Rugby processes and raise questions about the reasons for secrecy.

The request was turned down, and the hearing continued on a video conference call. Frikkie flew over to be my legal representative and we sat in separate rooms at the hotel. The proceedings were private, but they weren't secret, and the Judicial Committee later released details of the evidence, the findings and the reasons for those findings. The full details of my disciplinary case can be easily accessed online.

They heard my evidence, as well as that of Nic Berry, Ben O'Keeffe, Joël Jutge, Russell Belter, Jurie Roux and Jaco Peyper.

In the meantime, the Springboks flew to the UK for the end-of-year tour, and I joined them a day later. Despite the result of the Rugby Championship, I thought the team was looking okay, having lost three matches by only two points. We beat Wales 23–18 in Cardiff, and Scotland 30–15 at Murrayfield the following weekend.

Four days later, the Judicial Committee handed down their decision. I was found guilty on all six charges.

An important ruling they made up front was what was meant by me having 'published or permitted to be published' or 'published or caused to be published'. World Rugby argued these words meant causing the video to be uploaded to Russell's Vimeo platform and sharing the link. Both SARU and I said the concept of publication must be interpreted more widely to mean disseminating the video to the public at large, which I denied doing. We lost that argument and the Judicial Committee members said that the words 'published or permitted/caused to be published' did not have the wider meaning.

Being found guilty of publishing or causing the publication of the video resulted in people thinking I had been found guilty of leaking it. That wasn't the case. By asking Russell to upload it to his Vimeo account, emailing the link to five people, and then WhatsApping the link to the Springbok players, I *had* caused it to be *published*. But it did *not* mean I had *leaked* it.

Unfortunately, the widespread belief that I *had* leaked it would not go away.

World Rugby rejected my argument that I had made the video for a limited audience and highlighted five occasions where I said I didn't know where the video was going or that SuperSport might use it, which satisfied them that I had intended it to have a large audience.

I was suspended for two months with immediate effect, starting on 17 November 2021, from all involvement of any kind in Rugby Union, and suspended with immediate effect to 30 September 2022 from match-day involvement, including coaching and direct or indirect contact with team management or players on match day. I was banned from going to stadiums where games were being played or communicating with match officials on match day. I wasn't allowed to engage in any feedback sessions with match officials. I was also banned from talking to the media. Finally, I had to apologise to the match officials, which I did.

For me the big issue was the way Siya had been treated. The Committee said:

We recognise the exceptional sensitivity of race in South Africa. We found that none of the match officials deliberately or consciously treated Siya Kolisi differently from any other player. Nothing they did was motivated by race. That RE [as I was referred to] believed his captain was treated differently does not get close to justifying the content of his video. We also note that only two of the clips concerned that topic and there were a further four or so references to the Springbok players being disrespected.

The Judicial Committee members took a dim view of my lack of apology to Berry and my failure to acknowledge that the video was 'abusive, insulting and/or offensive', which meant I couldn't expect much leniency from them in sentencing. They accepted I had no prior findings of misconduct against me and they recognised my 'very significant contribution to the Game, as a player and coach, which reached its zenith in Japan at RWC 2019'.

The Committee said it had:

… no hesitation in concluding that RE's misconduct is much more serious than any of the cases cited to us. This was an especially serious and egregious example of offending of this kind. It involved premeditated, multiple abusive and insulting comments and attacks on the officials' integrity in the course of that 62-minute video. That is compounded by three further facts (as we find them to be):

a. The Erasmus video was made for wider public dissemination.

b. It was made public by or at the behest of RE.

c. RE threatened the referee.

We planned to appeal the decision, but a week later we decided instead to withdraw our appeals and considered the matter closed. We'd had enough of this fight. World Rugby had heard us, and it was time to move on. Once the Judicial Committee decided on the narrow interpretation of the word 'publish', there was no chance of being found not guilty of publishing the video. I caused the video to be published when I asked Russell to upload it to Vimeo and when I sent the link to the people I wanted to see it. I couldn't argue otherwise. The issue was already a distraction, and the Springboks were trying to prepare for a Test match against England. I didn't want any more sideshows around the team.

The disciplinary was about how and why I produced a video that insulted the referees and brought the game into disrepute. But it was also about the treatment of a black captain who captained the World Champions. A year before the Lions series, World Rugby put out a statement with #BlackLivesMatter. They said:

> Rugby is a sport for all with a spirit of inclusivity, unity and diversity at its heart. Everyone has a role. Everyone has a voice and everyone has a right to be equals off the rugby field as they are on it. In partnership with our unions and the International Rugby Players, we know we must continue to play a leading role in positive, meaningful action to eliminate any form of racial discrimination. We will listen to all members of our community, and work closely with International Rugby Players, unions and other bodies to better understand the challenges faced by everyone in the game and take appropriate steps to drive continued positive change in our sport.

That was the real issue I was dealing with.

Since the suspension started immediately, I wasn't allowed to attend the Springboks' final game of the end-of-year tour, against England at Twickenham, which we lost in the final minute 26–27. It was the third Test match in 2021 that the Springboks had lost by two points or fewer. I later saw in the media that some fans went to the game wearing masks of my face – a small thing that made me smile.

I had expected a fine, but I didn't expect to be banned from all rugby for two months, and from match days for a year. It seemed to be a punishment not only for me but also for women's rugby, the EPD Pathway, and SA Rugby. I understood the match-day ban, and that one really stung because rugby was what I lived for. It was tough not being with the team on a Saturday. That ban really hit hard.

It felt strange, when I got back home, not to go to the office. I didn't miss anything because the Cape Town Sevens from 9 to 11 December was cancelled due to challenges caused by Covid-19, and the SARU office was closed from 16 December to 10 January. Within a week of the office reopening after the Christmas and New Year break, I was back at work.

While I was at home, I posted some fun videos on Twitter of me relaxing and enjoying a kuier and a few dops with friends. I also posted videos of my bulldog Frank, and there were messages of support, which helped keep my spirits up. I was particularly pleased with a video from an Irish online sports show in which former Leinster and Ulster coach Matt Williams gave a fair analysis of the Erasmus Video.

I was criticised in the media and abused on social media, where I was portrayed as some kind of monster. What hurt most was seeing how upset my mother was when people at her old-age home showed her negative articles about me. My sister was exposed to a lot more of the criticism in the English media because she and her family were in Reading, England, where she's a social worker for the National Health Service. She felt that her family were the only people inside the UK who didn't hate me.

As I look back, I ask myself, 'What if I hadn't made that video?' It's an exercise I do in camp with the Springboks, asking, 'What if …?' What could we change and do better?

On reflection, I would probably still make the video. If you want to achieve something you've never achieved before, you have to do something you've never done before. I wanted to catch the attention of Jutge and World Rugby. I achieved that, receiving a reply from Jutge in which he agreed with our comments.

Looking back, I do, however, regret my comment, 'I don't know where this will go' and suggesting the video could possibly end up at SuperSport. The remarks were perceived as threatening and I'm sorry for using those words.

After the leak, I gained nothing and lost a lot. Things didn't go the way I had intended. When the video was leaked, it seriously damaged my reputation, the Springboks and South Africa, and I deeply regret that. I fucked up. No question about it.

On 17 January 2022, the two-month ban came to an end, and my three daughters posted an amusing, tongue-in-cheek message to World Rugby on Twitter: 'We just want to say thank you so much for only making it two months. Honestly, thank you. We are so tired of having him at home. We have received enough life lessons and advice about everything. It's enough and we think it's time for him to go back. We are grateful the day has arrived for him to go back to work.'

The year-long match-day ban was still in force, though, and I missed the three-Test home series against Wales in July 2022, as well as the Rugby Championship, which New Zealand won narrowly, despite the Springboks' incredible 26–10 victory at Mbombela Stadium in Nelspruit. Those were the games that I desperately missed attending.

23

BY THE TIME THE SPRINGBOKS' end-of-year tour came round in November 2022, the World Rugby suspension was over, and I was back with the team on match day. Our first Test was against Ireland at the Aviva Stadium in Dublin, a contest between the World Champions and the number-one ranked team in the world. World Rugby assigned Georgia's Nika Amashukeli as the referee. He had taken charge of South Africa's first Test against Wales in July, which the Springboks won 32–29, but he was still new to the Tier One level of competition. Our game against Ireland was his seventh at that level. In a tense battle, we lost 16–19, with both sides scoring two tries.

Afterwards I tweeted a video clip from the game, saying, 'Surely was a game of big battles, but small margins.' I didn't mention Amashukeli. I showed an incident where an Irish player kicked the ball out of a ruck and Ireland scored from the advantage gained. In the TV broadcast, the player's foot couldn't be seen kicking the ball. I used a video clip from a camera on the opposite side of the field, which clearly showed the Irish foot kicking the ball clear. It also showed that the referee had a clear view of the incident, but he didn't penalise it. I also showed how the Springboks were blown up for exactly the same thing, so Amashukeli clearly knew it was against the law.

Our next Test was against France at Orange Vélodrome in Marseille, with Wayne Barnes as the referee. It was always going to be an epic battle as the French were going for their 12th win in a row. In the 11th minute Pieter-Steph was sent off after a diving headbutt on Jonathan Danty. Despite being a man down, we did well to trail 10–16 at the break after Siya scored a try.

Seven minutes after halftime, France were down to 14 players when their captain Antoine Dupont got a red card for tackling Cheslin in the air. Cheslin and Faf took over the kicking duties from Damian Willemse and did a great job kicking tricky penalties and conversions. Then Kurt-Lee Arendse scored a try to give us a 26–22 lead. But, without giving a warning, Barnes showed Deon Fourie a yellow card, which gave France a numerical advantage up front, and they immediately capitalised as their prop Sipili Falatea forced his way over. Another penalty by Thomas Ramos gave France the win: 30–26.

There had been a number of questionable moments in the game, one of which seemed quite suspicious. We felt Falatea had done a double movement in scoring his try, but surprisingly, Barnes's radio communication with the TMO went down, and the try was never reviewed. It seemed too convenient.

The next day, I posted eight tweets and seven video clips of contentious moments in the game. I showed a video clip where Barnes shouted 'Joue-le!' (Play it!) to Faf, and I attempted to make a joke and tweeted in isiXhosa 'Xolo asisiva isiFrench' (We don't speak French). How must our players know what Barnes was saying when he gave us instructions in French?

In another tweet, I showed a clip of a long pass from Willie to Damian, which Barnes blew up for being forward. My comment was 'Learning! Those long passes just have an optical illusion attached to it, we will work hard at it!!' I was then accused of being sarcastic.

All hell broke loose over the tweets, with Barnes and his wife getting terrible abuse on social media. I had no immediate idea of the trouble the tweets had caused and was sitting in a restaurant when Jurie phoned me.

He said, '*Rassie, watse kak het jy nou weer gemaak?*' (Rassie, what shit are you causing again?)

I said, '*Jurie, ek het tweets getweet van fokken footage wat op die TV was, en ek het nie die ref se naam genoem nie, en ek sê nie die ref is kak nie*' (Jurie, I sent tweets using fuckin' footage that was on TV, and I didn't mention the referee's name, and I'm not saying he was shit).

At a news conference on the Tuesday before the Italy Test, I said my tweets were aimed at the fans and weren't intended as criticism of the referee. I said, 'We have always been really close to our fans. If you go and read the tweets, they are actually for South African supporters to understand that there are some things that guys are doing really well, which we don't understand. People then form their own opinions and I understand that. They read the tweets and want to add something to the narrative that they want to put out there. It's obviously something on our side that we have to fix. I think South African supporters would like to understand that, and if people then put a narrative to that, I can't control that unfortunately.'

I said, 'It's not having a go at the referee, because I didn't think Wayne Barnes would make all those bad decisions. He is the number-one ranked ref in the world with more than a hundred Test matches.'

World Rugby reviewed my tweets and, two days later, banned me for two games. In a statement, they said they condemned 'any public criticism of match official selection, performance or integrity, which undermines their role, the trust-based coach/match officials feedback process and the values of integrity, respect, solidarity and discipline that are at the heart of the sport'.

The ban meant that I missed the Springboks' games against Italy and England, both of which we won. I was also banned from engaging with the media and using social media.

We didn't follow the protocol about challenging refereeing decisions after the Ireland game because we weren't getting anywhere. I decided not to send the mistakes to World Rugby because the process was unsatisfactory; instead, I put the video clips on social media and let the public judge if I was wrong. I was dead serious when I said we would have to adapt if I had made a mistake. If the referee was correct, then we had to get it right.

I was accused of being sarcastic, and I'll concede that I was frustrated and allowed sarcasm to creep into my comments. But I deliberately didn't take on the referee. Nigel Owens, a top referee whom I respect, said I had brought the game into disrepute. Jutge told a French newspaper that World Rugby was disappointed I was using social media to comment about the referees and called my tweets 'counterproductive and totally inappropriate'. He accused me of 'open[ing] the door to violent behaviour' and said the tweets were 'extremely dangerous'.

I was upset at the abuse aimed at Wayne and his family and tweeted, 'Like myself the referee of the French test & his family have received threats & abuse. Apparently it's partly due to my tweets which is totally unfounded. Tweets were not aimed at the officials, but to our [South African] fans on what we should do better. Have a go at me not the ref!!'

The response did little to convince people on Twitter that I was genuine in my comments, and I was accused of being sarcastic and disingenuous. I was getting used to this kind of response. People had made up their minds about me, and nothing was going to change that.

My actions had got me another ban, but they also caught the attention of the CEO of World Rugby Alan Gilpin and the Director of Rugby Phil Davies, and I asked to meet them in London. I now had the chance of a face-to-face meeting with the game's hierarchy to tell them that, in my opinion, the system wasn't working.

It was a very fruitful discussion. Both Alan and Phil were open-minded, understood my concerns and listened carefully to what I had to say. From my side, I understood why they were unhappy with the way I had tweeted the video clips. I saw their concerns and apologised for my behaviour and for the tone of my comments. I knew I had made mistakes. I was sorry

Wayne Barnes was abused and appalled that his wife had been caught up in the fallout.

I made the point that the players also had to be respected in getting clarity on refereeing decisions. The joint statement issued after the discussions said:

> There was agreement that further dialogue was needed in terms of enhancing the process that operates between teams and match officials to ensure all can play their part in creating great spectacles and avoid frustration but in a way that underpins the respect for match officials, coaches and players.

It was important that 'coaches and players' were included in that last sentence. I was very happy with this outcome because it meant I could go back to the players and tell them World Rugby could see what we could see.

I only had one meeting with Alan and Phil, but it paved the way for a much better relationship with World Rugby. Our communications have improved, Jacques sits on the High Performance Committee, and they share a lot of information with us.

I retweeted their statement issued after our talks, with the message, 'Thank you WR [World Rugby] and let's move on!!'

I'm embarrassed about being banned. I never want to be suspended, because rugby is my life. I absolutely hated being away from the team at the side of the field. It was a very effective punishment.

A good example of how people apply their own narrative to my tweets is when Eddie Jones was sacked as the England coach. I posted a screen grab of a WhatsApp conversation between Eddie and me when I had been banned by World Rugby. In the conversation he says he hopes I'm okay and called me 'a good rugby man'. My tweet said, 'Enough said! He's a man who has rugby in his heart.' I appreciated that he had made the effort to check in on me when I was at a very low point in my life. But the tweet was completely misunderstood. People presumed I was the one checking in on Eddie after he'd been sacked. They mixed up who was asking after whom. The result was I came across as trying to draw attention to myself as a good person. What I actually intended was to show what a good man Eddie was. That's all. It backfired on me.

After the Six Nations match between Italy and Wales in Rome in March 2023, Italy's coach Kieran Crowley was very outspoken in his post-match interview after his side lost 17–29. He was extremely critical of the ref Damon Murphy on live television and said, 'There's a lot of bloody frustration.' He questioned how Italy could be penalised 17 times and not be warned once, and complained that Italy hadn't been awarded what he felt was a legitimate penalty try because the play hadn't been sent upstairs to the TMO. He said he was 'sick' of World Rugby's protocols, which meant teams had to send their feedback about the referee to Jutge for him to provide feedback and get a response that says, 'Sorry, we got it wrong.' He also raised the issue of inconsistencies in the refereeing, with an Italy player getting a yellow card for challenging in the air, but Wales getting away with a similar incident.

These were exactly the same complaints I had raised during the British and Irish Lions tour.

To this day, people still talk about me leaking the video as if it's a fact. My friends will tell me, 'You had balls to leak that video.' It's difficult to persuade people that I didn't. When the suspensions ended, I found it tough to walk into stadiums because people would hurl abuse at me, calling me a 'fucking cheat'. I tried to ignore them; it would do me no good to get into a row with people like that.

24

RUGBY WAS ALWAYS GOING to be an important part of my life. My love for the game was inspired by the people of Despatch, who lived for rugby and supported their club with passion. Rugby was everything to them and became everything to me. It was impossible not to feel passionate about rugby in Despatch, and I started playing at an early age.

At first, all I wanted to do was play for Despatch. Then, as I grew up and my world got larger, I wanted to play for the Springboks and win the Currie Cup. When I achieved that, I wanted to be the Springbok coach by the age of 50 and win the World Cup. I became coach when I was 45 and won the World Cup three days before my 47th birthday.

I don't consider myself to have been a special rugby player, but I had an ability to see things other players couldn't see. I knew if I just did what the other boys were doing on the field, I wouldn't be any better than them. I had to find a way to do things differently. I wasn't the biggest or the fastest person on the field. But I could anticipate and react quicker, and that made me a better player. As I started establishing myself, I bought my computer and started coding and analysing the games. By doing that, I could see patterns that others couldn't see. I wasn't afraid to try things that would complement my physical size and my speed. Sometimes my ideas were a disaster, but other times they worked brilliantly.

I didn't consider myself to be a special coach either, but I came with a wealth of experience on and off the field. I had learnt many life lessons as a player, which I brought into coaching. I could tell my players about the dangers of excess and feeling entitled because I had been down that road. I understood what it was like to play the big games because I had been there.

In the introduction to World Rugby's Playing Charter, it says, 'The wide variation of skills and physical requirements ... mean[s] that there is an opportunity for individuals of every shape, size and ability to participate.'

I had simple philosophies in my approach to coaching. If our team's shapes and sizes fitted a certain game plan, then that's the way we played. We were big and strong, so we played physical rugby. We had fast, innovative backs, so they were given the chance to run. The fans and some analysts have suggested that I fundamentally changed South African rugby by introducing a running game into the traditional Springbok game plan. That isn't the case. We stuck with the tried-and-tested hard, physical game up front, but we created opportunities for the backs and encouraged them to run.

I wouldn't change our game plan just to please those who wanted flamboyant, running rugby. We didn't expect small, fast teams to play hard, physical rugby and wouldn't complain that they were too quick for us when they won.

A lot of teams have incorporated a number of our key strategies into their game, particularly in defence, where the backs come up on attack with speed and tackle their opponents from the outside in, forcing the attackers closer to the forwards and improving the chances of a turnover.

We were often criticised for kicking too many high balls. If we were guilty of anything, it was that we kicked too many bad high balls. If our box-kick is accurate, it's anybody's ball when it's in the air and we have a 50% chance of winning it back. As the attacking team, we're running forward, and we've practised time and again jumping up to take the ball, with support players ready to dive on it if it goes loose (we call it 'the scraps'). Once we've secured the high ball, we're behind their lines and they have to scramble back in defence. A bad high ball means they get the ball immediately and can do what they like with it. A high ball has to be contestable, where we have at least a 50% chance of winning the ball back.

I am a participant in an exciting project regarding computer software for coaching rugby called Outfox. Coaches traditionally use a whiteboard to draw up their moves and plays, and I realised there had to be a more modern and effective way of doing this. I started working on my Outfox concept with software developers 12 years ago and, over the years, I have continued to develop and improve the program.

Players use a controller to move their corresponding icons in simulated formations on a screen. Once they have perfected their drills in a classroom environment using Outfox, they can practise them on the field, saving a lot of time. The software is a unique coaching tool with several other benefits.

Outfox is legally protected, with extensive security features. The Springboks have used it with great success, particularly at the 2019 World Cup. It can be adapted for any team sport and will go on the market soon.

As we approach the 2023 World Cup, Jacques announced that he would leave his position as Springbok head coach to take up a job at Leinster. His contract ends after the tournament, so there was no reason for us to stand in his way. Our personal relationship is unaffected by his decision. It just means that, after so many years together, we won't be coaching the same team any longer. I have no plans to follow him as my contract with SARU ends in 2025 – as long as I don't get fired!

The three Springbok assistant coaches Mzwandile Stick, Deon Davids and Daan Human, as well as head of athletic performance Andy Edwards, signed contract extensions for another four years, and they will stay with the Springboks until the end of the 2027 Rugby World Cup in Australia.

Our preparation for the World Cup hit a setback in April when Siya suffered a crippling knee injury playing for the Sharks against Munster in a United Rugby Championship match at Kings Park, four months before South Africa's opening game of the World Cup against Scotland. He consulted specialists before undergoing surgery on a torn anterior cruciate ligament.

Time will tell whether or not Siya is ready for the World Cup, but he is one of the toughest players around. With intensive rehabilitation, there's a good chance he can take up his position as captain of the team. He came back from a knee injury in 2019 to lead the Springboks to victory. He can do it again in 2023.

So what's next?

My dad used to say, 'If you love something and can't contribute any more, you must love it enough that you can step away.' When I can't contribute to rugby in a way that's meaningful, then it'll be time to move on.

CEOs or management boards don't fire coaches, the fans do. As long as I have the support of the players and the fans, and the impact to achieve winning results, I will continue to do my job.

As we prepare for the 2023 World Cup, I'm confident we have the majority of South Africans behind us. I'm satisfied that our game plan is good. If the fans still want me after the World Cup, that's fantastic. If they don't, then I'm willing to step away in the interests of the game I love. I'm open-minded about this.

I've been through some dark times, feeling down and out. There were days when I could only sleep, and nights when I could not sleep at all. The lows were very low, rock bottom. Banned from all rugby, sitting at home while the Boks were in Australia and New Zealand, and missing the incredible atmosphere when we beat the All Blacks at Mbombela Stadium in Nelspruit. Being verbally attacked by people on the street who told me I had buggered up, and I just didn't have the energy to defend myself every single time. Reading abusive comments on social media. Having people make up their minds about what kind of terrible person I was.

But the highs have been incredibly high. Playing for the Springboks and winning 17 games in a row, playing against the British and Irish Lions on debut, playing in the 1999 World Cup. Coaching the Springboks, implementing my vision, taking the team from seventh to first in the world, winning the series against England as rank underdogs, and winning the 2019 World Cup.

My greatest moment in rugby wasn't lifting the Webb Ellis Cup – it was watching my Springboks create and score tries in the World Cup final with ease. They trusted each other and were comfortable with each other. They understood that it was a privilege to represent their country and they did it all with a smile, despite the unbelievable pressure they were under.

My biggest achievement has been the creation of the EPD Pathway. I get immense pleasure from watching young players, who might otherwise not have had opportunities, become Springboks and play in a World Cup final.

I remember going to Border with Jacques to help their coach in 2013, and we saw this young centre, Lukhanyo Am. I told Jacques we had to keep him on our radar. Six years later, he was winning the World Cup. Those are the moments that stay with me.

I often get accused of being a political animal, doing the bidding of my political masters, because of the way I handled transformation and selected my Springbok teams. Let me be very clear – not once in my Springbok coaching career has anyone ever told me who to select based on political considerations. My selections have been my free choice, in consultation with my assistant coaches. I can almost hear people who want to believe I play political games shouting 'Bullshit!' when they read this. I can't change their minds. I've tried, but I realise some people don't want to know the facts. I'm being honest when I say I made Siya captain and picked a group of young black players against England, not because I had to make up quota numbers, but because they were the right players for the job. And, without question, they all proved themselves worthy of their selection. I did the groundwork to fix rugby all those years ago with the introduction of the EPD Pathway. When it started producing fruit, I didn't have to worry about transformation targets, because the right players were ready for the big time. Transformation is not a matter of white player out, black player in. It's about fair and equal opportunities. But first we had to create those opportunities.

I think the average person on the street knows I'm a normal boykie. They'll tell me, '*Ons staan agter jou*' (We stand with you). Tannies come up to me saying, '*My kind, kom hierso dat ek jou net 'n drukkie gee*' (My child, come here so I can give you a little hug). I love chatting to people who stop me in the street, or shaking a young boy's hand.

I take great pride in watching how rugby has changed from being supported by a minority of people in South Africa to a sport embraced by all its people. Rugby has shown how South Africans, no matter what race we are, what language we speak, or what background we come from, can all work together. We can beat countries more powerful and richer than ours if we stand together and use all our resources.

I look back on my rugby life, with its achievements and its mistakes, with a degree of satisfaction. I played in big Test matches and I coached even bigger ones. I hope my lasting contribution is having provided opportunities to people who stepped up and took them. Anyone can play rugby if they are just given a chance.

You can be a boy from Bishops in Cape Town, Grey College in Bloemfontein, or Paul Roos Gym in Stellenbosch. You can be a boy from Hoërskool Brackenfell near Kraaifontein, Jim Mvabaza Senior Secondary in King William's Town (now Qonce), or Ntyatyambo Primary in Zwide.

Or you can be a boy from Hoërskool Despatch in Despatch.

Test matches as Springbok player (1997–2001)

DATE/VENUE: 5 July 1997, Ellis Park, Johannesburg
OPPONENT: B&I Lions, Lions tour
RESULT: Won, 35(13)–16(9)

INFO: Debut for **RASSIE ERASMUS**
TRIES: Montgomery, Rossouw, Snyman, Van der Westhuizen
CONVERSIONS: De Beer (2), Honiball
PENALTIES: De Beer (3)
CAPTAIN: Gary Teichmann
COACH: Carel du Plessis

MISSES
DATE/VENUE: 19 July 1997, Ellis Park, Johannesburg
OPPONENT: New Zealand
RESULT: Lost, 32–35

RASSIE ERASMUS replaced by Ruben Kruger

DATE/VENUE: 2 August 1997, Suncorp Stadium, Brisbane
OPPONENT: Australia
RESULT: Lost, 20–32

RASSIE ERASMUS replaced by Ruben Kruger

DATE/VENUE: 9 August 1997, Eden Park, Auckland
OPPONENT: New Zealand
RESULT: Lost, 35–55

RASSIE ERASMUS replaced by Ruben Kruger

DATE/VENUE: 23 August 1997, Loftus, Pretoria
OPPONENT: Australia, Tri Nations
RESULT: Won, 61(18)–22(15)

TRIES: **RASSIE ERASMUS**, Andrews, Brosnihan, Dalton, De Beer, Montgomery (2), Rossouw
CONVERSIONS: De Beer (6)
PENALTIES: De Beer (3)
CAPTAIN: Gary Teichmann
COACH: Carel du Plessis

DATE/VENUE: 8 November 1997, Stadio
Renato Dall'Ara, Bologna
OPPONENT: Italy, tour match
RESULT: Won, 62(22)–31(20)

TRIES: **RASSIE ERASMUS** (2), Du
Randt, Muir, Rossouw (2), Small (2),
Swart
CONVERSIONS: Honiball (7)
PENALTIES: Honiball
CAPTAIN: Gary Teichmann
COACH: Nick Mallett

DATE/VENUE: 15 November 1997, Stade de
Gerland, Lyon
OPPONENT: France, tour match
RESULT: Won, 36(19)–32(9)

TRIES: Dalton, Montgomery, Muir,
Rossouw, Small
CONVERSIONS: Honiball (4)
PENALTIES: Honiball
CAPTAIN: Gary Teichmann
COACH: Nick Mallett

DATE/VENUE: 22 November 1997,
Parc des Princes, Paris
OPPONENT: France, tour match
RESULT: Won, 52(28)–10(3)

TRIES: Honiball, Rossouw (4), Snyman,
Teichmann
CONVERSIONS: Honiball (7)
PENALTIES: Honiball
CAPTAIN: Gary Teichmann
COACH: Nick Mallett

MISSES
DATE/VENUE: 29 November 1997,
Twickenham, London
OPPONENT: England
RESULT: Won, 29–11

RASSIE ERASMUS replaced by
Andrew Aitken

DATE/VENUE: 6 December 1997, Murrayfield,
Edinburgh
OPPONENT: Scotland, tour match
RESULT: Won, 68(14)–10(3)

TRIES: **RASSIE ERASMUS**,
Montgomery (2), Rossouw, Small (2),
Smith, Snyman, Teichmann, Venter
CONVERSIONS: De Beer, Montgomery
(8)
CAPTAIN: Gary Teichmann
COACH: Nick Mallett

DATE/VENUE: 13 June 1998, Free State
Stadium, Bloemfontein
OPPONENT: Ireland, tour match
RESULT: Won, 37(13)–13(10)

TRIES: Andrews, Terblanche (4)
CONVERSIONS: Du Toit (3)
PENALTIES: Du Toit (2)
CAPTAIN: Gary Teichmann
COACH: Nick Mallett

DATE/VENUE: 20 June 1998, Loftus, Pretoria
OPPONENT: Ireland, tour match
RESULT: Won, 33(19)–0(0)

TRIES: **RASSIE ERASMUS**, Dalton, Rossouw, Teichmann, Van der Westhuizen
CONVERSIONS: Montgomery (4)
CAPTAIN: Gary Teichmann
COACH: Nick Mallett

DATE/VENUE: 27 June 1998, Loftus, Pretoria
OPPONENT: Wales, tour match
RESULT: Won, 96(29)–13(6)

TRIES: **RASSIE ERASMUS**, Hendricks, Montgomery (2), Otto, Rossouw (3), Skinstad, Smith, Terblanche (2), Van der Westhuizen, Venter (2)
CONVERSIONS: Montgomery (9)
PENALTIES: Montgomery
CAPTAIN: Gary Teichmann
COACH: Nick Mallett

DATE/VENUE: 4 July 1998, Newlands, Cape Town
OPPONENT: England, tour match
RESULT: Won, 18(12)–0(0)

TRIES: Terblanche, Van der Westhuizen
CONVERSIONS: Montgomery
PENALTIES: Montgomery (2)
CAPTAIN: Gary Teichmann
COACH: Nick Mallett

DATE/VENUE: 18 July 1998, Subiaco Oval, Perth
OPPONENT: Australia, Tri Nations
RESULT: Won, 14(8)–13(8)

TRIES: Van der Westhuizen
PENALTIES: Montgomery (3)
CAPTAIN: Gary Teichmann
COACH: Nick Mallett

MISSES

DATE/VENUE: 25 July 1998, Athletic Park, Wellington
OPPONENT: New Zealand
RESULT: Won, 13–3

RASSIE ERASMUS replaced by Andrew Aitken

DATE/VENUE: 15 August 1998, Kings Park, Durban
OPPONENT: New Zealand, Tri Nations
RESULT: Won, 24(5)–23(17)

TRIES: Dalton, Skinstad, Terblanche, Van der Westhuizen
CONVERSIONS: Montgomery (2)
CAPTAIN: Gary Teichmann
COACH: Nick Mallett

DATE/VENUE: 22 August 1998, Ellis Park, Johannesburg
OPPONENT: Australia, Tri Nations
RESULT: Won, 29(16)–15(12)

TRIES: Garvey, Skinstad
CONVERSIONS: Montgomery (2)
PENALTIES: Montgomery (5)
CAPTAIN: Gary Teichmann
COACH: Nick Mallett

DATE/VENUE: 14 November 1998, Wembley
  Stadium, London
OPPONENT: Wales, tour match
RESULT: Won, 28(14)–20(14)

TRIES: Van der Westhuizen, Venter,
  Penalty try
CONVERSIONS: Smith (2)
PENALTIES: Smith (3)
CAPTAIN: Gary Teichmann
COACH: Nick Mallett

DATE/VENUE: 21 November 1998,
  Murrayfield, Edinburgh
OPPONENT: Scotland, tour match
RESULT: Won, 35(11)–10(7)

TRIES: Rossouw, Skinstad, Snyman,
  Terblanche, Van der Westhuizen
CONVERSIONS: Montgomery (2)
PENALTIES: Montgomery (2)
CAPTAIN: Gary Teichmann
COACH: Nick Mallett

DATE/VENUE: 28 November 1998, Lansdowne
  Road, Dublin
OPPONENT: Ireland, tour match
RESULT: Won, 27(7)–13(6)

TRIES: **RASSIE ERASMUS**, Skinstad,
  Van der Westhuizen
CONVERSIONS: Montgomery (3)
PENALTIES: Montgomery (2)
CAPTAIN: Gary Teichmann
COACH: Nick Mallett

DATE/VENUE: 5 December 1998, Twickenham,
  London
OPPONENT: England, tour match
RESULT: Lost, 7(7)–13(7)

TRIES: Rossouw
CONVERSIONS: Montgomery
CAPTAIN: Gary Teichmann
COACH: Nick Mallett

DATE/VENUE: 12 June 1999, EPRFU Stadium,
  Port Elizabeth
OPPONENT: Italy, tour match
RESULT: Won, 74(22)–3(3)

TRIES: Boome, Du Toit (2), Fleck,
  Montgomery, Paulse (3), Teichmann,
  Terblanche, Penalty try
CONVERSIONS: Du Toit (8)
PENALTIES: Du Toit
CAPTAIN: Gary Teichmann
COACH: Nick Mallett

DATE/VENUE: 19 June 1999, Kings Park,
  Durban
OPPONENT: Italy, tour match
RESULT: Won, 101(40)–0(0)

TRIES: Drotské, Fleck, Kayser (3), Marais,
  Montgomery, Terblanche (5), Von
  Hoesslin (2), Vos
CONVERSIONS: Du Toit (8), Van
  Straaten (5)
CAPTAIN: Corné Krige on debut
COACH: Nick Mallett

DATE/VENUE: 26 June 1999, Millennium
Stadium, Cardiff
OPPONENT: Wales, opening of Millennium
Stadium
RESULT: Lost, 19(6)–29(19)

TRIES: Montgomery, Swanepoel
PENALTIES: Du Toit, Van Straaten (2)
CAPTAIN: Gary Teichmann
COACH: Nick Mallett

MISSES
DATE/VENUE: 10 July 1999, Carisbrook,
Dunedin
OPPONENT: New Zealand
RESULT: Lost, 0–28

RASSIE ERASMUS replaced by
Corné Krige

DATE/VENUE: 17 July 1999, Suncorp Stadium,
Brisbane
OPPONENT: Australia, Tri Nations
RESULT: Lost, 6(6)–32(20)

PENALTIES: Van Straaten (2)
CAPTAIN: **RASSIE ERASMUS**
COACH: Nick Mallett

DATE/VENUE: 7 August 1999, Loftus, Pretoria
OPPONENT: New Zealand, Tri Nations
RESULT: Lost, 18(11)–34(20)

TRIES: Snyman, Van der Westhuizen
CONVERSIONS: Du Toit
PENALTIES: Du Toit (2)
CAPTAIN: Joost van der Westhuizen
COACH: Nick Mallett

DATE/VENUE: 14 August 1999, Newlands,
Cape Town
OPPONENT: Australia, Tri Nations
RESULT: Won, 10(3)–9(3)

TRIES: Fleck
CONVERSIONS: De Beer
PENALTIES: De Beer
CAPTAIN: Joost van der Westhuizen
COACH: Nick Mallett

DATE/VENUE: 3 October 1999, Murrayfield,
Edinburgh
OPPONENT: Scotland, World Cup Pool A
RESULT: Won, 46(13)–29(16)

TRIES: Fleck, Kayser, Le Roux, Van der
Westhuizen, André Venter, Brendan
Venter
CONVERSIONS: De Beer (5)
PENALTIES: De Beer (2)
CAPTAIN: Joost van der Westhuizen
COACH: Nick Mallett

MISSES
DATE/VENUE: 10 October 1999, Murrayfield,
Edinburgh
OPPONENT: Spain
RESULT: Won, 47–3

RASSIE ERASMUS replaced by Ruben
Kruger

DATE/VENUE: 15 October 1999, Hampden
  Park, Glasgow
OPPONENT: Uruguay, World Cup Pool A
RESULT: Won, 39(27)–3(3)

TRIES: Fleck, Kayser, Van den Berg (2),
  Van der Westhuizen
CONVERSIONS: De Beer (4)
PENALTIES: De Beer (2)
CAPTAIN: Joost van der Westhuizen
COACH: Nick Mallett

DATE/VENUE: 24 October 1999, Stade de
  France, Paris
OPPONENT: England, World Cup quarterfinal
RESULT: Won, 44(16)–21(12)

TRIES: Van der Westhuizen, Rossouw
CONVERSIONS: De Beer (2)
PENALTIES: De Beer (5)
DROP GOALS: De Beer (5)
CAPTAIN: Joost van der Westhuizen
COACH: Nick Mallett

DATE/VENUE: 30 October 1999, Twickenham,
  London
OPPONENT: Australia, World Cup semifinal
RESULT: Lost, 21(6)–27(12)

PENALTIES: De Beer (6)
DROP GOALS: De Beer
CAPTAIN: Joost van der Westhuizen
COACH: Nick Mallett

DATE/VENUE: 4 November 1999, Millennium
  Stadium, Cardiff
OPPONENT: New Zealand, World Cup third
  place
RESULT: Won, 22(16)–18(12)

TRIES: Paulse
CONVERSIONS: Honiball
PENALTIES: Honiball (3)
DROP GOALS: Montgomery (2)
CAPTAIN: Joost van der Westhuizen
COACH: Nick Mallett

DATE/VENUE: 10 June 2000, ABSA Stadium,
  East London
OPPONENT: Canada, tour match
RESULT: Won, 51(27)–18(10)

TRIES: Barry, Fleck (2), Kempson,
  Montgomery, Paulse (2), Vos
CONVERSIONS: Van Straaten (4)
PENALTIES: Van Straaten
CAPTAIN: André Vos
COACH: Nick Mallett

DATE/VENUE: 17 June 2000, Loftus, Pretoria
OPPONENT: England, tour match
RESULT: Won, 18(15)–13(10)

PENALTIES: Van Straaten (6)
CAPTAIN: André Vos
COACH: Nick Mallett

MISSES
DATE/VENUE: 24 June 2000, Free State
  Stadium, Bloemfontein
OPPONENT: England
RESULT: Lost, 22–27

RASSIE ERASMUS replaced by
  Corné Krige

DATE/VENUE: 8 July 2000, Docklands
  Stadium, Melbourne
OPPONENT: Australia, tour match
RESULT: Lost, 23(23)–44(17)

TRIES: Paulse (2), Swanepoel
CONVERSIONS: Koen
PENALTIES: Koen (2)
CAPTAIN: André Vos
COACH: Nick Mallett

DATE/VENUE: 22 July 2000, Lancaster Park,
  Christchurch
OPPONENT: New Zealand, Tri Nations
RESULT: Lost, 12(12)–25(19)

PENALTIES: Van Straaten (3)
DROP GOALS: Montgomery
CAPTAIN: André Vos
COACH: Nick Mallett

MISSES
DATE/VENUE: 29 July 2000, Stadium
  Australia, Sydney
OPPONENT: Australia
RESULT: Lost, 6–26

RASSIE ERASMUS replaced by
  Corné Krige

DATE/VENUE: 19 August 2000, Ellis Park,
  Johannesburg
OPPONENT: New Zealand, Tri Nations
RESULT: Won, 46(33)–40(27)

TRIES: Delport, Fleck (2), Swanepoel (2),
  Williams
CONVERSIONS: Van Straaten (5)
PENALTIES: Van Straaten (2)
CAPTAIN: André Vos
COACH: Nick Mallett

DATE/VENUE: 26 August 2000, Kings Park,
  Durban
OPPONENT: Australia, Tri Nations
RESULT: Lost, 18(6)–19(13)

PENALTIES: Van Straaten (6)
CAPTAIN: André Vos
COACH: Nick Mallett

MISSES
DATE/VENUE: 12 November 2000, River Plate
  Stadium, Buenos Aires
OPPONENT: Argentina
RESULT: Won, 37–33

RASSIE ERASMUS replaced by
  Corné Krige

DATE/VENUE: 19 November 2000, Lansdowne
  Road, Dublin
OPPONENT: Ireland
RESULT: Won, 28–18

RASSIE ERASMUS replaced by
  Corné Krige

MISSES

DATE/VENUE: 26 November 2000,
    Millennium Stadium, Cardiff
OPPONENT: Wales
RESULT: Won, 23–13

RASSIE ERASMUS replaced by
    Corné Krige

DATE/VENUE: 2 December 2000, Twickenham,
    London
OPPONENT: England
RESULT: Lost, 17–25

RASSIE ERASMUS replaced by
    Corné Krige

DATE/VENUE: 16 June 2001, Ellis Park,
    Johannesburg
OPPONENT: France, tour match
RESULT: Lost, 23(11)–32(16)

TRIES: Paulse
PENALTIES: Montgomery (6)
CAPTAIN: André Vos
COACH: Harry Viljoen

DATE/VENUE: 23 June 2001, Kings Park,
    Durban
OPPONENT: France, tour match
RESULT: Won, 20(14)–15(15)

TRIES: Krige
PENALTIES: James (5)
CAPTAIN: André Vos
COACH: Harry Viljoen

Test matches as Springbok coach (2018–2019)

DATE/VENUE: 2 June 2018, RFK Stadium, Washington DC
OPPONENT: Wales, friendly
REFEREE: Matthew Carley, England
RESULT: Lost, 20(3)–22(14)

TRIES: Ismaiel, Mapimpi
CONVERSIONS: Elton Jantjies (2)
PENALTIES: Robert du Preez, Elton Jantjies

DATE/VENUE: 9 June 2018, Ellis Park, Johannesburg
OPPONENT: England, England tour
REFEREE: Ben O'Keeffe, New Zealand
RESULT: Won, 42(29)–39(27)

TRIES: De Klerk, Dyantyi, Le Roux, Nkosi (2)
CONVERSIONS: Pollard (4)
PENALTIES: Pollard (3)

DATE/VENUE: 16 June 2018, Toyota Stadium, Bloemfontein
OPPONENT: England, England tour
REFEREE: Romain Poite, France
RESULT: Won, 23(13)–12(12)

TRIES: Vermeulen, Penalty try
CONVERSIONS: Pollard
PENALTIES: Pollard (3)

DATE/VENUE: 23 June 2018, Newlands, Cape Town
OPPONENT: England, England tour
REFEREE: Glen Jackson, New Zealand
RESULT: Lost, 10(3)–25(6)

TRIES: Kriel
CONVERSIONS: Elton Jantjies
PENALTIES: Elton Jantjies

DATE/VENUE: 18 August 2018, Kings Park, Durban
OPPONENT: Argentina, Rugby Championship
REFEREE: Ben O'Keeffe, New Zealand
RESULT: Won, 34(10)–21(14)

TRIES: Am, De Klerk, Dyantyi (2), Mapimpi (2)
CONVERSIONS: Pollard (2)

DATE/VENUE: 25 August 2018, Estadio Malvinas Argentinas, Mendoza
OPPONENT: Argentina, Rugby Championship
REFEREE: Angus Gardner, Australia
RESULT: Lost, 19(7)–32(27)

TRIES: Kolisi, Mapoe (2)
CONVERSIONS: Pollard (2)

DATE/VENUE: 8 September 2018, Suncorp Stadium, Brisbane
OPPONENT: Australia, Rugby Championship
REFEREE: Glen Jackson, New Zealand
RESULT: Lost, 18(18)–23(17)

TRIES: Mapimpi, Mbonambi
CONVERSIONS: Elton Jantjies
PENALTIES: Elton Jantjies (2)

DATE/VENUE: 15 September 2018, Westpac Stadium, Wellington
OPPONENT: New Zealand, Rugby Championship
REFEREE: Nigel Owens, Wales
RESULT: Won, 36(24)–34(17)

TRIES: Dyantyi (2), Kolbe, Le Roux, Marx
CONVERSIONS: Pollard (4)
PENALTIES: Pollard

DATE/VENUE: 29 September 2018, Nelson Mandela Bay Stadium, Port Elizabeth
OPPONENT: Australia, Rugby Championship
REFEREE: Jérôme Garcès, France
RESULT: Won, 23(20)–12(12)

TRIES: De Klerk, Dyantyi
CONVERSIONS: Pollard (2)
PENALTIES: Pollard (3)

DATE/VENUE: 6 October 2018, Loftus, Pretoria
OPPONENT: New Zealand, Rugby Championship
REFEREE: Angus Gardner, Australia
RESULT: Lost, 30(6)–32(6)

TRIES: De Allende, Kolbe, Kriel
CONVERSIONS: Pollard (3)
PENALTIES: Pollard (3)

DATE/VENUE: 3 November 2018, Twickenham, London
OPPONENT: England, end-of-year tour
REFEREE: Angus Gardner, Australia
RESULT: Lost, 11(8)–12(6)

TRIES: Nkosi
PENALTIES: Pollard (2)

DATE/VENUE: 10 November 2018, Stade de France, Paris
OPPONENT: France, end-of-year tour
REFEREE: Nigel Owens, Wales
RESULT: Won, 29(9)–26(16)

TRIES: Nkosi, Mbonambi
CONVERSIONS: Pollard (2)
PENALTIES: Pollard (5)

DATE/VENUE: 17 November 2018, Murrayfield, Edinburgh
OPPONENT: Scotland, end-of-year tour
REFEREE: Romain Poite, France
RESULT: Won, 26(20)–20(17)

TRIES: Kriel, Pollard
CONVERSIONS: Pollard (2)
PENALTIES: Elton Jantjies, Pollard (3)

DATE/VENUE: 24 November 2018, Millennium Stadium, Cardiff
OPPONENT: Wales, end-of-year tour
REFEREE: Luke Pearce, England
RESULT: Lost, 11(3)–20(14)

TRIES: Kriel
PENALTIES: Elton Jantjies, Pollard

DATE/VENUE: 20 July 2019, Ellis Park, Johannesburg
OPPONENT: Australia, Rugby Championship
REFEREE: Paul Williams, New Zealand
RESULT: Won, 35(14)–17(10)

TRIES: De Jager, Herschel Jantjies, Nkosi, Reinach
CONVERSIONS: Elton Jantjies (5)

DATE/VENUE: 27 July 2019, Sky Stadium, Wellington
OPPONENT: New Zealand, Rugby Championship
REFEREE: Nic Berry, Australia
RESULT: Drew, 16(6)–16(7)

TRIES: Herschel Jantjies
CONVERSIONS: Pollard
PENALTIES: Pollard (3)

DATE/VENUE: 10 August 2019, Estadio Padre Ernesto
Martearena, Salta
OPPONENT: Argentina, Rugby Championship
REFEREE: Romain Poite, France
RESULT: Won, 46(24)–13(13)

TRIES: Kolbe, Mapimpi,
Mbonambi, Pollard (2)
CONVERSIONS: Pollard (3)
PENALTIES: Pollard (5)

DATE/VENUE: 17 August 2019, Loftus, Pretoria
OPPONENT: Argentina, friendly
REFEREE: Luke Pearce, England
RESULT: Won, 24(8)–18(10)

TRIES: Nkosi (2)
CONVERSIONS: Elton Jantjies
PENALTIES: Elton Jantjies (4)

DATE/VENUE: 6 September 2019, Sports Dome,
Kumagaya
OPPONENT: Japan, friendly
REFEREE: Nic Berry, Australia
RESULT: Won, 41(22)–7(0)

TRIES: Herschel Jantjies, Kolbe
(2), Mapimpi (3)
CONVERSIONS: Pollard (2),
Steyn (2)
PENALTIES: Pollard

DATE/VENUE: 21 September 2019, International
Stadium, Yokohama
OPPONENT: New Zealand, World Cup Pool B
REFEREE: Jérôme Garcès, France
RESULT: Lost, 13(3)–23(17)

TRIES: Pieter-Steph du Toit
CONVERSIONS: Pollard
PENALTIES: Pollard
DROP GOAL: Pollard

DATE/VENUE: 28 September 2019, Toyota Stadium,
Toyota
OPPONENT: Namibia, World Cup Pool B
REFEREE: Mathieu Raynal, France
RESULT: Won, 57(31)–3(3)

TRIES: Am, Brits, Gelant,
Kolisi, Louw, Mapimpi (2),
Mbonambi (2)
CONVERSIONS: Elton Jantjies
(6)

DATE/VENUE: 4 October 2019, Shizuoka Stadium,
Fukuroi
OPPONENT: Italy, World Cup Pool B
REFEREE: Wayne Barnes, England
RESULT: Won, 49(17)–3(3)

TRIES: Am, Kolbe (2),
Mapimpi, Marx, Mbonambi,
Snyman
CONVERSIONS: Pollard (4)
PENALTIES: Pollard (2)

DATE/VENUE: 8 October 2019, Kobe Misaki Stadium,
Kobe
OPPONENT: Canada, World Cup Pool B
REFEREE: Luke Pearce, England
RESULT: Won, 66(47)–7(0)

TRIES: Brits, De Allende,
Gelant, Malherbe, Nkosi,
Reinach (3), Steyn, Willemse
CONVERSIONS: Elton Jantjies
(8)

DATE/VENUE: 20 October 2019, Tokyo Stadium, Tokyo
OPPONENT: Japan, World Cup quarterfinal
REFEREE: Wayne Barnes, England
RESULT: Won, 26(5)–3(3)

TRIES: De Klerk, Mapimpi (2)
CONVERSIONS: Pollard
PENALTIES: Pollard (3)

DATE/VENUE: 27 October 2019, International Stadium,
  Yokohama
OPPONENT: Wales, World Cup semifinal
REFEREE: Jérôme Garcès, France
RESULT: Won, 19(9)–16(6)

TRIES: De Allende
CONVERSIONS: Pollard
PENALTIES: Pollard (4)

DATE/VENUE: 2 November 2019, International Stadium,
  Yokohama
OPPONENT: England, World Cup final
REFEREE: Jérôme Garcès, France
RESULT: Won, 32(12)–12(6)

TRIES: Kolbe, Mapimpi
CONVERSIONS: Pollard (2)
PENALTIES: Pollard (6)

Awards and achievements

1990	Hoërskool Despatch Rugby Player of the Year
1992	Defence Force (Free State) Rugby Player of the Year
1996	South Africa A Most Promising Player
1997	Free State Rugby Player of the Year
1998	Free State Rugby Player of the Year
1999	Nominated for Golden Lions Rugby Player of the Year
2000	Nominated for SA Rugby Player of the Year
2001	Cheetahs Most Valuable Player
	Super 12 Players' Player of the Year
2002	Cheetahs Most Valuable Player
2004	Cheetahs Most Valuable Player
2005	Free State Coach of the Year
2006	Free State Coach of the Year
	Sports Illustrated Coach of the Year
2008	Nominated for SA Rugby Coach of the Year
2017/18	Pro12 Coach of the Year
2019	World Rugby Coach of the Year
	SA Rugby Coach of the Year
	SA Sports Awards: Coach of the Year (for 2018)
2022	SA Sports Awards: Coach of the Year (for 2019/20/21)
	DStv Mzansi Viewers' Choice Awards: Favourite Sports Personality

Acknowledgements

A T THE TOP OF MY LIST of acknowledgements is the game that shaped my life from early childhood and continues to rule my world – rugby. It has been at the forefront of almost everything I have done and continue to do. Without rugby, I would not have been the person I am today.

I acknowledge all those – far too many to name individually – who have been on this incredible journey with me, from my teammates and coaches at school, the army, university and junior rugby to the Cheetahs, Cats, Lions and Springboks. I acknowledge a similarly large group of people who have travelled with me on my adventures as a coach at the Cheetahs, Stormers, Munster and the Springboks. If I could, I would name you all individually.

My neighbours in Despatch, the Human family, cared for me, influenced me, and nurtured my love of sport. I am eternally grateful to them.

I would like to single out one man who unselfishly shaped me at an early stage of my life – Gideon van Rensburg. He was the first to spot my potential as a rugby player and took me under his wing, not because he felt obliged to or was asked to, but because he wanted to. He expected no accolades and applause, but quietly imparted his passion for rugby to me. I owe him more than I can say.

In particular, I would like to thank Jacques and Elmarie Nienaber for their constant support and friendship. Jacques has been like a brother to me ever since we met as youngsters in the army. We have experienced the exhilarating highs and devastating lows that come with rugby. I value having him alongside me throughout.

Frikkie Erasmus has been my rock. He is more than a friend. He is my family. His guidance, advice, support and friendship have kept me going through good and bad times. Without him, I wouldn't be half the man I am today.

I would like to thank David O'Sullivan for writing this book. He has taken me on a wonderful journey of nostalgia, filled with great memories and deep emotions. I enjoyed every minute of our many conversations.

But my biggest thanks goes to my family. To my mother, Maria, who provided so much love during difficult times as I was growing up and instilled in me a love of sport. To my sisters, Martlie and Gerda, who loved and protected their little brother. To my wonderful, beautiful wife Nikki, thank you for understanding that you married a man who was also married to rugby, for your unflinching support as I moved the family from Bloemfontein to Cape Town, to Castleconnell and back to Cape Town as I followed my rugby dreams. I know it hasn't been easy, but your love means more than I can say. And to my incredible children – Nikki, Carli and Jani. You are the centre of my universe.

RASSIE ERASMUS
Cape Town
June 2023

I MET RASSIE ERASMUS at De Grendel Wine Estate on a hot day in January 2023. Back then, I thought I knew all about him from having reported on his career as a player and a coach. After three months of intense conversations, as he took me into his confidence and laid his life bare, I realised I had known very little about him. My thanks to Rassie for immediately entrusting me, a complete stranger, with his story. He is a deeply private man, who strays way out of his comfort zone when he allows the public to scrutinise him. Yet he allowed me to dig into all the nooks and crannies as we peeled back the many layers of his life. It never felt like work as we spent hours in conversation shaping his book. I can only hope I've done him justice.

I'd like to thank Jacques Nienaber, Nick Mallett, Frikkie Erasmus and Russell Belter for giving up their time to chat to me and share their insights into this mercurial person. Thanks also to Ken Vernon for his recollection of a terrible time in South Africa's turbulent past.

I am indebted to transcriber Vivien Wray, who worked with great speed and accuracy, and enhanced her work with insights, observations and links to articles for future research.

My thanks to Dr Emile Gouws for providing rugby books from his large library, as well as dozens of articles about Rassie from his vast collection of rugby magazines. His incredible ability to instantly recall where to find the articles amazes me.

My thanks, too, to Terry Morris and Andrea Nattrass of Pan Macmillan for their confidence that I could write this book, as well as for their insights and advice. Thanks to my dear friend and colleague Mandy Wiener, who has been down the author's road so many times, for sharing her wisdom and advice. I'm also indebted to editor Sean Fraser and proofreader Wesley Thompson, whose input and unerring eye for detail has produced this fabulous final product.

Finally, my love and thanks to my wife Jacqui, who happily took a backseat to Rassie as I disappeared to Cape Town for another round of interviews or spent endless hours in my study bashing out a manuscript. I can do the school run again. And to my boys, Michael and Tom, you can make a noise again without hearing the words 'That's your first warning ...!'

DAVID O'SULLIVAN
Johannesburg
June 2023

Index